Meaning Inc.

Meaning Inc.

The blueprint for business success in the 21st century

Gurnek Bains with Kylie Bains

and Damien Anciano, Jane Anderson,
Rani Bains, Jock Encombe, Claire Garner,
Miriam Javitch, Nik Kinley, Carmel Pelunsky,
Rachel Robinson and Ken Rowe

P
PROFILE BOOKS

First published in Great Britain in 2007 by
Profile Books Ltd
3a Exmouth House
Pine Street
Exmouth Market
London EC1R 0JH
www.profilebooks.com

A CIP catalogue record for this book is available from the British Library.

ISBN-10: 1 86197 883 9
ISBN-13: 978 1 86197 883 7

Text design by Sue Lamble
Typeset by MacGuru Ltd in Stone Serif
info@macguru.org.uk

Printed and bound in Great Britain by Bell & Bain Ltd, Glasgow

Contents

About the authors

Gurnek Bains is a founder and the CEO of YSC. He has worked for the past twenty years at senior levels within a range of global companies, advising them on people and cultural issues.

Kylie Bains is a director of YSC with seventeen years' experience of working with business leaders on individual and organisational development. She has a particular interest in issues of trust, alignment and political behaviour in organizations.

Damien Anciano is a managing director of YSC. He has managed some of YSC's biggest accounts, partnering with chief executives and HR directors to get the best out of their people.

Jane Anderson is a director of YSC. She has been involved in a wide variety of sectors, working in partnership with clients to build organizational, team and individual effectiveness.

Rani Bains joined YSC in 1995 with a background in occupational and clinical psychology. She has a special interest in the area of personal development, as well as maximizing individual and leadership potential.

Jock Encombe is the director of YSC Scotland. He has a particular interest in relationship-based approaches to individual and organizational change.

Claire Garner joined YSC in May 2001, moving to Hong Kong in October 2005 to co-found YSC's first Asian office.

Miriam Javitch is a director at YSC, leading the development of the Global Organization Change Practice for the firm.

Nikolas Kinley joined YSC in 2002. His interests include process facilitation, developing coaching techniques, and group dynamics in teams.

Carmel Pelunsky joined YSC in 2002. Previously she worked for Monitor Company, the Harvard-based strategy consultancy. Carmel has a special interest in working with teams and broader groups in addressing organizational change.

Rachel Robinson is a director of YSC with fifteen years' experience of working with business leaders. Her areas of expertise include the role of work in people's broader life as well as the development of high-potential individuals.

Ken Rowe is a managing director of YSC. He helped to found YSC in 1990.

Acknowledgements

It is customary to claim somewhat platitudinously that a book is a team effort. This one, however, is genuinely the fruit of an extensive collaboration within YSC, a global corporate psychology consultancy, and beyond. About two years ago a number of us started to meet to pull together some of the findings that were emerging from our interviews. Gradually, these findings were distilled into the themes and concepts outlined in the book. As with much at YSC, the initial efforts were rich in ideas and intent but lacked structure and cohesion.

The group process, we concluded, could only take things to a certain stage. Eventually I decided to go to Australia for a few months with my wife, Kylie Bains, and we both pulled everything we had into a coherent whole. We continued, however, to work closely with the YSC team. In particular, the following colleagues contributed to different sections: Chapter 4 on Leadership, Kylie Bains, Jock Encombe and Carmel Pelunsky; Chapter 5 on Purpose, Damian Anciano; Chapter 6 on History, Values and Continuity, Nik Kinley; Chapter 7 on Branding, Claire Garner; Chapter 8 on Impact, Ken Rowe and Miriam Javitch; Chapter 9 on Personal Growth, Rani Bains; Chapter 10 on Belonging, Kylie Bains; Chapter 11 on Rebalancing, Kylie Bains and Rachel Robinson.

In addition, Jane Anderson provided important interview material and played a key role in pulling things together and checking our material with clients. Apart from the core writing team, we were assisted by the researchers Jessica Lee and Hayli

O'Rourke. Claire Viney, my assistant, also worked extremely hard typing up the manuscript and wrestling with umpteen amendments and redrafts.

We would also like to extend a massive thank you to all the clients who have agreed to be featured in the book. These include ALJ, AOL, BP, Cadbury Schweppes, Diageo, Goldman Sachs, J. Sainsbury's, RBS, Rio Tinto, Starbucks, Tesco, Westpac, Whitbread and Yell.

In addition, we would like to thank the many others who have agreed to be interviewed and give us their views. There are too many people involved to be mentioned individually. However, this does not mean that we are not massively indebted to everyone who has provided us with support. One of the observations in our book is that, when you are engaged in something meaningful, it magnetically draws people to your cause. We have certainly found this in the writing of this book.

Last, but not least, we have had a very productive relationship with our publishers. Stephen Brough and Paul Forty of Profile Books have established a truly collaborative relationship with us as the book has evolved. We also owe a huge amount to our editor, Stuart Crainer. Stuart's constructive criticism has led to a massive improvement in the quality of our ideas and their presentation. The book has gone through a frighteningly large number of redrafts and it is to Stuart's credit that he has stayed on the game and pushed us to make it better and better.

Gurnek Bains
London and Brisbane, 2006

Tables and figures

Tables

Figures

Introduction

"I never make predictions, especially about the future."
Sam Goldwyn[1]

What will businesses that flourish in the 21st century look like? How can leaders continue to drive ever loftier performance goals without something giving? What will employees, consumers and governments require of companies in the future? And most importantly: How do you create an organization that will thrive in the new world? In addition, does any of this have implications for how we should live our lives or on wider social issues? These are the questions that are addressed in this book.

We believe these questions are incredibly important. Business corporations wield ever greater power and influence. The turnover of many global corporations exceeds the GDP of individual nations. For example, Wal-Mart's revenues in 2005 of just over $287 billion would make it the 22nd richest country in the world, beating over 170 sovereign nations. A study by the World Bank and *Fortune* magazine reports that close to two-thirds of the world's 150 largest economic entities are corporations rather than countries or public institutions.[2]

Although anti-globalization protesters would baulk at the assertion, this power has yielded some incredibly positive results.

Since China and India opened up their economies, a full 600 million of their citizens, over 10 per cent of the world's population, have been pulled out of the World Bank's definition of poverty in less than twenty years.[3] This change did not come about because of politicians or bureaucrats (state planning in both countries yielded miserable results), because of World Bank or IMF economists (the latter in particular seem to have had at best a very mixed record with any country that came within their grasp) or, however well intentioned, because of the activities of charities or trade unions. It has been local and international business working day by day, little by little, that has transformed people's lives.

The impact has not just been in the poorer countries. Goods and services that would have been seen as luxuries thirty years ago are now within the reach of large swathes of the population of developed countries. Things for which you would have needed to save for months, or even years, can now – for many – be bought on a whim. This shift has not been achieved by redistributive taxes, however useful they may be, but by businesses' relentless pursuit of innovation, efficiency and cost reduction.

However, the significance and impact of business is not matched by the way it is regarded. A survey by Public Agenda in 2004, for example, put business leaders second from bottom, just above politicians but below journalists, in terms of public regard. Only 20 per cent of the population trusted them.[4] Business leaders languish at the bottom of the list in many similar surveys. Worryingly, a 2005 Global Survey by the World Economic Forum (Davos) shows that the standing of global companies has fallen and reached the lowest levels since tracking began in 2001.[5] Barely a day goes by without some kind of scandal over the amounts of compensation received by a top leader. Films like *The Corporation* talk about the "pathology" of modern business. In the eyes of many, corporations are empty legal shells intent on maximizing shareholder value – more interested in the latest management fad than in improving the lives of those who work for them or in making a positive impact on society.

Internally, the world of organizations is also bedevilled by cynicism. After all, the biggest selling business book of all time is *Dilbert*.[6] Organizational life is routinely pilloried and parodied – witness the observational brilliance of the television series *The Office* and its highly successful American adaptation. Recent books such as Jill Andresky Fraser's *White Collar Sweatshop* and Madeleine Bunting's *Willing Slaves* paint a Dickensian picture, reflected on to a middle class canvas, of modern corporate life.[7] The French bestseller *Bonjour Paresse* extols the virtues of laziness and lack of commitment to work.[8] You could summarize it as one big, dismissive Gallic shrug at the world of work.

The reality is that both views of corporations have some truth in them. Collectively, business has had a much more profound and positive impact on the world than its detractors would allow. However, increasingly there are issues that companies need to think deeply about if they are to retain the trust of the public.

When you talk to people in business, and by that I mean really talk to them and get under their skin, you discover layers of attitudes. On the surface people demonstrate the kinds of corporate "good citizen beliefs" that you would expect of them. Dig a bit deeper and you find many are more critical and less accepting of what they see around them. They don't buy everything they hear. They are weary of management fads. This is the world of business that is derided in the popular media. It is an easy world to make fun of. The implicit message in this critique of business is – "It's all rubbish, just keep your head down. Play the game but be cynical inside." However, a closer examination reveals another vein of attitudes. Work is quite simply too important to be put in the "get through it cynically" bin. People care about their work. They want the issues that concern them to be tackled. They want to feel good about a part of their life that takes up over 50 per cent of their waking hours. In short they want their work to be meaningful.

These issues can't just be ignored. Organizations are where the vast majority of us spend our lives. We work in organizations, buy from organizations, borrow ideas and practices from them, look to them for help and information, and much more.

Forward with meaning

When we first thought about this book, it was going to be called *The Crisis of Meaning*. But as we researched it, we found there was much more to be positive about than we had originally thought. What's more, it seemed to be wrong to criticize from the sidelines without getting close to the pressures and intentions of leaders who have to juggle an increasingly intense and contradictory set of pressures.

Underneath all the negativity and cynicism we found something more positive going on – the rise of what we term here the Meaning Inc. company. Business leaders are not universally avaricious machines solely intent on lining their pockets or blindly driving shareholder value. The vast majority – like their employees – want to feel good about what they are doing. The most forward-looking are creating organizations that are invigorating and meaningful for employees, customers and other stakeholders. What's more, these leaders are not just being nice for the sake of it. Most are also discovering it works and helps them achieve results. The Meaning Inc. themes identified in this book are increasingly the only viable recipe for long-term success in the modern world, for companies like Tata, Starbucks, Virgin, Apple, Orange, ANZ Bank, Southwest Airlines, Genentech and many more. An even larger group of companies – we believe and hope, the majority – are aware of the need to move in this direction. Companies like Diageo, BP, Sainsbury's, Whitbread, Cadbury Schweppes and Goldman Sachs, to name a few, are all focused on Meaning Inc. themes as key drivers for delivering sustained performance.

This movement is built on a number of important realizations. First, what worked for leaders in the 1980s and 1990s is not working any more. The old recipes can no longer be rehashed. Leaders have recognized that the old tools and thinking are creating cultures that are increasingly destructive and incoherent, and which fail to deliver results. In such organizations, true commitment and engagement are fragile and worsening, accentuated by the fact that what people want out of their work has shifted.

A growing number of forward-thinking – and financially successful – companies realize that, for 21st-century companies, the key to raising levels of performance is to create a sense of meaning for their employees. By this we mean a sense of meaning that is real as opposed to going through the motions of creating statements of purpose and values or launching worthy initiatives. Genuinely listening to what people want and responding to it authentically is what we understand by "creating meaning". We believe this will be one of the most important tools for driving business results in this century. Meaning can and will give businesses a genuine competitive edge as well as making leaders feel good about what they are doing.

Future-proofing

In this book we explore the characteristics of Meaning Inc. How does it differ from the Dilbertian-world of cubicles and the Brentian nightmare of ennui, jargon and ego? How will it change the way we work and the way we think about work? How will it change our lives?

Sam Goldwyn would not have approved of what we are trying to do here. It's worth quickly explaining our methodology and the data upon which our conclusions are based.

Meaning Inc. is based on our experience of working with executives in organizations throughout the world. Over the past ten years, we have interviewed over 20,000 senior and middle executives in the UK and other parts of Europe, the US, and Asia-Pacific countries. Therefore, we can be reasonably confident about our conclusions and, in particular, about our predictions for the future. Over 10,000 of these interviews have taken place over the past five years. We talked to people about their personal values, their career histories, what they feel about their work, what energizes them, what frustrates them and what they want to see and do going forward. On average, we spent over four hours with each person to really understand their true feelings about their work. These interviews convinced us that there is a growing crisis of frustration developing among senior leaders. The old levers are just not working. There is also a lack of genuine engagement and commitment among a large section of the working population. Meaning Inc. is our attempt to make sense of what is happening to these executives and to provide a blueprint for what needs to happen for them to become genuinely engaged and committed to truly 21st-century organizations.

As we talked to people, certain companies would crop up repeatedly as positive role models. We started to look at these companies more closely to identify themes and lessons, and we studied their performance – typically, these companies had delivered stunning results. Slowly but surely the themes that were going to become increasingly dominant in the business world began to emerge. We believe they are going to become dominant because they reflect what leaders and people in business want and because they work. They also reflect what the general public and political stakeholders want of business. Too good to be true, perhaps. But here's the hard bit: these themes are not simple or straightforward to put into practice. It is easy to kid yourself that you are already implementing them when in actual fact you are light years away. There is a subtle alchemy involved here between getting it right and wrong.

The logic behind this book should be made clear. We started by looking at what leaders and people were frustrated by and wanted going forward. We then looked for companies that were trying to provide these things already. Only then did we look at the performance of these companies. This is different from looking at highly successful companies and trying to find out what makes them work. It is also different from starting with a theory in mind and testing it. There is value in all these approaches. We hope that our stance of focusing on what people want and what they think will happen gives the views outlined here a forward-looking focus and helps to future-proof the conclusions.

But before we get carried away, a word of caution. As I was writing my contribution to this book my eight-year-old son, Akal, came up to me to ask what it was about. I said we were writing about what companies might look like in the future. After a moment's thought he said, "So you're writing fiction then." "No," I replied, "we are writing about real stuff." But this response didn't pass the test with him. He insisted, "No one knows what's going to happen, so you don't really know what you're saying is going to be true do you?" At this point my six-year-old daughter Aman added, "Yeah, if you know what's going to happen you could just go and win the lottery."

These young children had intuitively understood that making predictions about the future is fraught with difficulty. If it's difficult enough to predict what you're going to have for dinner, how much more problematic is it to say how the world is going to evolve? This is all the more difficult with anything that touches on people. The inanimate world doesn't read books or get swept away by fads or fashions. The problem of reflexivity – people internalizing predictions and altering their behaviour as a consequence – also makes any confident statements about future social behaviour problematic.

The above notwithstanding, however, we do believe that there is sufficient evidence of the themes we outline here being practised – and increasingly being required. We are not simply engaged in an elaborate exercise of crystal-ball gazing.

While the future is unknowable, it is worth noting that looking backwards is not always the complete answer either. Perhaps the most famous exercise in looking back is reported in *Built to Last* by Jim Collins and Jerry Porras.[9] This extremely rigorous work, published in 1994, looked at what had sustained eighteen companies that had achieved prolonged success over a seventy-year period or so. The book was extremely well researched and the authors adopted a stringent set of tests to establish which would be the eighteen companies. Bizarrely, however, almost as soon as the book was out, a number of the companies studied hit a brick wall. Disney, Hewlett-Packard, Sony, Ford, Johnson & Johnson, to name a few, have struggled over the past decade. Shares in the eighteen *Built to Last* companies have appreciated by less than 150 per cent in the ten years since 1995. This compares with an appreciation of the Standard & Poor's and Dow Jones indexes of over 250 per cent over the same period. This is sobering since the eighteen companies had been selected precisely because they had had a track record of outperforming the market decade after decade. Meanwhile, shares in the Meaning Inc. characteristic companies mentioned on page 4, that have a 10-year quoted stock history, have gone up close to 600 per cent.

Let's be clear here about what we are saying. We are not questioning the *Built to Last* themes. In fact, we agree with many, although not all, of them. Some of the themes identified (e.g. having a core purpose and clear values) are actually even more relevant in the 21st century than they were when the book was written. However, as is clear from the lacklustre subsequent performance of some of the companies, such themes have to be constantly refined and reinterpreted in a fresh way in order to make them relevant to current realities. The world does not stand still. It is not enough just to have a core purpose and clear values: your core purpose and values have to be invigorating and relevant today and in tomorrow's world. Indeed, while there are many potential reasons for the problems encountered by some of the *Built to Last* companies (e.g. changes in the structure of their industry), we believe that a common issue was that, organizationally, many failed to keep their culture and values updated and relevant. In short, many of them started to look old-fashioned. Conversely, many of the Meaning Inc. companies look fresh and inviting and have interpreted some of the same themes in a contemporary manner. Interestingly, only three of the *Built to Last* companies appear in the *Fortune* 100 Best Companies to Work For survey of 2006. It may be a coincidence, but collectively these three show stronger performance than the other fifteen. By contrast, virtually all the Meaning Inc. companies regularly appear in their country's lists of best places to work.

The natural question is, What is cause and effect here? Doesn't success just make companies great, meaningful places to work? Hold this thought. We will visit it later and hopefully show that there is compelling evidence to suggest that the relationship is complex and very definitely not just one way.

The purpose of this book

In writing this book, we have a number of objectives in mind. First, we want to share what we have learned about the thoughts, feelings and frustrations of people at all levels in business. We also want to pull this together and suggest ways forward. We believe there are incredible examples out there that everyone can learn from. We also want to change the way leaders think about what they are doing and change the way business acts in the world and is perceived. Despite its power, societally we detect that business is on the back foot and we want to lift the confidence and spirit of those who work within it. The public is quite prepared to take the benefits of business (e.g. oil for their cars, cheap goods and services delivered when and where they want) but then take a big stick to the very same businesses for polluting the environment or not treating their employees as well as they might. Businesses should handle these issues better, but the public needs educating too. Finally, and most importantly, we want to share our experience of implementing solutions and the practical issues associated with becoming a Meaning Inc. company.

How does what we say relate to other theories and existing work? Stuart Crainer and Des Dearlove review the history of management thinking in their *Across the Board* article, "Whatever Happened to Yesterday's Bright Ideas?"[10] They describe a chaotic current world of fads and fashions, with new ideas coming and going at bewildering speed. In fact, it appears that, as with the tenure of CEOs, the life expectancy of a new business idea is shrinking fast. A new idea now takes a paltry 2.6 years to reach its peak, down from a robust 14.8 years in the 1950s. One is reminded of the market scene in the Monty Python film *Life of Brian* where ad hoc gurus and prophets hawk their wares. Caught in a tight spot, Brian assumes a guru persona and hastily strings together a stream of nonsense which finds a large audience, albeit for a brief period of time.

What we have presented in this book are the ideas that we think will work in the 21st century. Sometimes they are an elaboration of what has been said before. We make no apologies for this. Great ideas are timeless as they are built on fundamental truths. Indeed, we believe that meaning is a lens through which much valid advice to managers can be seen. Seeing it in this way allows people to make fine-grained judgements about what is likely to work or not. At other times, the ideas are genuinely new. However, even when they are not, we have worked to identify how certain concepts can be authentically interpreted in the world of tomorrow rather than that of yesterday.

Chapter One sets out our overall argument and looks at the characteristics of Meaning Inc. companies and the rapidly emerging pressures that are driving businesses in this direction. Chapter Two lifts the cover on what leaders and employees really think about their work and how increasingly the pursuit of once necessary change themes is now becoming unhealthy and leading many organizations to run on empty. Chapter Three looks at the different features of Meaning Inc. cultures and how these come together to create success. The remaining chapters look practically at what companies have done and can do to develop the vibrancy and success that comes from being Meaning Inc. Running throughout the book are examples taken from work with our clients and practical tools and models you can use to assess your situation and make improvements. Once we have put our argument forward, the focus is on what you can actually do in each area of meaning creation. We've tried not to be too academic or ponderous.

What we write about can be applied at any level. Indeed much of it can be applied to yourself as an individual outside of work. The authentic creation of meaning is not just a task for leaders but for all people in a business. Furthermore, it's not just a task for corporations, but also applies to public sector organizations, nations and individuals. In each section we also devote some attention to, in particular, the implications for individuals and nations.

1. Back to the future

In the middle of the nineteenth century a young Indian named Jamsetji Tata visited England. He saw a country in the throes of a mighty industrial revolution. Almost overnight new conurbations had appeared, generating unimagined wealth for some, but for others, in almost equal measure, dislocation and squalor. Tata was also aware of the impact on his country of what was happening in England. India had been, through the ages, an economic engine for the world – in 1750 it accounted for close to 20 per cent of world industrial production. Now it was effectively being de-industrialized, largely as a consequence of the movement of textile production from Bengal to Lancashire. As a result, India's industrial economy, by the latter half of the nineteenth century, accounted for less than one per cent of total world production.[1] Jamsetji Tata was particularly taken by a lecture in 1878 given by Thomas Carlyle, in which he stated: "The nation which controls iron, soon acquires control of gold."[2] Hearing this, Tata decided that he would devote his life to setting up India's first steel plant. Having witnessed the condition of working people in the factories of Manchester and Liverpool, he also made another resolution – the lives and conditions of the people working on his steel project would be different.

Fighting cynicism from the British that at times lapsed into outright hostility – as well as apathy on the part of his fellow Indians, many of whom thought he was a starry-eyed dreamer – Tata began working on the venture. At that time, nobody even knew whether India had any iron ore or coal deposits! The British were not encouraging. Sir Frederick Upcott, India's railway commissioner and an important potential customer for the steel, vowed to "eat every pound of rail steel they succeed in making".[3] Jamsetji Tata turned to others to help. A German geological report was used to identify iron ore sites. He visited America and commissioned the help of engineers and metallurgists there. When a prospectus for the company was eventually launched in London in 1906, it generated virtually no interest. The Tatas turned to fellow Indians in the independence movement and within a year 8,000 people had rustled up the necessary financing for the project.

Thus was born Asia's first steel mill, constructed in the unlikely environment of the jungles outside Calcutta. A fledgling plant that many thought was bound to fail started producing steel in 1912 and went from strength to strength. The success of the project, to quote R. M. Lala, author of a book on Tata, galvanized others: "When the first steel plant opened, men came to learn and to work from North and South Bihar, from far away Punjab and Madras … In Jamshedpur they were welded into a nation."[4]

This was how India's Tata Group was born, a unique concoction of the drive for industrial strength and efficiency allied with Indian nationalism and a paternalistic attitude towards employees. Tata is an early example of what we term a Meaning Inc. company. Before we define this term, let's take a closer look at some of Tata's attributes.

Steely purpose

The core purpose of the Tata Group – to focus on "what India needs next" – has guided its business direction for over a hundred years. It has led Tata to breakthroughs and important innovations in sectors as diverse as airlines, hotels, financial services and chemicals. Tata was the first company to produce a wholly Indian-designed car – the Indica – and, true to its philosophy of focusing on what matters to ordinary Indians, plans to launch a $2,000 people's car in 2008. Much earlier than many family-run companies in India, the Group decided to professionalize its management – a step that was thought necessary to achieving its core purpose. Today executives from Tata are some of the most sought-after in India, although it is often difficult to entice them away from their employer.

The original values so dear to Jamsetji Tata are also evident in the attitude the company adopts towards its workers. As early as 1912, Tata fixed the working day at eight hours when, even in England, the limit was twelve hours. Throughout its history, Tata has not just treated its people well, it has been an innovator in employee benefits – for example, introducing paid leave in 1920 and funded benefits in 1923. Tata Steel, a constituent company of the Group, has not had a strike for 75 years and, while it has cut a substantial proportion of its workforce in recent years, it did so by agreeing to pay all ex-workers their salary until retirement. The company has had the courage to stick to these principles through thick and thin. During the Wall Street crash of 1929, despite a great deal of pressure it refused to alter its conditions for employees, saying it was short-sighted to do so.

Employee development is almost a religion at Tata. From the start, the company focused strongly on training and today it funds a myriad of development facilities and educational establishments. Over the years, a paternalistic approach to employee development has given way to humane HR policies that give people more choice over how they develop. The success of this is clear as the Tata Group regularly wins awards for its treatment of people.[5] A particularly distinctive feature of the Group is the focus on community involvement in order to foster the development of its employees. Each Tata Group company has facilitators who coordinate and encourage community involvement. This is not a mere PR exercise. The company backs up its professed values with money and close to 30 per cent of Group profits after tax are spent on supporting social causes.

A concern for the environment has also been a core feature of the Tata way. As early as 1902, Jamsetji Tata said when advising planners on the proposed steel city: "Be sure to lay wide streets planted with shady trees, every other of a quick-growing variety. Be sure there is plenty of space for lawns and gardens. Reserve large areas for football, hockey and parks. Create space for Hindu temples, Mohammedan mosques and Christian churches."[6] In 1969 JRD Tata inaugurated the Tata Ecotechnology Center to look at the environmental impact of the Group's activities.

These positive social and human values co-exist with a strong drive for excellence and rigorous measurement of individual, functional and departmental contributions. Tata has always taken performance management extremely seriously. Tata Consultancy Services provides advice to a range of international clients on this area and in 2005 the company formed a partnership with Hyperion, a leading US firm in the field of performance management. Tata Teleservices, meanwhile, has a performance evaluation system that requires all individuals to be rated within their function first by everyone at the next level and then by all people at the next level in other functions. Ratings are then plotted on to a normal distribution and relative rankings are given. This focus on fairness and transparency is common to all Group companies. Performance management is made easier because the business is disaggregated into 90 or so different units.

To many Western business analysts, Tata would appear to be an anachronism. Indeed, even in India, the company was until recently felt to be an out-of-date institution which would be surpassed by newly emerging companies, often led by MBA-educated Indians who had imbibed the best of Western ideas. But Tata defied these predictions and has gone from strength to strength. It is by most standards one of India's most successful company, having repeatedly achieved exemplary rates of growth. It has diversified into a range of businesses and now has 93 businesses in 7 sectors, accounting for close to 10 per cent of the value of all companies on the Indian stock exchange. Its percentage share of national wealth exceeds that achieved by Wal-Mart and GE in the US. Once exchange rates are adjusted for purchasing power parities, the company's total revenue achieves levels attained by some of the US's biggest corporations – a not insignificant achievement given the size of the Indian economy. This seemingly old-fashioned industrial conglomerate also boasts India's largest outsourcing company. In short, Tata has not just survived, it has thrived.

In a 2005 survey by the *Financial Times* and Pricewaterhouse-Coopers of the views of 1,000 of the most significant CEOs across 25 countries, Tata was ranked as one of the most admired companies in the world for its sense of corporate responsibility.[7] Indeed, *Newsweek* has pondered whether Tata should be considered a model for companies everywhere.[8]

Meaning Inc. in unusual places

Tata is unusual but it is not alone. A number of what we label Meaning Inc. companies are fast emerging. For us, this term refers to companies whose success is founded on creating meaning for their employees, as well as for their customers and other stakeholders. Typically, the following key attributes are present in such companies:

- An invigorating sense of purpose that goes beyond business success and which makes people feel they are changing society as opposed to just servicing needs.

- The courage to set extremely stretching goals and to be ground-breaking in the pursuit of the core purpose.

- An innovative approach to benefits and the treatment of people which makes them feel special.

- A culture that allows people to be themselves and to feel they are personally making a difference and utilizing their distinct talents.

- A rigorous, at times almost aggressive, approach to evaluating performance and contribution.

- Clear and authentically grounded values which are lived through thick and thin.

- A concern for the wider and, particularly, the environmental and societal impact of business activities.

- Through all the above, an excellent reputation with consumers and other political and social stakeholders.

- Excellent long-term performance coupled with a preparedness to sacrifice short-term gains if their achievement conflicts with the core purpose and values.

More and more of the world's most successful companies show, or are trying to develop, these Meaning Inc. characteristics. To illustrate this, we have chosen companies from industries that you would not necessarily think would have these characteristics. Just take a look at what is happening in the oil sector, in the pharmaceutical industry, in investment banking, retail banking and in some global companies that are routinely criticized by anti-globalization protesters. When you lift the lid you find there is much of value going on in businesses where you would least expect it.

As we were writing this book, our eyes strayed to an important soccer match in the UK. Among the usual half-time ads for beer was a commercial from BP which focused on the company's commitment to alternative sources of energy. The advertisement highlighted BP's strong environmental credentials and ended with a definition of BP: "Beyond Petroleum". For BP, this was not a one-off exercise but reflected the company's firm embrace of progressive values. Lord Browne, BP's CEO, was the first chief executive of an oil company to acknowledge the reality of global warming and to develop supporting policies for dealing with it. Indeed, his efforts in this area were recognized by his receiving a United Nations prize for contributions to the environment – a bizarre accolade, one might think, for an oil company head.

While BP's conversion to environmentalism attracts the most public attention, this has probably been less of a significant feature in the evolution of the company than its strong commitment to the concept of what Lord Browne calls "mutual advantage". This, in BP's terms, means genuinely operating in a way that balances the interests of key stakeholders and, in particular, the countries where oil is located. In a lecture to students at Stanford Business School Lord Browne said: "Gone are the days when a foreign country could come in and – with a bit of brawn – impose its will on a foreign government. This type of relationship is no longer possible – and even if it were would be considered wholly undesirable."[9]

But while mutual advantage is an easy thing to say, it is harder to deliver. It requires sensitivity and empathy for the needs of others. To quote Lord Browne: "Every person is different, every place is different, every nation is different, every culture is different. In global business, it's very important to listen and learn. Nothing should be presumed ... To create the best business globally requires doing business which creates mutual advantage locally."[10] He went on to acknowledge, "People don't instinctively trust business executives or business. I always tell students to be humble, but be confident. Out of humility can come strength. Always remember that business has a very noble role in society."

One might think that these soft values could hamper BP in its competition with more aggressive players in the highly competitive oil market. Not so. BP has swallowed Amoco and Arco as well as a host of other smaller US oil companies. Shell, a company with a reputation for a much more aggressive culture, has been hit by a number of reputational crises, including the well-publicized furore over its over-statement of its oil reserves.

BP has also been notably successful in making acquisitions and finding reserves in difficult places, and persuading other companies and countries to partner it. For example, a key driver of BP's current success is a joint venture with the Russian company TNK to develop the vast Russian oil reserves. In landing this delicate deal, BP's soft values and commitment to diversity have been an astute play by Lord Browne which have, in particular, kept political authorities onside. The strongly political nature of the deal was evident from the fact that both Vladimir Putin and Tony Blair were present when the deal was signed in London.

Consequently, from being a relatively modest player in the oil business, BP is now the second biggest oil company and, by market capitalization in 2006, the seventh biggest company in the world. In a 2005 *Financial Times*/PWC survey, BP was voted the seventh most admired company in the world and Lord Browne the fifth most admired leader by 1,000 of his global CEO peers.[11]

There is, however, a sting in the tail that serves to illustrate the point that if you are going to go down this route, it is important to be thorough and consistent. Even in the early days, BP's efforts at environmentalism attracted cynical comment. When he received his UN award, Lord Browne was also presented in absentia with an "academy award" from Greenpeace for his convincing "acting". Some of these doubters felt vindicated by the well-publicized problems that BP had in 2006 in Alaska and the safety issues in one of its Texas refineries. The strong adverse political reaction to these events, particularly in the US, illustrates the importance of keeping public and governmental stakeholders onside. While, on the whole, BP profited when it was perceived to be getting it right, the virtuous cycle risked going into reverse as it stumbled.

● West Coast pioneers

Meaning Inc. companies cannot be easily categorized by industry sector. Look at the biotech company, Genentech, considered by *Fortune* to be the best company to work for in the US.[12] Genentech is renowned for the focus it puts on creating an environment that will allow its workers to discharge its mission of innovative drugs research. Close to 20 per cent of revenues in 2005 went into R&D, and researchers are given extensive time to spend on adjacent projects. Giant posters of patients who have been helped adorn the company's campus-like site and patients are regularly called in to provide a tangible example of why the company's work is important. There is a strong sense of informality, freedom and, at times, an irreverent and playful culture. Like Tata at the turn of the twentieth century, Genentech is an innovator in the 21st century with respect to employee practices. On-site day care, adoption assistance, domestic partner benefits and a service called Lifeworks, which sorts out any problems that are bothering people, all help to create a sense of being cared for. Flexibility is key and the company has won awards for being one of the best places for working mothers to work.

Yet in spite of, or rather, because of these soft values, Genentech is a star performer and one of the few companies in its field able to challenge the big pharmaceuticals because of the growth it has achieved. In 2005, *Fortune* judged Genentech to be the 30th most successful company in the US as assessed by profit, sales growth and total return.[13]

This focus on Meaning Inc. attributes is increasingly evident in most of the highly successful companies that are emerging today. Starbucks, for example, while attracting the wrath of anti-globalization campaigners for reducing individuality and choice in the market-place, is an organization that operates according to a forward-looking and positive set of values. These values are quickly evident when you walk into Starbucks' headquarters in Seattle. Within seconds you know not only that Starbucks' business is coffee and hospitality, but that they are passionate about it. There is a buzz and the culture smacks of openness of communi-cation. Most company meetings start with a coffee-tasting and a lesson on the attributes of the blend being consumed. More profoundly, the company expressly puts the interests of coffee growers and employees above all other considerations. Starbucks as a consequence pays almost 25 per cent more for its coffee beans than the market rate. This alone costs the company billions off its bottom line. Unusually for an American company, Starbucks gives stock options to part-time workers, as well as health cover. This costs the company even more than the higher prices it deliberately chooses to pay for its coffee.

Starbucks' managers are given huge discretion to do what is needed to live the company's values. Leaders have been given discretion to pay for the funerals of employees who have passed away, if their families needed the help. The result is a company that is quirky, and at times ill-disciplined, but at least one that tries to take its people with it. There is a genuine commitment to the core values and senior leaders joining the business are expected to spend time working in the outlets doing just about every job there is. They are allowed to throw out the rulebook to do the decent thing. Tolerant in many areas, Starbucks does not hesitate to remove leaders – even strongly performing ones – if they don't live the core values.

Listen to how Phil Broad, CEO of Starbucks UK, describes his interview process for joining the company. "I met Howard Schultz in his office and he asked me about myself, my values and what I found important in life. I met him again in Pike Place which is the first Starbucks ... we were having a meeting there at night and he opened the door with his key. He goes there and touches the wood every now and again to check he is making the right decisions."

This focus on values has served Starbucks well. It has over 10,000 outlets worldwide and since 1992 its shares have increased in value by 6,200 per cent.

Reinventing investment banking

One would think that the New York investment banking fraternity would be one of the last places to look for Meaning Inc. values. Certainly books like *The Bonfire of the Vanities* and *Liar's Poker*, as well as "greed is good" films like *Wall Street*, don't immediately suggest a world where the kinds of things that drove Jamsetji Tata would necessarily flourish. And then we encountered Goldman Sachs, 26th in *Fortune*'s Best Companies to Work For 2005 rankings and the only investment bank on the list.

Talking to people at Goldman Sachs, the first thing that surprised them was the restrained, almost cerebral tone of the bank, in an industry where flamboyance and ego tend to flourish, and hefty payments to employees at the receiving end of bad behaviour are routine. At Goldman Sachs, however, insiders describe a culture of teamwork, where excessive individualism is frowned upon. The story of a young talented manager who wrote his first memo and was told by a senior leader "This is fantastic, but can you change every *I* into a *we*" is illustrative of this sentiment, as is Goldman Sach's unusual tendency towards having co- or tri- heads of many of its business areas.

The bank encourages a strong sense of stewardship ("leave the firm a better place than you found it") and historically has been driven by a powerful sense of excellence and a view that doing the right thing and building strong, enduring relationships with clients works out in the end. "Long-term greedy", they call this orientation. "We would rather be the best than the biggest" is another mantra at the firm. The company builds loyalty and tries hard to remain in touch with ex-employees, many of whom move on to involvement in government or other public institutions.

Like many of the other companies with Meaning Inc. tendencies, these values have not held Goldman Sachs back. On the contrary, the firm has achieved extraordinary success. In particular, it has been the leading innovator in derivative financial instruments, an area that has transformed the industry. Over the five years to 2005, Goldman Sachs increased its revenue by close to 12 per cent compound growth a year. It is held in awe on Wall Street. During this same period, the firm experienced explosive growth, which certainly presents challenges for preserving and perpetuating its time-honoured culture as it continues to expand globally. But its success to date is a testament to the fact that the Goldman Sachs leadership never take things for granted and speak of the firm's culture all the time.

Retail banking responds to public pressure

On the other side of the world, in Australia, there are examples of banks on the retail side who have had to think hard about Meaning Inc. principles. Australians are quick to sense and speak up if they feel they are being ripped off. For Australian retail banks, things hit an extreme low in the late 1990s when perceptions about excessive fees, rural bank closures and a host of other issues led to what they called at Westpac (one of the largest banks in Australia) "growing community outrage". A real wake-up call for Westpac was when some staff began to avoid wearing their Westpac uniforms on public transport, only changing into them at work, to avoid being publicly associated with the bank. Both Westpac and ANZ, another key player in the industry, were forced to confront the issues, but did so in slightly different ways. Westpac focused primarily on shifting both its internal and external image by embarking on a broad-based corporate responsibility programme. The company developed and published a set of values and set out the behaviours that stakeholders could expect. It confronted perceptions head on and published a social impact report in 2000 that had a picture of a squashed tomato on it to represent what people had metaphorically been throwing at the bank. "This is what you thought of us," was the message, and the report dealt with how Westpac was going to change perceptions. A series of internal and external initiatives were launched to engage staff and the community and a "Barbeque book" was given to staff to help them field and answer the brickbats the Australian public typically threw at the banks.

To restore pride and morale, Westpac initiated a scheme whereby its 25,000 staff were given one paid day a year each for involvement in community projects. Flexible working arrangements were put in place to enable staff to contribute to causes of their choice. The bank also introduced a matching gifts programme in which it matched individual donations to worthy causes dollar for dollar. The impact, according to employees, has been a massive uplift in morale and engagement which has had a discernible impact on business results. Westpac's performance now places it in the top echelons of the industry as opposed to close to the bottom. ANZ, for its part, tackled the issues by embarking on a fundamental transformation of its internal workings and culture, of which we will talk more later (see pages 216–18).

It would be rash to say that the Australian public has full confidence in the banks these days, but things have changed. What Westpac and ANZ were forced to confront was an early manifestation of what many businesses are likely to face in the future as the public becomes more and more judgemental of the ways companies operate.

The fashion is spreading

Look around and you will see that Meaning Inc. themes are evident in a range of companies across all sectors of the economy, including Southwest Airlines, Gap, Virgin, W. L. Gore and Orange. Such companies show a desire for authentic purpose, positive impact and focus on employee well-being, coupled with strong business success. In Silicon Valley, in particular, a range of companies, such as Apple and Google, are pioneering ways of operating that will eventually seep into other business areas, just as the early methods at Ford became the model for businesses everywhere in the last century. An even greater range of companies in our consulting experience are aspiring to these attributes and recognize the importance to their future of embracing them. Companies like RBS, Diageo, AOL, Tesco, Cadbury Schweppes, Whitbread, Sainsbury's, ALJ and many more in our experience are working hard to embed Meaning Inc. attributes. The relationship between these attributes and success is, we believe, not coincidental. These principles represent the keys to success in the modern business world. The world has changed and companies that have recognized this are ahead of the curve and are reaping the benefits of being so.

The purpose of these examples is not to demonstrate that the Meaning Inc. companies are perfect in every respect or, indeed, that they are necessarily virtuous. Many, for example, may have embraced certain principles simply because they drive long-term business success. All could be criticized in a number of areas. BP, despite its "Beyond Petroleum" advocacy, is still an oil company, and one that has experienced problems recently. Starbucks minimizes any sense of local culture with its corporate imprint. Unlike the Tata Group, all of the above Western companies have been forced to lay off workers routinely at different points in their history and to make difficult decisions to satisfy the financial markets. However, all these companies have thought deeply about why they exist, what they do, how they project themselves and how they treat their people.

Why Meaning Inc. companies are on the rise

A number of significant trends are coming together to drive companies in the Meaning Inc. direction. In particular, the rise has been driven by shifts in what key stakeholders of a business want going forward (see Figure 1).

First, and perhaps most importantly, there have been sharp shifts in what drives employees. In our view, many companies are experiencing a latent crisis of commitment and meaning. Literally thousands of our deep-structure interviews (see Appendix), which probe behind the surface to establish what people really feel about their work, have led us to this conclusion. These views have begun to be widely supported by more orthodox survey data. The evidence for our concept of running on empty and the reasons behind it are the focus of Chapter 2. But for now let's just say that what people want from their work has shifted.

This extends all the way to the top of organizations. As the baby-boomer generation moves to significant positions of leadership, questions about what an organization is about and how things are done have moved from being peripheral concerns to centre-stage issues. People do not just want to work in businesses that are successful; they want to feel they are engaged in something worthwhile and that they are able to make a difference. This shift in motivations comes at a time when businesses need, more than ever, intense and deep levels of commitment to deliver performance in a world where the easy wins have mostly been banked.

Secondly, as McDonald's and Wal-Mart are now discovering, the way you operate and engage the external world also has a

Figure 1 ● Forces creating the Meaning Inc. company

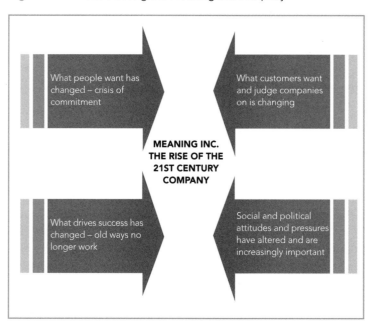

big impact on how consumers see you and on their preparedness to buy your products. Both these icons of corporate success
have now been hit by significant issues affecting the way the
public perceives them. For example, questions about the health
of McDonald's products have always been in the air but, in his
book *Fast Food Nation*,[14] Eric Schlosser closely examined how fast
food companies operate and, in particular, how they treat their
suppliers. The popularity of the book illustrates that people are not
just interested in the cheap price of a product, but want to know
what lies behind it. Wal-Mart, too, has been hit by a strong flow of
critical newspaper articles looking at the way it treats its employees
and deals with its suppliers, and the leaders of the company have
noted these concerns and publicly stated their commitment to
addressing them. Both McDonald's and Wal-Mart have taken
these changes in public sentiment seriously. When one looks at

their recent initiatives, it is clear that they are doing a surprising amount to tackle the problems that have been identified.

● Consumers' drive for personal meaning

The increasing reaction against big global brands stems from the sense of personal meaning that people seek as consumers.

A survey by the Co-operative Bank on consumer behaviour in the UK, for example, found that over half of consumers had boycotted a brand or a global business over the past year because of ethical reasons. The survey also found that, over a three-year period, businesses that projected themselves as having a strong ethical orientation increased their market share by 30 per cent. The survey found strong support for the increasing importance of how companies operate and the values that they project to consumers.[15] A global survey of consumers[16] by GMIPOLLS spanning seventeen countries found that 36 per cent of consumers were boycotting brands for ethical reasons. Nike, Coca-Cola, McDonald's and Nestlé were the most boycotted brands.

A significant factor driving this new consumer awareness is the speed with which information can now be disseminated. A host of websites now provide a platform for various consumer boycotts and, more rarely, positive endorsements for particular products. Recent campaigns include a boycott of De Beers for dislocating Kalahari Bushmen. The actress Julie Christie's warning, "Boycott De Beers or have the destruction of the Bushmen on your conscience," has led to a veritable rush of "beautiful people" distancing themselves from the company. The most notable of these defections has been the model Iman quitting as "the face of De Beers". In India, a highly public campaign against Coca-Cola for depleting underground drinking water led to a 14 per cent collapse in sales in one quarter. Other boycott campaigns include: Adidas for using kangaroo skin; Bacardi for riding on its Cuban heritage despite being active in anti-Cuban groups; Caterpillar for selling bulldozers used to destroy Palestinian houses to Israel; Wal-

Mart for its massive donations to George Bush; Esso for its role as an oil company with respect to climate change; Dolce & Gabbana for using a chimpanzee in an advert; and Nike because of concerns about its labour force in third world countries.[17]

In the past, businesses might have got away with ignoring these campaigns as the activity of a small number of disgruntled outsiders. Not so today. The list of companies which have been forced to rethink what they do is large and growing. Nestlé has had to make significant changes to how it markets its infant feeding products. After a campaign, Staples, the office supplier, agreed to ensure that 30 per cent of the content of its products was from recycled resources. Triumph, the motorbike manufacturer, has withdrawn production from Burma because of a campaign about the country's political situation.

Companies have a choice: listen to consumers or risk losing a potentially hugely damaging 5 per cent of sales. What's more, in our experience, more and more leaders sympathize with the motivations of the campaign organizers. Many of the latter are often surprised, and possibly sometimes disappointed, to find that, instead of a prolonged battle with their unethical enemy, they are pushing against an open door. Distant memories of their own activities as students in the 1960s and 1970s make many business leaders reluctant to play hardball with younger reflections of themselves. Coming back from a meeting with some senior business leaders, a member of an NGO was heard to remark: "It was a love-in – I honestly thought at the end they were going to pull out a joint!"

The bigger picture

In addition to the changing motivational reality and the rise of consumer activism and awareness, a third factor driving Meaning Inc. behaviours is the increasing importance of how wider stakeholders view a company and the permission that they give it to operate. Joel Bakan, in his book *The Corporation*[18] (also an award-winning documentary), poses an extreme view of companies, but one that finds increasing resonance with people.

"What would the world be like if its rulers were insane?" he asks. "The most powerful class of institution on earth, the corporation, is by any reasonable measure hopelessly and unavoidably demented. The corporation lies, steals and kills without hesitation when it serves the interests of its shareholders to do so. It obeys the law only when the costs of crime exceed the profits. Corporate social responsibility is impossible except in so far as it is insincere."[19]

One might think from the above statement that those criticising corporations are more detached from reality than the businesses they despise. However, it is clear from the reaction to Bakan's work that such views are shared by many. One of the conclusions of the book is that corporations need to be constrained by society and government if they are to be prevented from wreaking havoc across the globe. A common complaint from CEOs in the US is the amount of time that they have to spend managing their image and responding to the rapidly increasing regulatory requirements that governments are placing on them. Sarbanes-Oxley, a new and demanding regulatory regime imposed on US companies following scandals such as Enron, is an obvious example. This establishes new and stringent requirements for corporate boards and audit committees, as well as accountability standards, punishable by criminal penalties. Many industries across the globe are now facing increasing regulatory and public scrutiny that inhibits their scope for manoeuvre.

For some, these restrictions are a bureaucratic straitjacket. For others, they provide an opportunity. Companies that have thought hard about what they do and frame their objectives in a positive way with reference to society have benefited tangibly from the leeway that this has given them.

Tata, for example, is famous for its ethical standards of operation in a country that has a strong reputation for political and bureaucratic corruption that inhibits many aspiring companies. One of the reasons that Tata is able to be successful is that its core purpose and connection to the Indian freedom movement has given it support at the highest governmental levels. Similarly, the leaders of Sony have commented on how helpful the Japanese telecommunications ministry was to its growth at a period when most other departments of government were acting against the interests of commercial companies. The main reason for this was that Sony was explicitly engaged in an enterprise aimed at the restoration of Japanese national pride.

Increasingly, as companies become global, the permission to do business in politically sensitive environments becomes more and more important. According to an executive from an oil company, the real business it was in was not extracting oil, but the management of political relationships. Mining companies, too, are acutely aware of what they need to do to give them the licence to operate. In particular, governments are sensitive to the benefits that foreign nationals who extract profit bring to their countries. Critical among these are: how they treat and develop their employees, their concern for the environment and the wider societal values that they hold.

A range of initiatives is now under way to assess companies on these dimensions. As long ago as 1997 John Elkington, in his book *Cannibals with Forks*,[20] suggested the "triple bottom line" measure for assessing company performance. This adds, to the traditional metrics around economic and financial performance, measures around environmental impact and social impact. Developing this thinking, he quotes Professor Tom Gladwin of New York University who suggests that all boards should have three empty chairs – one for a fish to represent the natural environment, one for the poorest person on earth to represent the disadvantaged and one for a representative from the year 3001. Although these ideas did not immediately catch on, there are now a number of global initiatives to measure companies on wider dimensions. An important one is the UN's Global Compact initiative launched in 2001 which seeks to hold companies to core values around human rights, treatment of employees, environmental considerations and anti-corruption practices. By 2006 over 1,500 organizations had signed up to this document. The increasingly high standards being set in this area are illustrated by the fact that NGOs have criticized the compact as simply providing a cover for big companies to carry on as before.

The final factor driving the rise of Meaning Inc. attributes is quite simply the build-up of compelling evidence that it works and produces results. This is especially the case with respect to the enactment of a business's customer promise and the retention of customers. Viral marketing in the business community has led to leaders absorbing the lessons from some of the most successful companies around – many of whom display Meaning Inc. characteristics. But perhaps the most powerful reasons are that the old ways are just not producing the goods. Leaders are becoming increasingly aware of problems in commitment and, through a process of experimentation, are realizing that the creation of meaning is key to the future. Essentially the following pennies are beginning to drop:

What worked in the 1980s and 1990s is not working any longer

Over the past two decades, many businesses have transformed themselves through a variety of organizational initiatives. Defining and setting stretch goals, injecting new talent, organizational restructuring, process re-engineering, introducing more aggressive performance-related pay and getting people to work harder – these are all things that helped turn sleepy businesses into aggressive performance-oriented machines. For many companies, however, the benefits of these interventions have already been mined, and in a world where the challenge is to find strategies that grow the top line organically, they are less and less relevant. Continuing to rely on such techniques and approaches is now having a counter-productive impact on organizations. The chief sign of this is a growing feeling of chaos, cynicism and an erosion of people's sense of meaning.

In Chapter 2 we review the evidence that suggests that profit growth in recent years been based on an unsustainable share of productivity growth going to the corporate bottom line. We also argue that median salaries have been squeezed to achieve recent profit targets in a way that just cannot continue.

The markets are reflecting an awareness of these issues. In the 20 years up to 2000, the big US corporate stocks returned over 15 per cent a year. Since then they have returned a measly 2 per cent with dividends included. Big corporations have been hit most; the returns on the Standard & Poor's smaller companies index has shown returns of close to 15 per cent over this period.

There is an important dynamic here which is worth outlining. In the 1980s and 1990s, the price/earnings ratios of big corporations reached historically high multiples. The markets were betting that corporate profits would carry on rising fast. For companies simply to maintain their share price they have to deliver on these stretching expectations. In order for share prices to rise significantly, they have to *exceed* these expectations. Today's executives are, in fact, picking up the bill for the stock appreciation and bonuses earned by a previous generation of leaders in a world where the easy levers for improving performance have already been pulled.

A consequence of this is the increasing pressure that leaders face to find answers. Biological analogies are relevant here. When an animal experiences a new problem that it cannot deal with, its best option, if it keeps its head, is to develop a new adaptive response. However, when such a response is not easy to find, two other reactions can be observed. The first of these maladaptive reactions is to panic and to thrash about between different responses in the hope of finding anything that works. A second response is to persevere with behaviours that have previously worked and to stay rigidly fixed on them. Obsessively repeating what worked in the past in the hope that it will start to work again is not solely the preserve of the animal world. Indeed, in organizations we see all three of these adaptive and maladaptive responses (see Figure 2).

In the 21st century a surprising proportion of companies are in panic mode. They are desperately thrashing around for something that works. This is leading to the emergence of companies suffering

Figure 2 ● 21st-century organizational types

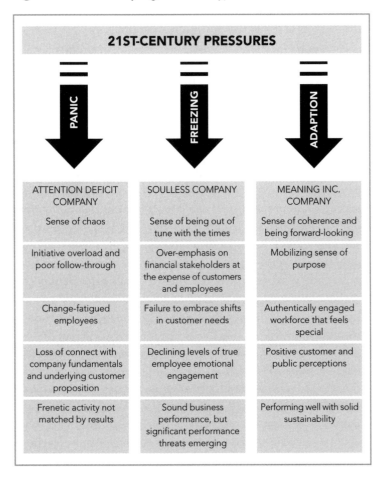

from what we term *Attention Deficit Syndrome*, when businesses engage in frantic, usually uncoordinated, activity – characterized by initiatives rarely being seen through to completion and an inability to stay focused for a sustained period. Attention deficit companies are hives of activity that make little or no progress. Such companies exhibit a high level of change fatigue – a weariness in the workforce associated with very low expectations of the latest initiative achieving anything.

Another syndrome is the development of the *Soulless Organiza-tion*. This occurs when companies try to block out the changes that are taking place around them and focus more and more narrowly on things that have worked in the past, so leading them to becoming steadily divorced from their people, as well as potentially out of synch with their customers. Performance in such companies can still be strong, but it is achieved through means which leave employees questioning whether they want to be a part of what is going on. Soulless organizations are characterized by a steady erosion of people's true commitment. They are also prone to a tipping point in terms of customer's reaction to them.

The above two syndromes are not mutually exclusive. Some companies have the unfortunate distinction of being both at the same time. For companies to resist slipping into either of the above, it is important for their leaders to keep their heads and respond to the pressures by finding adaptive responses. This is what Meaning Inc. leaders do: they coolly find the right responses to the unusual situations and challenges they face.

Archie Norman, well-known business figure in the UK because of his role in turning around the retailer Asda (now owned by Wal-Mart), has observed that financial re-engineering of businesses is now a commodity and that it is the quality of management and operational effectiveness which distinguishes successful organi-zations. We would argue that traditional approaches to manage-ment and execution have also become commoditized and that true competitive advantage now comes from doing things that lie outside the rulebooks of the 1980s and 1990s.

If you are wondering where your company sits with respect to the above categories, try answering the questions below? You can also apply them to your bit of the company.

Table 1 ● Which one are you?

Attention deficit	Soulless	Meaning Inc.
Is the amount of effort and energy people are putting into their work failing to be matched by the results that are being delivered?	Are there increasing question marks being asked about maintaining performance into the future?	Is your performance strong and robust when looking to the future?
Is there a lack of integration with the right hand not knowing what the left hand is doing?	Does your internal environment feel old-fashioned and constraining?	Do customers and external stakeholders have a positive view of you?
Is there loose measurement of people's impact and performance?	Is the main focus on driving results and delivering the numbers?	Is there an invigorating sense of purpose shared by all?
Are there a lot of change initiatives that do not build on or which are even a reversal of prior initiatives?	Are relationships transactional and lacking in openness and trust?	Do people feel that the best is yet to come?
Are people weary and change-fatigued?	Is turnover rising when you look at your better performers?	Is there a tolerance of individuality and self-expression?
Is there strong external pressure to deliver results that internally appear unrealistic?	Is there a fear culture in which people are afraid to openly be themselves?	Do people get pulled up if they violate core values?
Has there been significant churn at the top and a high level of staff turnover?	Have you been getting adverse external publicity?	Do the different parts of the business feel integrated and aligned?

Virtually all companies have elements of the above and the themes are certainly not mutually exclusive. However, there is often a tendency towards one of the above types in many companies we have seen. Of course there can also be extremely high levels of variation within companies.

In organizations that have not recognized that old tools and thinking no longer work, true commitment and engagement are fragile and worsening

There is growing evidence that engagement levels in many organizations are not as strong as they should be and are getting worse. Indeed, many organizations have achieved performance gains by squeezing their employees both psychologically and materially in a way they cannot continue to do.

This trend is particularly apparent when one looks at deep measures of engagement as opposed to surface indicators, such as time and energy spent at work. People have more profound needs from their work than has perhaps been acknowledged or recognized in the past, and these needs are coming to the surface as the importance of many other social institutions that traditionally provided for these needs has declined.

Today what people want from their work has changed. This has coincided with certain trends in corporate life that have served to erode a wider sense of commitment and engagement. In short, the gap between expectations and reality is growing because people are conscious of wanting more in a context where some significant trends in organizational life mean they are getting less. There is a growing body of evidence that employees are also less prepared to accept the gap between what they want and what they are getting.

Senior business leaders are often not aware of this situation. They can fool themselves into thinking that they are tackling the problem of commitment when they are not. The reality is that many initiatives aimed at increasing levels of commitment and engagement are received cynically and do not truly capture people's hearts. Employees can quickly spot the difference between authentic and inauthentic attempts to get them on board. Sadly, as our discussions with individuals illustrate throughout this book, a lot of what businesses do in this area falls into the latter category.

In 21st-century organizations, the key to raising levels of commitment will be to create an authentic sense of meaning

Much of what is happening in organizational life is creating a gap in meaning for employees. We will define meaning more fully later on, but for the moment, let us say that meaning arises when people are able to connect what they are doing to things that matter to them. It is increasingly difficult for employees to achieve this or find something that they can genuinely commit to and hold on to in an authentic manner. Exhortation will not raise commitment levels of businesses any longer, nor will fear or compensation serve to increase the productivity of workers. *Creating a sense of meaning for people will be what makes the difference.* Profound differences exist up, down and across organizations with reference to commitment and engagement. Individual leaders can make a huge difference. Organizations and leaders that get this right intuitively understand that what people are looking for in their working lives is *a sense of meaning*. Although they may not label it as such, this is what they are doing.

We have therefore developed a model of meaning which looks at the main aspects that need to be addressed for people to feel a renewed sense of connection. Each chapter of this book will look at a different slice of the meaning that people want in the new world, drawing out the issues in each area and, in particular, trying to understand how meaning can be eroded or enhanced.

While the creation of meaning has profound and positive effects, it is a subtle and elusive quality that can easily be lost without anyone being aware. We will argue that this has been the problem with some of the companies identified in *Built to Last*, companies which subsequently hit difficult times. A crucial issue, given that many organizations are making an effort to create meaning, is the distinction between authentic and inauthentic responses. There is a difference between going through the motions and actually doing something, for example, about improving the work–life balance. Similarly, it is quite easy to have a purposeful and meaningful mission statement but much more difficult to ground it in reality and make the hard choices that make it real for your people. The reality is that trade-offs are often necessary between a declared purpose and more prosaic market and financial considerations.

Creating meaning will be one of the most important tools for driving business results in the future

A focus on meaning creation will help to generate coherence in organizations and counter the powerful forces which are pushing companies into the attention deficit and soulless conditions identified on page 32. It will also be necessary to create the authentic and deep levels of commitment that will be needed to drive the next waves of the performance cycle for many businesses.

But just what is the relationship between meaning and success? All of the companies cited as striving for Meaning Inc. attributes earlier (Tata, BP, Starbucks, Genentech, etc.) have delivered exceptional results. Many companies in *Fortune*'s best employer list are also star performers. For example, two of the best performing food retailers in the US – Wegmans and Whole Foods Market – also feature high up in the list. If you ignored all share pundits and dutifully invested your money in the US 100 best employers list, and liquidated every year money in companies that fell out of the list and put it into the new entrants instead, you would have made a return of close to 15 per cent annually for the period 1998–2006. This compares to under 5 per cent for the S&P 500 index over this period. This is a profound and significant difference. In the UK, the *Sunday Times* survey in March 2006 of the best companies to work for also demonstrates that companies which treat their people exceptionally well have a significantly better performance record than those which do not.[21]

Of course, such relationships beg the question; what comes first – the chicken (being nice) or the egg (doing well). A natural conclusion is that successful companies can afford to look after their employees. While there is certainly some truth to this, the relationship is definitely not just one way. Many of the companies that embody Meaning Inc. or which appear on best employer lists had these values from the start. This is true of Tata, Wegmans, Google, Whole Foods Market and many more. They didn't reinvent how they dealt with employees because they were successful. However, their success did allow them to reinforce and maintain these values.

With other companies that did not start out embodying Meaning Inc., the relationship is more complex. Many, including BP, Westpac, and ANZ, had to sort out performance issues before embarking on the quest for meaning. In our experience this impetus is necessary as it helps create time for the more long-term meaning measures to work. In conclusion:

- If you are setting up a company, do so on Meaning Inc. principles.

- If you are underperforming, sort out some short-term issues and then pull the Meaning Inc. levers.

- If you are performing well, use Meaning Inc. principles to take you to another level.

- If you are performing well and feel you embody Meaning Inc. values, beware. Stay paranoid, as meaning is a fragile flower which can easily and unknowingly be crushed.

Success and Meaning Inc. principles feed off each other, but the route to this dynamic varies according to the position your company is in.

What is the mechanism by which meaning delivers results? Quite simply, the creation of meaning directly drives commitment and engagement and this has a tangible and demonstrable impact on business results. This is particularly true when the focus is on the medium- and long-term sustainability of results. Delivery of strategic intent, the brand proposition or a customer-centric culture requires employees who are emotionally, rather than just intellectually, committed to doing what is being asked of them.

The creation of meaning, however, is also crucial in giving companies competitive edge in their dealings with consumers and in ensuring that a business is protected against the kinds of adverse publicity that can have a catastrophic impact on sales at short notice. Anyone who doubts this view need only look at how Reebok, Nike, Gap and Levi Strauss & Co have fought to manage their image following concerns around child labour. This has not been a side issue for these companies, but an area over which they have fought tooth and nail to gain competitive advantage. As the examples cited earlier suggest, the rapidly burgeoning values criteria against which more and more consumers judge businesses means this is an area that cannot be ignored.

Nor can the views that political and other stakeholders have of a business be ignored. The ability to make acquisitions, the right even to do business in different countries and to have freedom of manoeuvre, are all critically dependent on how a company is seen to operate and treat its employees. As the world democratizes, politicians in more and more countries find themselves caught in the maelstrom of public reactions to business and are forced to use their power either to hinder or assist their activities.

It is not uncommon for people looking at businesses to blame the company leaders for their short-term preoccupation with results at the expense of other criteria. When one talks to the leaders themselves, they frequently pass the buck to the financial markets. The latter certainly wield great power, as recent books on the destructive impact that financial markets can have on organizations, such as Don Young's *Having Their Cake*, demonstrate.[22] However, even here we detect changes in attitude. Partly these are driven by the insurance industry. The crisis at Lloyd's in the 1990s was to a substantial extent driven by claims in relation to asbestos poisoning. This helped create in the financial markets an awareness of the potential disastrous consequences of ignoring environmental considerations.

Fund managers are similarly shifting their position as evidence mounts that the long-term success of businesses requires a broader perspective. A study by the Social Investment Forum[23] estimates that in ten years the amount of money going into socially responsible investments has quadrupled to over $2 trillion – a staggering amount. In Australia, the investment bank Macquarie has started to report employee engagement scores achieved by businesses that it is analysing as part of its assessment of their strength, because of the powerful impact that turning around employee commitment had on the performance of the likes of Westpac and ANZ.

Applying Meaning Inc. to nations

Just as companies can ask themselves, to what extent they meet Meaning Inc. standards, so, too, can nations. The questions are slightly different but follow the same themes.

Is our country Meaning Inc.?

- Do we have a unifying sense of national purpose?
- Do we have a drive to make a contribution to the world that goes beyond our own national interests?
- Do we have a shared set of core values which unite pretty much everyone?
- Are we recognized by others for authentically living our espoused values?
- Do most sections of our society feel they have a stake?
- Does being part of our nation make people feel special or distinctive in any way?

Although it would be a digression to go into the history of different countries, our view is that nations surge forward positively during phases when they embody Meaning Inc. attributes, but fractionate internally at home and lose their influence abroad when this is not the case. For example, in the early days, when the Soviet Union thought that it was a pioneering nation for a new world order, it achieved astronomic rates of industrial and economic growth. During the 1920s and 1930s, the outside world failed to appreciate the strides that the Soviet Union had made economically. Subsequently, this led to a profound miscalculation on the part of the Nazis. Hitler felt that the predominantly agrarian Soviet Union would collapse like a house of cards in the face of the German onslaught. The subsequent Soviet victory at Stalingrad arose more from the impact of thousands of fresh tanks and planes (produced by a myriad of factories in Siberia) being unleashed than from the exhaustion of the Germans or the rigours of the Russian winter.

Similarly, India achieved very high economic rates of growth in the period immediately following independence when it saw its world mission as being to spearhead the non-aligned alternative to the West and the Communist blocs. India was forced to abandon its high-profile championing of this initiative following its wars with China and Pakistan, which required it to develop alliances as opposed to pursuing a more independent path. It is interesting that rates of growth in both the Soviet Union and India plateaued after each country had lost its sense of belief in its global mission.

Stepping back to ask questions on these dimensions is therefore an important component of the underlying psychological vitality of nations. In our experience, companies are most in danger of losing sight of their values either when they have their backs to the wall in terms of performance, or when they are at the top of their game. In recent years, the US has paradoxically experienced both these mindsets. Winning the Cold War gave the country a sense of omnipotence, but then being subjected to attack on 9/11 added to a sense of being under siege. In this situation, there is a tangible risk of the US losing sight of its higher-level values and being less questioning of its modus operandi.

Does this matter? Yes, because, just as with companies, loss of Meaning Inc. attributes can lead to long-term problems. In particular, a nation can lose the kind of soft power or attitudinal buy-in that is crucial for political, commercial or even military success. The loss of internal cohesion can also become a significant issue when countries lose their Meaning Inc. attributes. If you start to feel bad about yourself or question what you are about, with countries as with companies, this eventually starts to show in terms of performance.

Applying Meaning Inc. to yourself

The Meaning Inc. questions can also be applied to individuals.

Am I Meaning Inc.?

- Do I have an invigorating sense of purpose that ignites my passions?
- Do I have aspirations beyond living a high-quality and pleasurable life?
- If others were asked would they be able to identify my core values?
- Do I have a distinctive set of strengths that make me feel unique?
- Do I feel I connect in a meaningful way with others around me?
- Do the aspirations and goals that I have stretch me?
- If my current dreams were to come true would I feel that I have lived a worthwhile life?

For the moment, we will leave you to ponder these questions. The following chapters will delve deeper into the above areas and offer some solutions if, as expected, you have emerged less than fully Meaning Inc. as a person.

Going back to go forward

In short, therefore, businesses, nations and individuals cannot afford to ignore questions of meaning. For companies, there is an element of "back to the future" in all of this. Just as with

Jamsetji Tata, many nineteenth-century industrialists reacted to the conditions in the new "satanic mills" with a drive to better the conditions of working people. Consequently, there was a strong philanthropic element to some of the companies that emerged in the latter stages of the industrial revolution, such as Cadbury's, Fry's, Unilever and many others. Visionary leaders then and today have had the imagination to look beyond the short term, but the professional managers who take the helm later in a company's development often lack the imagination or courage to stick to the founder's original values. In the recent past, the influence of the financial markets, particularly in Anglo-Saxon countries, has accentuated this trend. The Indian cyclical view of the world says that everything that passes away inevitably returns, but in a different form. Meaning Inc. companies are the new expression of these earlier sentiments.

Yet the rise of the Meaning Inc. company is not without dangers. In her book *Willing Slaves*,[24] Madeleine Bunting complains of the drive within organizations to own someone's soul. She decries the rise of what she calls *missionary management*. Indeed, there does seem to be something Orwellian about the rise of large corporations pretending to be saviours of mankind. More prosaically, efforts by businesses to move in this direction run the danger of appearing inauthentic and attempting to provide a cover for their pursuit of self-interest. Skin deep and, at times, contradictory and half-hearted efforts to create meaning are, as we will show later, all too common in the corporate world. They risk raising the appetite for something which business may not be able to deliver.

Nevertheless, authentically striving to create meaning and doing so in non-formulaic ways are skills that successful leaders will need to develop. Doing so is likely to be more an art than a science that can be applied with a ready-made set of recipes. Apart from creating organizational health and driving success in the marketplace, perhaps the best reason for striving to create meaning is the impact that it has on the well-being of workers. People spend up to 50 per cent of their waking lives in the workplace, so the question of what they get out of that time is fundamental. Trying to make a third of somebody's life more productive and meaningful is a good goal to have. Short of attacking world hunger or the AIDS crisis, there are few goals that are more worthy and important – or indeed more meaningful.

Before we turn to how companies can start doing this let's look at some of the issues and problems inside businesses that are making such a shift necessary and how a company can assess where it stands on the themes we have described.

2. Running on empty

"Unreal city,
 under the brown fog of a winter dawn,
 a crowd flowed over London Bridge, so many,
 I had not thought death had undone so many."
T. S. Eliot, *The Waste Land*[1]

"The wheel is still spinning but the hamster is dead," is how a middle-ranking executive wearily described his working life. The quip illustrates an increasingly widespread theme in corporate life across the globe – intense effort and commitment to work on the surface are coupled with growing psychological detachment and an increasing cynicism about the point of it all on the inside. It is increasingly clear that many business people feel, like T. S. Eliot's hordes, that they are going through the motions without feeling fully alive inside.

At the top there is also frustration. "It used to be the case that when I pulled a lever of influence within my organization things happened. Nowadays, the lever just falls off in my hand," a CEO told us. He is not alone. There is growing recognition of this problem among senior executives who, faced with the task of achieving ever more challenging goals, struggle to get the responses and reactions they want from their organizations. The old levers, such as organizational restructuring, process re-engineering, setting aggressive targets for employees and injecting new blood no longer work.

The sentiments outlined above are two sides of the same coin. Frustration experienced by senior leaders as they struggle to find new ways of pushing performance forward arises in part because people's hearts are not as engaged as one might think from their surface behaviour.

What people really think

At work, driven by ambition, fear or genuine belief, workers tend, on the whole, to wear their enthusiasm for a company's goal on their sleeves. They learn to parrot with energy the latest purpose or vision statements that are floating around. They talk enthusiastically about "killing the competition" and express surface passion for a company's products or brands. After enduring a gruelling year pushing themselves and others hard to achieve targets, the ambitious ones sign up even more enthusiastically to next year's breakthrough goals, whatever thoughts they might have about realism or attainability.

In the past five years, we have seen the tone and content of people's reactions shift significantly. In particular, we have seen considerable underlying disquiet develop in many people. More recently, we have seen the green shoots of more positive reactions as well, virtually exclusively in companies which are trying to develop Meaning Inc. attributes. We will talk about the more positive sides that we have seen recently, but for the moment let's focus on some of the issues that are arising.

Scratch the surface and you find that the psychological uniform people are expected to wear in corporate life is just that, a uniform. Table 2 summarizes some of the key negative shifts taking place in today's corporate world. While obviously the split into pre-2000 and post-2000 is somewhat artificial, there has been a gradual shift over time in people's views.

Table 2 ● Attitude shifts in employees

Pre-2000	Post-2000
● Excitement at having leaders thinking positively about purpose and values	● Cynicism that it's all been an empty exercise
● A sense of freshness and enthusiasm about future plans	● Staleness and a sense that old recipes are being recycled
● Anxiety, but engagement, around organizational change	● Change fatigue; exhaustion from weathering pointless change
● Finding work hard but reasonably rewarding	● Finding that work is hard and just getting harder
● Wanting to fit in and be part of what's happening	● Resentment at having to play the corporate game
● Seeing a big corporation as a challenging and worthy career goal	● Feeling that there's more excitement and possibility outside corporate life; planning escape routes
● Sense of confidence about future business performance	● Feeling increasingly challenged to keep up with ever-demanding growth targets

Here are some of the things that people have said to us:

"There have been three restructures in two years. I've survived them all. When the last one happened, I was actually offered a promotion but I just said to my manager I want out."

"Internally I got a great job – 200 people applied. But I found I could make no decisions. It came to a head when I had a meeting with a senior manager about the promotion of a toothbrush in Europe. He wanted an orange toothbrush. I said it wouldn't work. He said his hands were tied. This all took ages. My head was telling me I had a great job but my heart said if you can't even get a sensible colour for a toothbrush what's the point of staying. I left."

"Everyone around me was cynical. At first I resisted but after a while I realized they were right. It was all a game, a sham. Everyone was just doing what they could to keep their head down and save their jobs."

"They think because we get some of the crumbs off the table, it's OK. It's not. Last year I worked night and day and when I saw what they got and compared it to my bonus, something inside me died."

We could go on and on. To be sure, over this period we have also unearthed many positive attitudes. But we have definitely seen the frequency and tone of comments shift markedly in a negative direction over the past five years.

These observations are reinforced by many studies of engagement within businesses. The Gallup Organization has periodically conducted surveys of worker engagement inside businesses across the globe.[2] Gallup categorizes responses to its survey into three clusters:

- Engaged Employees: those who are loyal, productive and find their work satisfying;

- Not Engaged Employees: those who lack psychological commitment to their roles and who may leave if an opportunity presents itself;

- Actively Disengaged Employees: those who are disenchanted with their workplace and are overtly vocal and negative in their attitude.

In the US, Gallup found in 2003 that only 27 per cent of workers surveyed fell into the engaged category. The figures for other countries were: Great Britain (19 per cent), Germany (12 per cent), France (12 per cent), Japan (9 per cent) and Singapore (6 per cent). In Great Britain, Gallup found that over 80 per cent of British workers lacked any real commitment to their jobs. A full 20 per cent were defined as being actively disengaged; this was a higher figure than the 19 per cent identified as engaged.

Recently, Steven Covey reported on a Harris Interactive survey of 23,000 workers in the US about their work.[3] Here are some of their findings:

- Only 20 per cent were enthusiastic about their team's and organization's goals;

- Only 9 per cent felt very highly energized and committed;

- Only 15 per cent felt that their organization fully enabled them to execute key goals;

- Only 20 per cent felt their organization honoured its own values and commitments

- As few as 22 per cent felt valued by their organizations.

There is mixed evidence around what changes there have been in engagement levels over time and there appear to be some interesting differences across cultures. Most studies show either stable or slightly declining levels during the 1980s and 1990s across the world, but in the US there appears to be some sign of a small improvement post-2000. However, in Europe, things have continued to decline at a sharper pace than before since the turn of the century.

Professor David Guest of King's College, London, has surveyed people's attitude to work since 1996 for the UK Chartered Institute of Personnel and Development.[4] Historically, he resisted claims that engagement levels have worsened. However, over the past five years he has reported an alarming deterioration of attitudes in the private sector. Work satisfaction, engagement levels, trust and sense of autonomy are all showing a sharp downward trend. (In the public sector things are better, perhaps as a consequence of the Labour government pumping badly needed money into the system.) The UK Workplace Employee Relations Survey of 21,000 people also confirms the picture of a sharp decline across a range of areas.[5]

What does this tell us? At best, engagement levels are stuck at disappointingly low levels despite all that organizations have done in an effort to inspire and motivate people. Certainly, employee commitment in most organizations is not at the levels required to deliver the extremely stretching performance goals that businesses have to achieve just for their share price to stand still. Something bad has happened to people's experience of work, particularly, over the past five years. A positive is the slight improvement in the US. It seems that in countries where the 1980s and 1990s themes continue to drive business, engagement levels are declining but, in the US, where these methods have had their day, we are beginning to see the green shoots of a new way of engaging employees.

The ambivalence of departing

Woody Allen once remarked that 80 per cent of success in life was due to simply showing up. At the height of the internet boom, however, many businesses, consultancies and investment banks were surprised by the sheer number of their high flyers, even highly talented graduates from MBA programmes, who simply did not want to show up for a big, established enterprise but instead wanted to work for a start-up company or a dot-com. Clearly many were motivated by the chance to make a quick buck. However, this was not the motivation for most. A study of the people who joined the consulting firm Razorfish, for example, found that their primary driver was a desire for autonomy and to be close to the action.[6] Even with a majority of these ventures failing, one thing stands out: how few of the people who shifted out of corporate life want to go back. As one executive described it: "The dot-com stuff pushed me to make a decision I should have made a long time ago. It [the job change] was like a veil lifting and while my start-up experience was horrendous, I would never go back."

Take the case of Andrew Penfold, a highly successful investment banker, who worked, until recently, for a top firm in their Asian market. He describes the environment of intense commitment and 20-hour days as being "like working in the boiler room 24/7 without getting above deck ever". What is worse, much of this effort was sandwiched with flying around "everywhere like a leaf caught in a cyclone". Some businesses send employees who get married a bunch of flowers or a bottle of champagne. On their honeymoon, however, Penfold's bank chose to send a large box of documents for him to work on. At one level Penfold found his time at the investment bank stretching and fulfilling, but when asked how much meaning he had got out of his work, he said, "Virtually zero. The only motivation I had was to make money as quickly as possible to give me choices about the future."

Eventually, after he had "done his time", he decided to leave. He thought long and hard about what he wanted to do. As a youngster, he had been rebellious and had risked "going off the rails". Help and guidance from mentors had kept him from doing this. Because he felt so deeply about his experiences, he decided to set up a project to help native Australians, who tend for the most part to fall through the system, to get good-quality, high-school education. Today he raises money for this project, visiting many people he got to know from his investment banking days. He has come out of meetings with $100,000 personal cheques, and he is surprised by how many people from his previous world want to help him. "It's so personal for me – it's more of a buzz than any deal I ever did." Penfold kept himself going and gave his existence meaning through the investment banking years by having a clear plan to do something else. When the time came, he did not just snatch at anything, he thought long and hard about what mattered to him, to find a meaningful way forward.

He is not alone. A colleague of mine recently visited Ibiza and was surprised at the growing numbers of people who are opting out of gainful careers at an early age and moving to live there – for little or no pay but also for less stress and for more meaning in their personal lives. In the past, such desertion only tended to happen with investment bankers, who have a high rate of burnout and who, like Penfold, are often able to make enough money to do something else relatively young. However, this trend is now increasingly hitting people who work in consultancies, businesses and, in some cases, the public sector. It is increasingly getting good just to get out.

More often the case than not, people now have some sort of escape plan which helps keep them going. The general rise in incomes, especially at the top, makes the opting-out option available to employees in more and more types of job. There are also less positive reasons for such plans. Managers are aware, for example, that although one is expected to be intensely committed, at some point the axe just might fall on you, perhaps capriciously and often with little warning. The controversial British politician Enoch Powell once remarked that all political careers end in failure. Increasingly, senior leaders in business feel this and are resigned at some point to meeting their corporate Waterloo.

Hence, career commitment is replaced by career ambivalence, at best – career apathy, at worst. Those around you may wear the mask of dedicated corporate loyalty, which makes your own shadowy feelings of ambivalence or apathy that much more intense, that much more painful.

Does this matter? Yes and no. At one level it is helpful for people to find ways of keeping themselves going. But businesses also need to ask some questions. What happens to employees' motivation once these dormant plans take hold? Is it right for people to separate their lives into "doing time" and "escape" phases? Should we not try to make people's current reality more meaningful so they don't feel they are wasting a large portion of their life?

But it is not just people leaving or constantly thinking about leaving organizations that is the problem. Young people are increasingly turning their backs on established companies that they do not believe will offer them meaningful employment.

Attracting and retaining new talent has become more problematical for many organizations. For young graduates, the values of a company, the sector it is in and whether it is making a positive contribution to society trump most other considerations. A mining executive noted how much less attractive a career in mining now appears to be for young people compared to when he was starting out decades ago. While his mining company is increasingly working hard to transmit the message that it is committed to the environment and local communities (issues of concern to young people), the impact of such efforts is small. The recruitment problem is looming ever larger. At the same time, another friend, who has made the decision to work in the voluntary sector, describes how frantic the competition is for the few, relatively low-paid jobs that are advertised in this sector of the economy.

Semi-detached leaders

The fact that many people choose to mask their true feelings about the company they work for means that there is a significant risk of senior leadership becoming detached from the thoughts, feelings and attitudes of people lower down. In fact, surveys routinely report more positive results about organizational health when leaders are questioned relative to the experience of the "led". We believe the pressure to present a positive front, when coupled with the internal disquiet people are experiencing, increasingly lulls leaders into a false sense of security. Because of this, the gap between reality and leaders' perceptions is growing wider.

In addition to errors arising simply from wishful thinking, another reason is that leaders do have a different experience of work from others. For example, Karen McLeod, HR director of Rio Tinto, says: "The more senior people are in an organization, the more opportunities they have for fulfilment and self-expression. The work itself tends to be meaningful. They also have more freedom to decide on the balance of their personal and professional lives, where and how they invest their time and energies. Earlier in a career, people often feel their choices are more constrained, both professionally and personally."

Despite the fat-cat label they are frequently branded with, few leaders are driven primarily by money. They typically challenge themselves about how they can make a real difference and many spend substantial time and money on advisers and executive coaches to help them improve their effectiveness. However, the recognition that their efforts are not delivering the results they once did is serving to erode leaders' self-esteem and genuine sense of worth – despite the necessary bravado to the outside world. Many leaders also feel guilty about the growing demands they place on employees because of the pressure to deliver increased shareholder return. Internally, they may feel alone in their struggle – frustrated at not having the answers and feeling that other leaders do. As a result, their own needs for meaning, in different ways, are not being met. They, too, are feeling a sense of disconnectedness. Table 3 summarizes some of the shifts in the attitudes of leaders.

Table 3 ● Attitude shifts in leaders

Before 2000	Following 2000
● Enthusiasm about driving modern, empowered cultures	● Frustration at people not taking responsibility and feeling personally blamed for everything
● Confidence about how to make a difference	● Ambiguity, doubt and confusion about which levers to pull
● Belief in the importance of driving robust performance cultures	● Guilt that they're driving the organization too hard but not knowing what to do about it
● Assuredness that driving stretch goals will bring success	● A feeling that the goals they are imposing on others are unrealistic
● Driven by business success	● Concern about the legacy they leave behind
● Pride in their public standing	● Unease about how they are regarded by the external world
● Feeling challenged but coping with juggling multiple stakeholders	● Frustration at the pressure and external scrutiny that they experience

Again some quotes from company leaders are helpful to illustrate the point:

"I worry we are not doing enough. You can feel it – people struggle to find meaning in their work. I have made some mistakes which I regret, like simply telling people after a difficult year that it wasn't good enough. Some said it needed to be said but others were extremely resentful."

"There's too much expectation of leaders these days. I guess it goes with the rewards. It's tough and getting tougher. I wish I could relax or just say don't look to me for everything."

"Business leaders have a terrible reputation out there. Partly it's our fault. We've let stereotypes develop and not challenged them. Whatever we say in public, we do care about how we are seen."

What gives rise to these feelings around work both for leaders and employees? Companies are increasingly running on empty for three key reasons. First, the way companies now think and act has eroded people's sense of performing meaningful work. Second, this change has taken place in a social context in which what people want out of work has also shifted. Lastly, significant societal trends have led people to look increasingly to their workplace for things that traditionally they found elsewhere in their lives. Let's look at each of these in turn.

● Healthy pressures turn unhealthy

A complex range of organizational trends has led to employees losing their sense of authentic commitment to their work and to their organizations. At a broad level, a general trend seems to be that many of the initiatives that have driven organizational success in the past have now become counterproductive and are destroying rather than creating meaning.

In the 1980s and 1990s, many sleepy businesses were given a rude awakening by both financial stakeholders and customers, who demanded an improvement in performance. These pressures undoubtedly galvanized organizations and forced them to address the issues that had made them flabby and stodgy. In many cases, however, the low-hanging fruit has already been picked and the pressure is resulting in a lot of turbulence and increasingly frantic efforts to find *something* that will give people at least the hope that performance gains can happen. Given that this pattern is seen inside virtually every significant organization competing for top quartile returns for its sector, a large number of companies are left with a sense that they have failed. Though they may not have met their irrational goals, they might have done quite well by "normal" standards. The result? Morale can start to flag. Fast.

One consequence is that people are increasingly concerned about the true purpose of their company. Regardless of what is said, employees often feel senior executives are only concerned with the share price, their options and how they might look. Even when people feel that their senior executives are motivated in an authentic sense by company goals, many increasingly ask the question of whether driving brand X at the expense of a competitor's brand Y is really what their life should be about.

And then there is the sheer and relentless demand for performance expected of companies by the financial markets. People do not mind being pushed, but they resent striving to achieve stretch goals year after year – certain in the expectation that success will simply be met by a ratcheting up of what is asked of them. They also resent the almost exclusive emphasis that some businesses place on cost-cutting and restructuring as a means of driving financial success. A few cost-cutting and downsizing exercises may be acceptable, but an unending stream is a dysfunctional strategy which saps the confidence and resolve, even of the most committed.

Another trend is that endless mergers and acquisitions have created ever larger companies. Again, this consolidation has, in the past, been extremely effective at driving down costs and rationalizing businesses that overlapped to the point of duplication. However, the prevalence of mergers has made it increasingly difficult for employees to identify with one coherent enterprise. As companies grow, their people become dwarfed in the process. Added to this are the waves of internal change and restructuring resulting from such mergers, prompted in large part by the desire of top management to be seen by external stakeholders to be doing something dramatic. As a result, many initiatives for change, unless fully thought through and well integrated, add to an ongoing sense of confusion and chaos. Worse is the cynicism that may accompany change that moves a business in a diametrically opposite direction to a previous initiative. This occurs more often than one might think! And with leaders coming and going at a fast rate, many workers may not be sure if they themselves are coming or going. In time, they may not care.

It is hardly surprising, therefore, that there is increasing evidence of a plateauing of profit growth in the Anglo-Saxon (US, UK, Australia) economies relative to their European or Asian counterparts, where some of the themes originating in the 1980s and 1990s have still some way to run. For example, over the period mid 2003 to mid 2005 the earnings per share of major companies climbed by 100 per cent in Germany, 50 per cent in France and 70 per cent in Japan, but only 35 per cent in the US, despite the debt-laden boom in America. Stock market performance has followed, with the German DAX up nearly 40 per cent, France's CAC40 up 32 per cent and Japan's Nikkei up 37 per cent, but the US DJIA up only 3.3 per cent over the two-year period. The performance of Britain and Australia is characteristically in the mid-Atlantic range, i.e. between the US and Europe. However, it is in the US, where the 1980s and 1990s themes were first tried out, that they are now reaching the end of the road.

Mind the gap

Over the past five years, the US economy has grown strongly, recording upwards of 3.5 per cent growth on average. You might think that this would mean that the average US employee would be better off over this period. Not so. According to the Bureau of Labour Statistics, median household incomes have declined every year since 1999, leaving people on average 4 per cent worse off after adjusting for inflation.[7] If the gains of economic growth had been distributed equally, median incomes would have been expected to be higher by something close to 20 per cent in real earnings.

People have made up the shortfall by taking on debt amounting to a whopping 35 per cent over the period. This picture is a little better, but not very different, in most industralized countries, with the exception of Japan. What's going on?

One thing is clear: across the developed world, the share of national income taken up by corporate profits has increased dramatically, leaving less of the pie for employees. In the G7 economies, corporate profits as a share of national income are close to an all-time high. According to the Economic Policy Institute, a bigger share of increase of national income in the US is going to corporate profitability than at any time since World War II.[8] For example, close to 60 per cent of the increase in national wealth recently has gone to corporate profits despite the fact that profits only constitute 10 per cent or so of total income. The rise of low-cost providers of labour, especially in Asia, the decline of trade unions and the relentless pressure for increased profitability from the financial markets have all contributed to this relative escalation of corporate profitability at the expense of employee remuneration.

Another thing is also clear: median incomes are down because more of the wages pie is going to people at the very top. The top one per cent of Americans have, since the 1960s, doubled their share of national income from 8 to 15 per cent. In particular, since the 1980s and 1990s, there has been a dizzying growth in the compensation gap between people at the top versus the rest of the organization. While this trend was initially extremely useful in driving and motivating people, it is now having considerable counterproductive cultural consequences. In short, workers don't trust their leaders as they once did or feel that the rewards for improved corporate results are being fairly distributed.

Yet, this is only half the story. When one talks to senior leaders, the most frequent complaints are around the intense pressures that financial stakeholders place on businesses, which increasingly lead to executives being forced into making short-term decisions that they have to publicly embrace enthusiastically, but about which they frequently harbour serious reservations. In addition, CEOs are painfully aware of their limited margin of error and the feeling that things can unravel fast, even if they are going well on the surface. CEOs may be well paid, but we doubt that many sleep particularly well at night.

Despite the fact that life is not easy at the top, it is going to be increasingly difficult for organizations to continue to squeeze the earnings of ordinary employees by boosting salaries at the top, or by increasing the share of national income taken by corporate profits, without something giving. Employees are not statisticians, but they do make mental calculations of what they put in versus what they get out. A repeat of the pattern of the past five years is just not possible without serious physical or psychological desertion on the part of employees.

Having examined some of the factors that are eroding meaning at work, let's move to looking at some significant changes in what people themselves want from their work.

● Work is more important than we think

"*Lieben und arbeit*" (love and work), wrote Sigmund Freud, "are the keys to human happiness."[9] Both are important because they connect people with something beyond themselves. Loving is an important way of connecting oneself to another person. As it was for Freud, work is one of the most important mechanisms for keeping people tied to society and reality. It is easy to lose sight of the important function that work plays in this regard. In the amorphous global society that we live in, there are precious few mechanisms which connect us in a deep and true way to the society around us.

Curiously, another mechanism is probably provided by the entertainment industry – or more specifically, by the stars who inhabit it. Since anonymity is the fate of the majority of people, those who stand out in either entertainment or sport attract inordinate amounts of attention. Other than our immediate acquaintances, they are the only people who have any definition or character in the amorphous social world that we inhabit. We talk about such people endlessly and, in some senses, they form a part of our social fabric. It is this which partly explains why we envy, and put on a pedestal, people whose attributes in many senses are unremarkable.

Work, however, is a more essential mechanism for connecting us to society and a critical component to a happy life. Work gives us a place in the grand scheme of things. The extent to which work provides context, purpose and meaning for people is often overlooked, in large part, because it also services the more basic, transactional function of meeting our cash-flow needs. It is because it meets these more prosaic needs, and because we have little choice other than to work, that we frequently are not aware of the other inner drives that it satisfies.

Freud himself was surprised that, in spite of its importance, work was not more consciously prized by people as a source of happiness. One of his early students, Marie Jahoda, attempted to look at this further by examining, in the 1920s, the town of Marienthal in Germany, where a large number of men had been made unemployed by the closure of a mine.[10] Her haunting descriptions of the listlessness, lack of purpose and loss of self-esteem experienced by these men represents an early documentation of the psychological effects of unemployment. These men had tended to view their work as a means to an end but had not consciously realized the other functions it served. They were confused by the impact that unemployment had on them and at sea in finding alternative ways of meeting their need for engagement.

These days, even though people are more aware of the effects of unemployment, they still underestimate the importance of work for their well-being. Consider the case of an executive who left her job in the media to migrate with her husband to New Zealand. Despite having a fantastic lifestyle and a feeling of euphoria at initially escaping the rat race of London, she found herself experiencing a growing sense of internal frustration whose source she was unable to understand. She started to erupt when small things didn't go right in a way that her children and partner found perplexing. Despite a vibrant social life and a host of hobbies to keep her busy, things didn't feel right. She built up resentment towards her partner and was mystified that at times "he couldn't do anything right". Only later did she realize that it was the lack of a job in New Zealand that was the issue – it made her feel much less central to things than she was used to. Without such an anchor, she felt disconnected from the world around her. She eventually settled down, after taking on a part-time job, but still missed the sense of identity and centrality she experienced when she was fully employed.

All too often unconscious or dimly realized frustrations about work seep into other areas of life. Women who leave work to have children are particularly prone to this misattribution. Often the fractiousness and irritability they experience and direct towards their "particularly difficult" infants or unsupportive husbands is fuelled by the loss of some of the things that work provided for them.

In countless interviews with people who have left the "grind of a job", one thing is clear: unless they replace their work with other projects to give them a sense of purpose, there can be a surprising flatness of mood after the initial euphoria has receded. Even when it is financially possible, just opting out of work is not a viable psychological strategy for most. Even for women who leave to have children, it is less and less viable, as fewer are now prepared or able to gain a sense of identity primarily through looking after their family or vicariously through their husband's work.

The search for meaning

The neuroscientist Wolf Singer reported an interesting finding in the mid 1990s. He had identified a particular pattern of brain waves whose purpose appeared to be to connect different activities within the mind to create a sense of coherence.[11] Specifically, he found that when people perceived something as meaningful, clumps of neurons in disparate parts of the brain mysteriously engaged in synchronized firing in the 40-hertz range for a brief period of time. These high-level oscillations were, for example, seen when a meaningful word was sounded out to people but absent when something meaningless was said. It seems that these 40-hertz oscillations have the key function of making the flood of data hitting our brains meaningful. Interestingly, when people make new insights, there is a jump in the frequency of these "meaning waves". This form of brain activity is very different from the serial firing of neurons associated with other mental activities.

At about the same time, the neurologist V. S. Ramachandran found that when people were asked to think about spiritual matters or areas of life that were highly meaningful to them a particular part of the brain, in the temporal lobes, was activated.[12] In addition, he established that when this area in the brain is artificially stimulated, people experience a strong, overarching sense of connection and unity with the world, as well as a spiritual sense of purpose. For years clinicians had known that patients suffering from temporal lobe epilepsy sometimes experienced an overwhelming sense of spirituality and, at times, grandiose ideas about themselves and their goals, but the new research identified that a deep sense of meaning, purpose and unity could be produced in just about everyone when this particular area was stimulated.

The human brain, it seems, is designed both to work hard to create a sense of coherence and meaning and to respond positively to this sense when it arises. Why? The emerging consensus is that, from an evolutionary point of view, the drive for contextualization and coherence is an essential cognitive tool for dealing with a complex and bewildering environment. The drive for a sense of meaning through positive purpose is also seen to be a significant motor which creates in people a perpetual sense of dissatisfaction and which leads us to break new ground and strive to make something more, not just of ourselves, but also of the world.

The above findings would not have surprised the famed psychoanalyst, Viktor Frankl, who wrote more than fifty years ago that it is people's search for meaning (not pleasure, power, status or wealth) that defines human beings.[13] By this, Frankl meant that people are, in a fundamental sense, motivated to make sense of their lives and to find a purpose that goes beyond thinking about their own basic needs. People want to find answers to the questions: "Why?" and "What for?" Frankl believed that, if they answered these questions, individuals could bear many of the challenges that life would inevitably throw at them.

The manuscript for Frankl's first book on this topic, *The Doctor and the Soul,* was seized by the Nazi authorities as he was taken to a concentration camp. In the unlikely environment of the concentration camp, Frankl truly learned to test his ideas. He found that even in a situation where some of the most fundamental human needs – for security, shelter and food – were left unsatisfied, it was the creation of meaning which helped people survive. Frankl created personal meaning by giving himself the task of "administering mental support to the needy". He encouraged people to focus on the thought that "for everyone, something or someone is waiting". Even for those who believed that they would not survive the camp, he endeavoured to create a sense of meaning by asking them to think about what others, who might be waiting for them, would expect of their behaviour. He also encouraged people to visualize life beyond the camp, what they could learn from the experience and how they could put it to good use. In his book, he encouraged people to reframe their lives by telling them to "think less about what to expect from life but rather ask yourself what life expects of you".

Frankl survived the concentration camp and put his learning to good use by creating a therapy (logo therapy) aimed at overcoming people's psychological problems through focusing on the creation of meaning. A significant aspect of Frankl's thinking is that meaning does not drop down from a blue sky but is rather something which people have to continuously create and recreate in their lives. The creation of meaning is all about how people frame things and contextualize their activities. Frankl is fond of a quotation from one of his patients: "A person who assumes that life must consist of stepping from success to success is like a fool who stands next to a building site and shakes his head because he cannot understand why people dig deep when they set out to build a cathedral."

The psychologist Abraham Maslow took up some of Frankl's theories and developed them further. In his seminal paper on the hierarchy of human needs, Maslow argued that there is a certain set of base needs that people need to satisfy, namely: hunger, security and shelter.[14] However, beyond these, they strive also for companionship and belonging – and, then, ultimately, for self-actualization. It is by satisfying these latter needs that Maslow felt that people generated a sense of true meaning and fulfilment in their lives. Self-actualization, for Maslow, occurred when people connected with the unique aspects of themselves and were able to contribute to society in a distinctive way. Maslow's famous saying applies here: "A musician must make music, an artist must paint, a poet must write; if he is to be ultimately at peace with himself, what a man can be, he must be."[15]

According to Maslow, meaning comes from stretching yourself to be what you can be. It's not about having a quiet time or the right work–life balance. If you ask people for times when they have felt best about themselves, they frequently pick situations in which they were challenged and had to dig deep to find answers. It is also interesting to note that a common feature of many of the *Fortune* best companies to work for is that they are personally stretching and stressful cultures.

It is instructive to apply Maslow's hierarchy of needs to the evolution of values in Western society (especially in terms of work) over the past fifty years or so. Not unnaturally, the decades after World War II were relatively conservative, and a concern for the basics was evident in many societies. People knuckled down to solid, secure jobs that allowed many to aspire to suburban lifestyles and the increasing array of consumer goods that were just becoming available. Robust growth in the 1950s and 1960s, however, quickly enabled people to feel comfortable in terms of their job needs and shopping desires.

In the mid 1960s many of the younger generation started to focus, just as Maslow's theory would predict, on self-actualization.

Culturally the 1960s were perceived as a decade that was much more focused on individuality, acts of personal rebellion, and the desire "to find oneself". To a substantial extent, the oil crisis of the early 1970s and the shock that it gave the global economic system put an end to these themes.

Rampant inflation and unemployment once more pushed people to focus on the basics. Many of the concerns that people had agonized over were simply dumped as they engaged in the Darwinian race for survival in a competitive job market. The 1980s then became the decade of materialism, but in a more individualistic and flamboyant sense than the 1950s had been. From the mid 1990s onwards, however, the success of most Western economies was once again allowing people to think about the kinds of self-actualization concerns that Maslow identified. This has led to people increasingly asking more searching questions of their work and their lives in general.

During the twentieth century, traditional belief systems shaped by institutions such as the church, the hitherto "natural order" of society, and the traditional family were replaced by a confusing array of possible ways of living, and of allegiances. In the midst of all this, the sociologist Anthony Giddens argues that the quest for personal self-fulfilment and personal meaning has become almost the only universally shared value.[16] By way of support, he points to the myriad of self-help books now available.

The evidence that people are increasingly concerned with the issues at the top end of Maslow's hierarchy is all around us. Rock stars doing charity events like "Live Aid" watched by billions; Hollywood stars getting involved in the UN and other political activities; the growth of personal coaching and the self-development industry (as opposed to psychotherapeutics, which was aimed at solving more clinically-oriented problems); the growth of ethical funds; the popularity of environmental movements and anti-globalization sentiments; the reaction against branded goods: all are examples of this.

Is it any wonder we hear questions like these all the time:

- What's it all for?

- Do I believe in what I am doing?

- Is the way that I am operating truly reflective of me?

- Could I be more fulfilled doing something else?

There is a popular view that these concerns keep only the middle classes awake at night. We think this is simply wrong. For example, the rural poor of the twentieth century, whose stories are so movingly told by Ronald Blythe in *Akenfield*, found their work gruelling and felt downtrodden.[17] They looked first, therefore, to right the wrongs of the basic contractual agreements over pay and conditions – rather than to find meaning in their work. Nonetheless, it is interesting that Blythe also comments on the solace and connection they found by singing together as they worked and in the satisfaction of a job well done – the field ploughed to perfection. As the twentieth century progressed and conditions improved, the old industrial and agricultural struggles for enough sustenance were replaced by demands for self-actualization through education and meaningful work for all.

The importance of meaning for employees at all levels is graphically illustrated by the experience of the Australian bank, Westpac. Shifting the external perception of the bank by driving corporate responsibility initiatives had a massive impact on the commitment and pride shown by people on the frontline. According to those on the inside, the impact at lower levels was, if anything, stronger than with more senior executives.

In our experience, questions about meaning have gone from being side issues to taking centre-stage for just about everyone. A graphic illustration of this was provided in one of our programmes for young executives with high potential where we reviewed the companies featured in two seminal business books by Jim Collins, *Built to Last* (with Jerry Porras)[18] and *Good to Great*.[19] When the examples of successful companies featured in both books were presented, one person commented, "I know I should want to, but I just can't get excited by the thought of working for Walt

Disney, Wal-Mart, Gillette, Philip Morris or Wells Fargo." Once this high-potential participant spoke up, it was surprising how many other attendees enthusiastically echoed these feelings. What was interesting was that sheer success, which might have been motivational once, was not enough. All these organizations had clear core values, but again, this was not enough. What was important to the programme attendees was what the company values actually were and how these organizations were perceived by the public – and, most importantly, the direction and value of their social aims. For example, Abbott Laboratories (dedicated to health) was seen as much more attractive than Philip Morris (dedicated to tobacco). However, the most important reaction was the antipathy towards being a cog in the monolithic culture of an organization where the imposition of core values and discipline were key features.

The age of money

These trends in individual motivation have taken place at a time when other social changes have left people looking increasingly to work for things that they traditionally found elsewhere.

The Indian philosopher of history Prabhat Rainjan Sarkar proposes an interesting set of principles for looking at the evolution of societies.[20] Sarkar outlines four stages that he believes all societies go through repeatedly and to which he suggests that the history of most civilizations can be subsumed. This thinking is founded on the idea that there are four basic mental orientations to the world and these create different ages. Each stage is characterized by a preponderance of one of the four types: workers, warriors, thinkers and moneymakers.

The age of chaos is characterized by the rule and preponderance of the workers. It is a stage in society during which laws have broken down, individuals are following their own base instincts and needs and people get away with whatever they can. It is an unsubtle age in which crime is rampant and materialism permeates society. This age typically starts when a ruling class has oppressed ordinary people so much that structures break down and a rebellion occurs.

The age of chaos gives way to the age of the warriors. This occurs when key individuals with a military bent impose order in order to rescue society from the disorder associated with the age of chaos. In the age of warriors, physical prowess and military might are valued and authority becomes extremely centralized. Life is ordered and rules are imposed vigorously. However, while society functions smoothly, people search for something more. The stability provided by law and order means that other more spiritual needs come to the fore.

This gives rise to the age of the thinkers. In this era, religion, philosophy and science thrive. It is a time when intellectual pursuits are valued and enlightenment is sought. Church and religious institutions often predominate, although often indirectly, by manipulating those officially in power. Both the age of warriors and the age of thinkers create conditions for business and commerce to prosper. However, it is in the latter age that individuals who have a propensity for these activities increasingly accumulate wealth and come to the fore. The thinkers are sidelined as the age of money begins.

In this age, money progressively becomes the central value and a reference point by which everyone and everything is judged. However, inequalities increase as the powerful gather more and more wealth in this period. Values become eroded, and there is progressive commercialization of the arts, sports and religion. The rule of law and higher intellectual values are progressively eroded and made subservient to money. Eventually, either the impoverished rebel or society is made vulnerable to an external shock; and, thus, the age of money heads inexorably towards the age of chaos, thereby completing the cycle.

Western civilisation appears to have gone through two turns of the whole cycle over the past two thousand years or so. Europe endured a chaotic and turbulent period following the death of Alexander and the division of the Greek/Macedonian Empire into four units. This turbulence was put to a gradual end by the rise of Rome.

The Roman era and, particularly, the Augustan period for Western civilization is characterized as an age of the warriors. This was a period of strong central government and the rule of law based on Roman military might. Sarkar indicates that such a period is frequently a high point for many civilizations in terms of actual concrete accomplishments.

This age was followed by the rise of Christian values within the West and the progressive influence of spiritual leaders. In this age of the thinkers, the rise of the Church of Rome, and the increasing importance of Christianity across Europe, were significant trends. Eventually, this stage gave way to feudalism, an essentially economic system which can be construed as Europe's first age of money. Increasing inequality and pressures on society created by feudalism are seen to have led to a turbulent and chaotic period for Europe (age of workers), which was only ended with the rise of the nation states based on military force (another age of the warriors). The stability provided by this eventually gave rise to the Renaissance, a considerable period of intellectual and cultural achievement for Western Europe. Eventually, however, this age of thinkers gave way to the capitalist impulse in Western society and to a new age of money.

Despite the obvious dangers of trying to reduce the ebb and flow of human history to a frighteningly small set of concepts, there is a surprising amount of richness and explanatory power in Sarkar's view. My own perspective is that, while all societies go through cycles where a particular theme dominates, different societies have a predilection for some themes over others. Western society is, for example, more oriented to the warrior impulse; Indian society to the religious/thinker orientation and Chinese society to the money making/commercial theme. The complex future interactions that emerge between these three centres of global power will be subtly shaped by these different orientations.

Most people would quickly identify where Western society stands in Sarkar's cycle today. We live in the age of money, but at the latter end of it. Most agree there are some signs of the age of chaos beginning to emerge. Sarkar himself puts both Western and Indian societies in the latter phases of the age of money, with India slightly behind.

Sarkar's views are interesting, because he explicitly identifies some powerful tendencies that help to destroy values and meaning in the age of money. One of these is the short-term preoccupation with money at the expense of other areas of life. This has a corrosive impact on relationships, making many, including familial relationships, transactional. The age of money also destroys institutions associated with other stages. While these decline, the power and influence of business and commercial institutions flourish. However, the money imperative leads to much short-term and opportunistic behaviour on the part of these institutions, as well as rising levels of inequality in society. Eventually, the collapse of core values creates a chaotic free-for-all as people increasingly pursue their individual agendas.

According to Sarkar, a key attribute of the age of money is the decline in the power of historically important institutions and the rise of individualism. There is ample evidence of this occurring. Whether it is commitment to nation states, trade unions, political parties, the church or even the nuclear family – the trend is clear: allegiances are in decline. In the UK, for example, less than two per cent of the population attends church regularly. Even in the US, regarded these days as the centre for revival of religious practices in the Western world, the actual trend in religious affiliation and attendance is downwards – one per cent absolute decline a year. At these rates, US church attendance will start to match the low European levels in just over two decades.[21]

Related to this decline in commitment to institutions has been the growth of more individualistic, ad hoc forms of allegiances. Impromptu pressure groups have taken the place of political parties as the vehicle for affecting change for many young people. The decline in religious affiliation has been replaced by the sprouting of many more individualistic forms of spiritual belief.

People are attracted to Buddhism because it does not seem like an orthodox religion. In the US, the fastest-growing religious group is the Wiccans – more commonly known as Witchcraft – growing at 30 per cent a year.[22] Another fast-rising religion is that of the "Aralians", adherents to which share the view that they are unique and descended from aliens.

Perhaps one of the most unusual expressions of this "individualistic" form of social expression is the rise of the phenomenon known as "flash mobbing". Flash mobs are apparently spontaneous gatherings of people who come together quickly, engage in some collective, often bizarre, behaviour and then equally quickly disperse. They are coordinated through the internet, email and mobile phone technology – informing potential mobbers of precise locations, timings and activities. The world's first flash mob was in New York City in 2003 and was evidently inspired by Howard Reingold's book *Smart Mobs*. Since then they have emerged all over the world, engaged in activities such as: worshipping a fake dinosaur, having massive pillow fights, meeting in a large store and yelling loudly without using the letter "o"!

Recently I was sitting in the office of the CEO of one of Britain's largest companies and he described how he had just seen a large number of people all dressed up as Santa Claus suddenly appear and disappear in a square he had passed. "Have I missed something?" he said, "Isn't Christmas several months away?" We mused about flash mobs and I said: "Now you can see the kinds of people you are going to need to appeal to in your future recruitment." "It's a shame we are not in the mail order gifting business," he replied.

The decline in a sense of belonging and the loss of a sense of responsibility towards others is perhaps what is behind the rise of road rage, shopping trolley rage and a host of other ills, such as "happy slapping" where people are randomly attacked and the pictures transmitted over mobile phones. People, it seems are on edge, missing something and feeling disconnected from the society around them.

A natural consequence of the decline in the importance of institutions that used to help hold society together is that work is now, for many, the only thing that connects them to their wider environment. It plays an even more important role for people today than it ever has done. However, the rise of individualism means that people's relationship with work needs also to change. Like the young, high-potential managers described earlier, fewer and fewer people are willing to be cogs in an institutional machine. People need work more than ever to give them a sense of belonging but they don't want a traditional parent–child relationship with their employer.

Is my company running on empty?

How do you tell if your company is at risk of running on empty? The first point to recognize is that, before you can fix things, you have to openly and honestly face up to the truth. Try answering some of the questions below. If you answer "yes" to one or more, then your company may well be running on empty.

Signs of running on empty

1. Are we having problems retaining talent?
2. Have absenteeism or stress-related illnesses been on the increase?
3. Do things just not happen, despite surface energy and enthusiasm?
4. Have people become more overtly compliant and stopped exercising initiative?
5. Do we have splinter groups who say negative things which are easily dismissed but which could be true?
6. Have we been persistently raising the bar without compensation increasing proportionately?
7. Do we have a culture where people might sit on personal issues or problems?

Standard organizational surveys can frequently create a false sense of complacency in leaders because they don't probe deeply enough. What is needed are richer and more values-oriented surveys, supplemented by in-depth confidential interviews, to flush out what people are truly thinking about their place of work. Wearing the positive corporate uniform is so habitual that employees may need to be jolted into opening up. A variety of tools are available for these types of investigations (see Appendix).

The most important issue here is for leaders to recognize that before asking for the depth of commitment they typically are tempted to demand from their people, they have a responsibility to work hard to understand what their employees are really thinking and wanting themselves. Only in this way can empty, and these days frequently ineffectual, exhortation be translated into a more meaningful call to arms.

Running on empty across countries

Symptoms of running on empty can vary across countries. To illustrate, let's apply the concept to two countries at potentially different ends of the running-on-empty continuum: the US and Australia.

The US exhibits many of the symptoms of running on empty, but at the corporate level there are early signs of some companies trying to fix things. However, international surveys put US corporate employees high up on the list of dissatisfaction with respect to work–life balance.[23] Increasingly long hours, short vacations (by international standards) and resentment about not being rewarded for effort are all taking their toll. The US has also been a trailblazer, if that is the right word, in awarding sharp pay increases to people at the very top of the ladder. As noted on page 50, the US was one of the first to try the interventions that drove success in the 1980s and 1990s. It is not surprising that it is now one of the first to experience the problems associated with these particular interventions running out of road. Indeed, because of this, American companies have also been pioneers with respect to developing Meaning Inc. solutions and it is this which explains some of the improvements in engagement levels that are beginning to be seen in some companies.

Just as with work, there are advantages to be gained from stretching yourself as a nation. While Americans are stretched and, all too often, overstretched by work, their superior engagement scores suggest at least in part that some enjoy the pressure.

Australia is a country that prides itself on having a very healthy attitude to quality of life and to placing work in appropriate perspective. Although hours worked are comparable or even higher when compared to other countries, there is a culture of psychologically keeping work in perspective. In Gallup's international surveys, Australia comes bottom out of all Anglo-Saxon countries in terms of engagement with work, with only 17 per cent being highly engaged, compared to 27 per cent in the US. This can lead to interesting dynamics when the two business cultures collide. One Australian executive described to me how shocked people from his American parent company had been when he told them that to get people to come to business meetings they had to serve beer. The beer was banned for a while but, when the predicted collapse in attendances duly occurred, American bosses had to retract the decision. Talking to another group of executives in Brisbane, I was struck by how much time they spent working out how to extract various benefits, including social trips, from their American parent company.

More broadly, the low population density and excellent climate of Australia combine to provide for many a high-quality lifestyle. Australians call themselves "the lucky country". However, underneath all this there is a darker side. Rates of alcoholism, depression and gambling are high in Australia by Western standards. The suicide rate for men is 20.1 per 100,000 of population, which compares with 10.8 for the UK, a country from which many Australians come and which therefore represents a good point of comparison. One explanation for all this is that being comfortable and having a great lifestyle is just not enough. You also need to stretch yourself to achieve a sense of purpose. Without this, even an idyllic lifestyle can feel meaningless.

In short, while there are dangers of running on empty, if you push yourself too hard and unsustainably, there are also dangers in settling for the good life. Psychologically, both under- and over-engagement with work can be stressful. It is interesting to note in this context that a recent survey of high income individuals across eleven countries found that those from the US and Australia were the most highly stressed, with 66 per cent and 63 per cent reporting being stressed at least several times a week.

Having looked at why meaning at work is increasingly important and why a number of trends, both in the corporate world and in society at large, are combining to erode people's sense of meaning, let's now turn to what can be done and is being done to put things right.

3. Building a Meaning Inc. culture

"I used to think culture was an important part of the game. I now realize it is the whole game."

Lou Gerstner, CEO, IBM (1993–2002)[1]

The Indian city of Amritsar is home to the Golden Temple, the holiest shrine of the Sikh faith. The temple complex, an array of marble buildings, enclosed by vast pools of water, is one of the most hauntingly beautiful sights of India. The central temple, the Harmandir, a brilliant white building with a gold-leafed roof, is famous throughout the world. Opposite the causeway to the temple, however, is a five-storey building that is much less well known, but which is almost as important to the Sikhs – the Akal Takht. When the Sikh Gurus set up the faith, they created two centres of power. The Harmandir, the centre for spiritual power, and the Akal Takht, the centre for temporal or worldly power.

Early in their history the Sikhs learned the hard way that they had to fight for their beliefs and succeed within the harsh reality of the real world to have any chance of their spiritual values taking hold. The Akal Takht became the forum in which they planned their military campaigns and made political or economic decisions. Judgements, for the most part democratically made, at the Akal Takht were expected to be executed efficiently and with discipline. They could only be over-ridden by one institution – the Harmandir.

Ultimately, success and power could only be pursued in the world if it was consistent with the core principles of Sikhism.

This duality – the focused pursuit of results in the real world tempered by a constant awareness of core values – is exactly what Meaning Inc. business cultures look like. They are not *soft*. Indeed, frequently they are aggressive. But they know what they stand for and what the end goals of the enterprise are. Ultimately, these values have the last say. Most businesses have their version of the Akal Takht – rooms where critical business decisions are made and results reviewed. Only a few, however, think about how, in the hurly-burly world of competitive business, they are going to stay true to their values. Even fewer create Harmandirs – formal institutions to ensure that this occurs.

Other features of Sikh culture, in its early phase, illustrate additional Meaning Inc. attributes. It is worth briefly pointing out a few. The Sikh faith was founded in the fifteenth century on the principles of tolerance for other faiths and a fierce spirit of egalitarianism. But the Sikh Gurus did not just talk about these values; they took courageous and ground-breaking decisions to enact them in the real world. Antipathy to the Indian caste system was followed through by insisting that all Sikh males adopt a common surname – Singh – so that their caste could not be identified. While this makes looking up phone numbers in the Punjab directory somewhat challenging, this one act created a strong sense of belonging. This sense was accentuated by creating graphic symbols of adherence which makes Sikhs recognisable the world over. Followers were expected to eat together, violating existing religious taboos, and every Gurdwara (Sikh temple) was charged with the responsibility of providing shelter and food for anyone who came to its door. This was not a light undertaking in an era in which disease and famine were all too common. In fact, enormous kitchens, manned by vast armies of volunteers, had to be created to deliver on this commitment.

A belief in the equal status of women led to the banning of the veil and of "Sati" – a practice whereby women were expected to throw themselves on the funeral pyre of their husbands. Sikhism was the first major religion to allow women to be priests and, by the sixteenth century, a high proportion of posts in the new religion were held by females. To further enhance equality, all Sikh first names were made unisex. You can't tell whether a Sikh is male or female by their first name – something of a surprise given the warrior reputation of the Sikhs. Women played a part in Sikh armies and on occasion military units were led by female generals.

Many of these practices would be considered revolutionary now, let alone at the time at which they were enacted. They created a feeling of being forward-looking, as well as a strong sense of distinctiveness and belonging – all key features of a Meaning Inc. culture. These examples also demonstrate that you have to be bold, courageous, and ground-breaking to truly create a distinctive sense of meaning. Playing safe, the natural instinct for corporate leaders who have painstakingly climbed the corporate ladder, does not cut the mustard.

The early band of Sikhs faced the might and wrath of the Mogul Empire. Few gave them a chance of survival let alone victory. Yet barely two centuries later, the fledgling religion had carved out a giant state covering large tracts of North-West India. Another feature of Meaning Inc. cultures is that people flock to the cause and want to help it. The Sikh banner was carried to the gates of Kabul by a Muslim general – Shaikh Basawan. Hindus filled the ministries of the new nation. When the British encountered the Sikh state in the eighteenth century, they found French, Italian, American, German and even Scottish officers and personnel in its ranks.

History, however, also has a less positive tale to tell. Meaning Inc. cultures are fragile. The Sikhs lost to the British because they lost sight of their values. Caste distinctions began to creep into the community. The rulers became dynastic in their orientation. This led to disunity within a community renowned for vigorous debate, but also for cohesion in the face of external threats. It is worth pointing out also that the Mogul Empire that the Sikhs fought derived its own roots from the strong Meaning Inc. culture of early

Islam. Here, too, power had corrupted early ideals. In business, as elsewhere, the challenge of keeping the Meaning Inc. flame alive is constant. Purpose and value erosion when you are successful are not just likely but virtually inevitable.

The meaning of meaning

Before we talk about how companies can create meaning, let's establish what the word actually means. In dictionaries it is defined variously as "a sense of significance"; "the inner symbolic or true interpretation of a message"; "the purpose of an act"; or "the expression of some underlying intention".

The range of definitions suggests that the term is a hard one to grasp. Writers on meaning have rarely defined it so precisely that everyone in an audience can nod their heads simultaneously when hearing the term. A shared event can be meaningful for one person, less so, if at all, for the person next to them.

Here is a broad, yet precise, definition of the term: essentially the meaning of any word is directly related to the other words it connects with or the external reality to which it relates. It is this sense of connectedness with something that lies at the heart of meaning in a literal sense. We can extend this notion to the psychological experience of meaning. *Meaning is experienced when we are able to connect our thoughts or activities with something else in a way that creates a sense of relevance or context.* This definition has the virtue of being rooted in the concrete way the brain works physically to create meaning. The 40-hertz meaning waves described on page 61 create a sense of coherence by enabling, for brief periods, synchronized neuronal firing of disparate parts of the brain – essentially they connect things that previously were separate in order to create a new concept or to place an event in context.

The experience of meaning can, therefore, be construed as fundamentally arising from connectedness with something else. A strong and powerful sense of meaning is created when, in particular, we are able to connect our activities to something else which is significant and which matters to us. It is this sense of significant connection that lies at the root of activities that creates a psychological sense of meaning.

As a result, meaning arises when we act in such a way as to make a positive and profound difference to the world. Through the act, we become positively connected to our external environment. At a micro level, behaviour can also be meaningful when it has clear consequences and is connected to tangible outcomes that we value. In addition, activities on which historical or wider institutional context can be placed are meaningful because we are able to connect them to a wider whole.

Meaning can also arise when a particular act or behaviour connects us with a true, deeper sense of ourselves. This lies at the heart of meaning through self-actualization; we favour doing what most reflects and connects with our inner core. Meaningful relationships are those that go beyond the mere transactional, in which we are connecting in a deeper way with one or more other people.

In the corporate world, meaning arises when people are able to connect their own and their company's activities to things that matter and are significant to them. Note the fundamentally subjective nature of this definition. No one can prescribe what people do or should find meaningful. One person may find a dull and unrewarding job highly meaningful because of the social connection it brings. Another may find the same job a total turn-off because his or her social needs are met in other ways. Note also the importance of how things are framed and connected for the creation of meaning. The ability to do this either for oneself, or as a leader for others, becomes a key quality in the new world of meaning.

● A model of meaning

Despite the fundamentally subjective nature of meaning, however, in the workplace it can usually be put down to the presence or absence of one or more key dimensions. To pull these themes

Figure 3 ● Ways of creating meaning

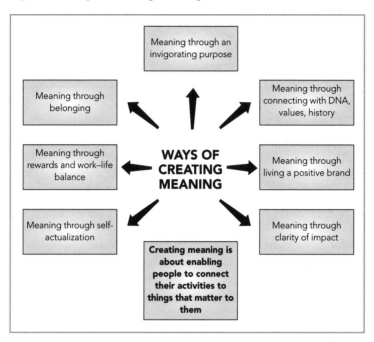

together, we have constructed a model that identifies the main factors that give rise to the experience of meaning at work. This model, outlined above in Figure 3, is by no means definitive, but it does capture the chief areas that signify meaning in an organization.

Below, we will briefly cover the essence of each of these areas. Subsequent chapters will examine each area in order to identify the critical issues, the barriers to success, what has been successfully done and what could be done in the future.

● Meaning through an invigorating purpose

The psychoanalyst Viktor Frankl said that if people can answer the question Why? and buy into it, they can bear much hardship and make sacrifices that would be unthinkable in other circumstances.

A compelling sense of purpose is therefore one of the most important ways of energizing and mobilizing a workforce. But it achieves more than that. When the sense of purpose is broad, or to use Apple's Steve Jobs's term, channelled to "making a dent in the universe", it forces companies to innovate and break the mould.[2] It can also allow companies to make ruthless and difficult decisions that much more palatable. People can accept a great deal if they are believers.

A number of things are clear from the outset. First, most people are not satisfied by the bland and rather generic reasons for existence that constitute most companies' avowed sense of purpose. It is not enough these days for a business to merely have a sense of its core purpose. The purpose needs to be one that ignites passion. Most people yearn for something bigger and bolder. In particular, they want to connect to the key emergent social themes of the day. As one executive put it, "I spend most of my waking hours at work and I have let a lot of my involvement in other things go. If I can't look back and see that my time here has changed the world, I'm wasting it."

A second common complaint is that, even when a company has painted an energizing picture of what it is about, there are real doubts as to whether it is taken seriously. Simply having a purpose statement is not the same as creating meaning through the purpose of your business. Frequently, employees feel the corporate purpose is just a statement on a wall or it is grafted on to a business by an aspirant CEO with little connection to the underlying DNA or reality of a business.

The flip side to this is the incredibly positive reaction that sometimes even small steps in this area can have. Philip Rowley, CEO of AOL Europe, describes how taken aback he was when he described to people initiatives that the company had launched, in association with the NSPCC, to make the internet safe for children. "When I told people at a Christmas party, many were really moved. They said things like 'It's so great' or 'I'm really proud we are doing this.' People have been putting a huge amount of effort entirely voluntarily into this. One guy shaved his head and came to the party as Mr T from the A-Team to raise money."

Similarly, Paul Walsh, CEO of Diageo, the world's largest drinks company, describes how incredibly proud and energized people are by the company's efforts to play a leading role in responsible drinking. He also recalls how a video of what the company had done to help the victims of the Asian tsunami had gone through the business "like wildfire".

This shows that there is a need within organizations which can be ignited sometimes with just the smallest of sparks. Most businesses, however, have only just begun to scratch the surface of what is possible.

The key questions, which are explored in Chapter 5, in this area are:

● What kinds of purpose do people find invigorating these days?

● How can a company construct such a purpose while at the same time remaining connected to the roots of its business?

● Is this equally possible in all sectors?

● How do you give people the sense that the purpose is authentic and drives decision-making?

● What do you do when the purpose conflicts with business reality – are you prepared to make the necessary sacrifices and trade-offs?

● And, how do you connect an overarching sense of purpose with more short- or medium-term goals?

● Meaning through connecting with organizational DNA, values and history

How do you make one person out of the four billion or so souls on the planet feel that their activity matters? Contextualization, contextualization, contextualization. Leaders must help people connect what they are doing to the enduring goals and values of a business and to what has gone before. I may be only one person, but I stand on the shoulders of others and some day others will stand on mine. A sense of continuity and history is a powerful way of creating meaning, but one that most business leaders, keen to make their mark and schooled in the art of change management, frequently simply miss.

These are powerful themes. People almost universally feel that their work activities lack coherence. Many feel they are disembodied actors in a swirling change drama that has no beginning, middle or end. To quote a manager in a large UK-based financial institution: "My work reminds me of the time I was caught in these huge waves when body surfing in Hawaii. I was rolled around until I had no sense of bearing. Every time I managed to stand up, another wave would just crash over me and knock me over. At work it's just the same except the weather is worse and you can't see the beach."

In short, people yearn to place their activities in some sort of context. The power of providing this contextualization is illustrated by the experience of Woolworths in the UK. Robin Mills, the HR director, describes the following:

"When the new CEO, Trevor Bish-Jones, arrived we did a bit of work with the executives on the history and values of Woolworths. There is a guy who has worked with us for about 20 years who is an amateur archivist. I got him to do a video about what it was like to work at Woolworths over the years. In the war we used to set up in markets if the store was bombed. When we first brought in Christmas decorations we bought up the supply for four years so the competition could not compete. There were lots of stories like this. We showed the video to the executive team. When it was finished, there was silence for several minutes. Everyone was thinking, 'what a heritage and now it is our watch'. It was an incredibly unifying experience for the people around the table."

A lack of attention to this area is often why poorly thought-out change initiatives that take a company away from its historical sense of itself create deep unease and, therefore, frequently fail. It is also the reason why surface enthusiasm for change is not always matched by actual results. Understanding the DNA of a business and, in particular, why people joined it in the past is crucial to understanding how change will be received.

The fall and rise of Snapple

The importance of connecting with DNA, values and history can be illustrated by the intriguing example of Snapple, a drinks company now owned by Cadbury Schweppes. Snapple was originally built from its New York home base in the 1970s and 1980s. It was a highly successful company and was eventually sold for $1.7 billion to Quaker Oats in 1994. From the start, the acquisition was a disaster, and sales plummeted. In 1997, alarmed by what was going on, Quaker Oats sold the business to Triarc, an entrepreneurial group sponsored by a set of venture capitalists, for barely a quarter of the price that it had originally paid. Triarc quickly rebuilt Snapple to its former glory and sold it after less than three years to Cadbury Schweppes in a deal worth $1.6 billion.

Jack Belsito was brought in by Triarc to turn Snapple around and is now with Cadbury Schweppes. Talking to him and some of his colleagues provides the inside story on how a company lost touch with what made it successful.

Snapple's original success was founded on the fact that it was a quirky, entrepreneurial and extremely irreverent company that constantly experimented with new methods and routes to market. The company wore its amateurishness as a badge of pride and had a strongly anti-corporate culture. New products were developed and taken to market on a whim. Market research consisted often of talking to one or two customers picked at random. Controversially, the company signed two "shock jocks" from radio shows, one an extreme right-winger and another a bad taste anarchist, to help with its PR.

It's not surprising that the "suits" at Quaker Oats looked at Snapple and thought that if it could do well under this chaotic style of management, what could it achieve under professional management? Dutifully, Quaker Oats imposed a very different business DNA on the company and, in particular, attempted to apply a highly professional model of marketing and distribution, based on its success with another drink company, Gatorade. This time, however, the recipe failed completely.

According to Jack Belsito, this was in no small part because it failed to gel with Snapple's internal culture and what lay at the heart of the brand.

One key mistake was that distribution was moved away from independents to Quaker's own channels. The new distributors had less enthusiasm for the brand than the independents, with whom its spirit of irreverence was a better fit, and who could focus on it more. The meaning of the brand was eroded in the market-place, but more importantly the people working for Snapple quickly began to feel out of synch with the new culture. The DNA of the business, as exemplified by the people, simply switched off or went out of the door.

It was only when ownership passed to Triarc that things began to turn around. On one thing Belsito is clear: they first had to fix some concrete issues like distribution. Then they started recreating the old "anything goes" ways to take the business to a new level of success. Setting the company on the right road was necessary before the cultural meaning levers could be pulled. Eventually, bit by bit, the original approaches to marketing and engaging the public were restored, with tremendous success. Belsito explains: "We had always hired smarter people who wanted to be the underdog, people who could outwit the competition by thinking on their feet." The marketing initiatives started to reflect this DNA. "We sent one guy off to NYC to upgrade our profile there and somehow he persuaded the authorities to turn the Empire State Building yellow for the day while we had our meeting there."

Not surprisingly, Cadbury Schweppes has trodden more gently than Quaker Oats since acquiring Snapple. In any case, Cadbury Schweppes typically gives its operating businesses a high level of autonomy. Its approach seems to be working and this time the acquisition of the business by a large corporate has not eroded Snapple's spirit or results.

What the Snapple story illustrates is the importance of seeing business opportunities and options, even hard-headed ones like acquisitions, through the lens of history. All companies have deeply embedded DNA that defines them and has led to particular people choosing to work for them. These building-blocks cannot be easily changed, nor should they be. This is not to say that companies shouldn't adapt, but they need to do so bearing in mind their core DNA.

The key questions in this area are:

- How can a sense of history and DNA be preserved while driving the changes necessary to keep businesses on edge?

- How can values be intelligently refreshed without losing their core meaning?

- How can executives provide the necessary sense of continuity in a turbulent world?

Relatively few corporate leaders understand, or have the ability to frame, change as part of an ongoing, unfolding history, one that connects today's workers to what has gone before and their corporate legacy. The need for this means that skills such as the ability to set context, tell stories or to be a cultural anthropologist are now coming to the fore. These are not things that conventional, analytically oriented training typically develops in people. The issues involved are dealt with in Chapter 6.

Meaning through living a positive brand

The social psychologist George Herbert Mead argued that we see ourselves principally through the eyes of others.[3] He didn't simply mean that how others see us influences how we see ourselves, but took the extreme position that we are totally dependent on external perceptions for our self-concept. Not all psychologists agree with this position but few would disagree that other people's views shape our self-esteem.

It is clear that since work is a key lens through which others view us, what others think of the organizations for which we work is incredibly important. This brings us directly to the issue of branding and external perceptions. These things matter much more to people than leaders typically recognize. Employees have a deep sense of how their company or even their sector of business is perceived. Recall the Westpac example, when employees stopped wearing their uniforms on public transport because of the reputation of banking in Australia at the time.

Or listen to Katie Selman, a senior brand manager with Green and Black's – an organic chocolate company – talking about why she finds her new company more motivating than her previous big corporate: "For me it's primarily about the brand. I get it. I have converted all the people I know. I love the fact that it is a cutting-edge brand. I love the relationship I have with it. I don't think I could ever now work for a brand which didn't reflect me in some way."

Imagine you are at a dinner party. If your company is mentioned do you experience an internal glow of pride or do you hide behind a wine glass? Or worse, do you rush to express the standard criticisms before anyone else does? Why does this matter? One of the most important things, outside of material rewards, people get out of work is the sense of personal identity it provides. In short, how others see your company influences your own sense of self-esteem and thereby the level of commitment and engagement you feel your employer deserves in return.

Frequently, the connection between meaning and branding is neglected in spite of the obvious truth that, for an external brand to live in the minds of customers, staff have to be aligned with it and act in accordance with it. Doing this also pushes the issue of authentic branding to the fore, as employees are quick to see through efforts at positioning a company with public words that do not resonate with reality. Whatever brand an advertising or marketing company may come up with for a business, its authentic delivery will depend critically on employees buying into the brand theme and believing it so much that they will make it credible for all to witness and believe in too. This leads to the importance of developing brand identity with your employees in mind – a theme that many organizations have failed to embrace. We call this "Inside-Out branding", and explore it in Chapter 7.

Meaning through clarity of impact

However worthy a company's purpose, history or brand, meaning at a local level only happens if people feel that their own activities are achieving something concrete and tangible. You might expect that the relentless pressure for results would provide ample opportunities for people to experience this feeling. But there is a real paradox here. While people feel overworked and under intense pressure to deliver, they also feel a large part of their time is spent on worthless activities that make no difference. Many corporations have more in common with *Alice in Wonderland* than you might think.

While there is often a genuine need for people to collaborate, work in teams and pull together, unless businesses rigorously manage it, an individual's unique contribution can be lost. Moreover, constant reorganizations and restructuring often mean that strategic initiatives fail to be grounded, and this can also lead to a strong sense of lack of impact. The sheer complexity of much of organizational life can make it difficult for people to define their role and contribution clearly.

The demand to look busy and of use to a business means that pseudo-activity moves into the vacuum that is created. One is reminded of the situation created by the two characters in *Waiting for Godot* by Samuel Beckett.[4] As they wait for what turns out later to be the non-arrival of Godot, they busy themselves with tasks that seem necessary but are patently worthless. At one point of reflective insight one says, "We always find something, Didi, eh, to give us the impression that we exist."

Businesses need to help create for people a sense that they are actually making a difference. Creating this clarity, while preserving the sense of collaboration and working across boundaries that is so essential to modern organizational life, is not always easy. All too frequently, well-intentioned initiatives can lead to unanticipated problems.

This can be clearly illustrated in the case of J. Sainsbury, a major UK food retailer that was exceptionally successful in the 1970s and 1980s, but which lost its way from the mid 1990s. Justin King was appointed in 2004 to turn the company around. It quickly became obvious that one of the things that had led to the company's decline was the disempowerment of store managers.

When Sainsbury's had flourished, the store managers had enjoyed high levels of responsibility and accountability. Various well-intentioned initiatives, such as the creation of a new centrally driven supply system and the establishment of strong functional control from head office, led to a palpable sense of disempowerment among store managers, who felt their roles had, to some extent, become meaningless. Reacting to the decline in commitment of store managers, the head office progressively put in place measures of their performance. By the time King arrived, store managers were being assessed and monitored on a plethora of different measures, to the extent that they felt they couldn't move without contravening the controls that had been placed on them.

This was graphically illustrated early on at meetings with store managers that King conducted on arrival. He had asked me to come and watch some of these meetings. After the gathering had finished, and while waiting for the next one, we reflected on the fact that the questions had seemed open and suggested a real spirit of independent thinking – something we had not been led to expect. At this point King noticed a typed sheet that one of the managers had left behind by mistake. On it were all the questions he had been asked, as well as instructions on who should ask them. The whole thing had been scripted by the senior management and the store managers had gone along with the charade because being micro-managed was what they now expected.

Not surprisingly, after experiences like this, King quickly moved to reduce and sharpen the head office and give power back to the stores. His moves have had a palpable impact on the motivation of managers and their sense of responsibility and accountability for what happens "on their watch" – one of the new leadership themes within the business. The impact of all this on performance is also clear – the business has started to regain market share after 15 years of decline.

A key question in this area is: How does one create focused clarity without sacrificing the cost efficiencies, cross-functional collaboration and consistency required in modern organizations?

A second question is: How do you make people accountable and focus on activities that add value without measurement getting out of hand? In particular, how can a sense of achievement be given to people in businesses where all too often the focus is on intangible, knowledge-based outputs? These tricky issues are explored in Chapter 8.

Meaning through self-actualization

The noted psychologist Martin Seligman, who became famous in the 1970s and 1980s for his work on depression, surprised the American Psychology Association, of which he was President at the time, by announcing that he felt the discipline had effectively been heading in the wrong direction for the past fifty years.[5] It had focused almost exclusively on people's problems and weaknesses rather than their strengths and on what made people happy. This was of greater relevance to the world than a negative preoccupation with pathology. Thus was born positive psychology – a movement that seeks to redress the balance. A key early finding was that happiness at the highest levels arose from people living meaningful lives in which they felt they were accessing their unique strengths.

At YSC we arrived at a similar point through a completely different route. A while back one of our clients John Dunn, at that time head of management and organizational development for Guinness, got into a conversation with us about the difference between people who were reasonably successful versus those who were exceptionally so. He had a view, based on previous experience, that highly successful people were not always well-rounded characters. In fact, he felt they were often decidedly weird. We decided to look more closely at this.

It is relatively easy to establish the kinds of attributes that make people do reasonably well in organizations – this is the standard stuff found in most leadership competency frameworks. But what does it take to be brilliant? We identified the most brilliant people we could think of, from all the thousands of managers we had seen, and started looking for themes.

While some common attributes did emerge, an overwhelming conclusion was that these people were all different, but all were unusual in some way. Some were almost pathologically obsessive and detail-oriented, while others were brilliant conceptualizers who would forget their secretary's name. Some were brilliant at connecting with people while others were painfully shy. But all were quirky and had at least one towering area of strength which made them distinctive in some way. More often than not this towering strength was associated with equally glaring weaknesses – which the more self-aware among them recognized and compensated for by putting complementary people around them. These observations led us to develop our "spike" model of top leadership (see page 113), which focuses on helping leaders identify and make Olympian their distinctive strengths while recognizing areas in which they need support.

This focus on strengths ties in with an important change in people's motivations that has been visible across organizations over recent years. There has been a sharp increase in the desire to assert one's individual identity and to be recognized for one's distinctive attributes. This shift is perhaps one of the most significant challenges facing large corporations, no matter how successful they are. It is the reason the idea of working for some of the most iconic, successful companies elicits, at best, ambivalent reactions. As many recruiters now tell us, the sheer cultural strength and clarity of values in these gigantic organizations can in fact be a turn-off for many people, who prefer to work for a smaller, messier and more chaotic business, where they can be themselves.

Most organizations have competency frameworks or other guidelines for defining the behaviours they value and the kinds of people they require. Used wrongly, these can easily be construed as dictating the psychological uniform all employees are required to wear. Driven too hard, such frameworks can create a feeling of stifling conformity that people are increasingly fighting against.

We will describe later how some businesses have recognized this and endeavoured to embed the notion of unique talents and individual spikes in the way they think about people and utilize their capabilities.

A key concern in this area is how one creates a sense of individuality while preserving the discipline and sense of cultural consistency that is also important for driving performance. How can you let creativity and individual initiative flourish without creating chaos. Another issue is how, in flat organizations, can people be given the sense of individual growth and development that is so important to their self-actualization. One of the most important complaints we hear from people is that their work is no longer stretching them or developing them, however intensely they may be working or driving performance. In our experience, while many businesses recognize the need to move their cultures to focus more on people's strengths, most experience difficulties in translating such ideas into action. These issues are dealt with in Chapter 9.

Meaning through belonging

The UK retailer Philip Green famously remarked that successful companies have parties and unsuccessful ones have meetings. This sentiment is not surprising coming from someone who has spent millions of pounds on his own toga-clad birthday celebrations. Richard Branson of Virgin would agree. Celebrations and partying are a crucial part of Virgin's company spirit.

A neglected side-effect of much organizational change is the disruption that it causes to the social bonds between people. The frequency with which people now move between companies and the relentless pursuit of organizational restructuring have also had a profound impact on this dimension of working life. The competitive nature of business leads to the fear that, if someone else in your workplace does not lose his or her job, then you might end up losing yours. Needless to say, this creates an unhealthy dynamic between workers in many organizations. Employees, and indeed many leaders, learn to deliberately distance themselves from their colleagues because they know that there may be difficult decisions and tough conversations on the way. Relationships can, in such circumstances, become transactional and superficial at best, distrustful at worst. Large numbers of people confide to us that they feel less and less able to be themselves at work.

In fact, surveys now routinely report extremely low levels of trust between colleagues. The Harris Interactive survey mentioned in Chapter 2 found that only 15 per cent of employees felt they worked in a high-trust environment.[6] In addition, David Guest's surveys since 1996 for the CIPD also report low levels of trust and even more worryingly, a steep decline over the past few years.[7]

A company must balance its determination to provide this sense of belonging without sacrificing the drive to promote talent or the capacity to make appropriate structural changes in response to business performance. For example, the options available to Tata in India – given the low wages in the Indian economy that allow it to keep workers through difficult periods or to give them pensions for life – just aren't realistic in other countries. However, when contemplating options or planning change, most executives fail to take into account the impact of their decisions on the sense of belonging among staff and the very real knock that their actions can have on performance.

Some companies do show an awareness of the importance of the social dimension for their success. Southwest Airlines, one of the most successful airlines in the viciously competitive US market, has pioneered a dynamic and fun culture which is high on commitment. The company explicitly encourages employees to bring family members into the firm because of the loyalty and commitment that this creates.[8]

The key questions in this area, which are dealt with in Chapter 10, are:

● How do companies create the sense of belonging in a world where people increasingly move around both within and between companies?

- How can this sense co-exist with the need to drive professional, meritocratic standards where people are dealt with objectively?

- And lastly, how do you create trust in a corporate world that has become less secure and more interpersonally competitive?

Meaning through rewards and work–life balance

It is wrong to glibly say that financial rewards or other tangible benefits cannot in themselves be important in creating a sense of meaning at work. Like it or not, in the age of money, what one earns is one of the most tangible manifestations of one's success in the game of life. This is meaningful – for some. Investment banks, for example, create extremely high levels of commitment by playing to this sense of meaning. Similarly, working in a soulless job can be highly meaningful if it helps people (through a big cheque) give their children the best opportunities in life. Rewards, therefore, are meaningful but generally not in and of themselves; they are much more meaningful when they connect with other things that a worker values.

A key issue is the balance that individuals perceive between inputs and outputs. As we argued earlier, over the past five years employees have put in more than they have got out. Quite simply, the average employee just has not benefited very much from the growth in productivity and profitability of their organization, and they know it. Until recently, there was a degree of psychological acceptance of this, in part because many ambitious employees kept themselves going by the prospect of hitting the compensation jackpot associated with the most senior roles. In recent years, however, we have seen a keener sense of reality set in – many have found out the hard way that the pyramid narrows sharply at the top and that career progression is not as automatic as it once seemed. To quote a senior executive in a global FMCG (fast moving consumer goods) business: "I don't accept that I should wait for the big prize at the end. These days you are just as likely to find the job you want has disappeared or been given to an outsider."

But it's not just what people get in tangible terms that counts. Positioning of rewards is key. One way to look at this is via real pay and token pay. People's capacity to use rewards to achieve goals that are meaningful is lowered if they see their compensation as merely collecting the tokens. Think about the investment banker who plans to build considerable wealth in order to launch a business venture, one that excites great personal passion. Such a banker experiences a much greater sense of engagement and meaning at work than someone who is just letting the money pile up without a compelling purpose. Most businesses do not think particularly deeply about how to develop programmes of reward that accentuate people's sense of meaning. And very few businesses help people develop the best strategies for maximizing the psychological value of hard-earned rewards.

Our interviews suggest that work–life balance is one of the biggest issues for people at work and also one of the most important criteria for young people when making career choices. This is confirmed by just about every survey on attitudes to work. But, a deeper examination of this concept reveals subtle differences in what people actually understand by work–life balance. Some want clear boundaries and to ensure that work does not filter into all areas of their lives. Others, including an increasing number of young people, are prepared to work intensely hard provided they get paid accordingly, and then have the option of doing something else afterwards. Both these seemingly contradictory attitudes are variants on a theme. People want to draw boundaries around their work either on a day-to-day basis or over a lifetime.

One of the reasons why work–life balance is such an issue in the first place is the fact that much of the time people spend at work is not as meaningful as it could be. It is one thing to be stressed-out and busy (that's bound to happen almost anywhere), while feeling that you are making a positive difference. It's quite another thing to be stressed-out and busy doing (what you feel) is meaningless work.

People are capable of extraordinary effort, even over sustained periods, when they are involved in an enterprise that engages their emotions. In such situations they may feel that their work–life balance is quite good, even though they are working very hard.

Meaning Inc. companies strive to make people feel special and show creativity in how they package rewards for people and help them achieve the right balances. In return, they get exceptionally high levels of commitment.

Genentech, a company with an exemplary reputation for looking after people (see pages 18–19), allows individuals to spend significant time on discretionary projects. Google does the same, allowing people to spend 20 per cent of their time on discretionary activity they think will add value to the business. Many of these companies' most innovative projects are first incubated during this free time. Genentech also gives people paid sabbaticals. A service called Lifeworks helps hard-pressed, often dual-income, family executives sort out a myriad of domestic issues ranging from finding nannies to dry-cleaning. Child care facilities are provided next to the offices and there is a concierge service at hand. Flexibility is paramount, and people are allowed to structure their time as they see fit. No wonder Genentech gets awards for being one of the best places for working mothers.

W. L. Gore, which also wins many awards for its treatment of employees, goes one step further – people don't have explicit roles or job descriptions at all, rather they are asked to do whatever they think will add value.

A key question in this area is how can organizations package rewards and help their people extract the most current and future psychological value out of them, while also protecting the interests of the business? Meaning Inc. companies are good at creatively developing win–win scenarios. In the future, genuinely addressing the increasingly burning issue of work–life balance is likely to be of considerable competitive advantage. These issues are tackled in Chapter 11.

● Diagnosing your meaning needs

Try applying the meaning model in Figure 3 on page 81 to your company or the part of it which you run or in which you work. It is a quick way of identifying the areas where you do or do not have a shortfall of meaning. As a check on your own views, give the model to others to fill in. You can also apply the model to yourself. Rate yourself on the seven dimensions and then perhaps get someone who knows you well or your partner to give you an external perspective. A variety of tools are available to do this (see Appendix).

One of the most useful ways of applying the above model is to consider whether significant change initiatives increase or decrease meaning in each of the areas outlined above. Simply asking these questions is enough to shelve many change initiatives; or at least to reconfigure them in a more meaning-oriented way. The specific questions that need to be considered are set out below.

- ● Can the objectives of the change be clearly linked to the achievement of the core purpose? Has this linkage been explained to people?

- ● Does the change build on other initiatives or is it disconnected from them in a way people might find confusing? Have we done enough to tell the story of change?

- ● Does the initiative positively or negatively affect the company's external image and therefore the sense of pride experienced by employees?

- ● Does the change make it easier or more difficult for people to experience a sense of personal responsibility or impact? Are significant numbers of people empowered or disenfranchised by the change?

- ● Have we involved people at all levels and given them the opportunity to contribute and experience a sense of personal growth either when envisaging the change or in driving its implementation?

- Have we clearly articulated the personal benefits of change for people or are we just asking them to embrace it with no discernible rewards?

- Will the changes enhance or damage personal bonds either within the business or people's dealings with customers? Will it increase or decrease trust levels in the organization?

This meaning filter cannot be applied only to significant initiatives it can also be applied on a day-to-day basis to any significant interventions that you make. Checking up all initiatives in this way can be wearing, but getting into the habit of seeing everything through the meaning lens is one of the most important things leaders can do for their business.

Of course, creating meaning is not just a challenge for people at the top of companies but for employees at all levels. One of the most common reasons that leaders give for not moving in a Meaning Inc. direction is the fact that, unless they are CEOs, they don't have the licence to do so. However, creating meaning is not impossible on a local basis, even in situations where senior leadership are not sympathetic. Remember, Viktor Frankl was able to do it for both himself and others at a concentration camp. A unit within the business can set itself the mission of changing the views of the leadership of a company by setting a particular example. Within their own units, leaders can package and sell change in a way that is meaningful given the local context. In addition, a strong sense of belonging can be created even in an environment that is ambivalent or hostile to what a group is endeavouring to accomplish.

While it is relatively easy to identify ways of creating meaning, true success comes from the subtlety with which these areas are handled. There are frequently a host of contradictory balances that need to be managed and some real challenges in distinguishing between authentic responses and merely convincing yourself that you are doing the right thing. In addition, a critical issue is the room leaders create for others to frame their own sense of meaning as opposed to imposing their own biases. At one extreme this means recognizing that some may not want a meaningful relationship with their work at all or, more accurately, that meaning may arise for some by keeping work in its place, collecting the cheque and focusing on other areas. Such individuals may find much of what we have talked about irritating or plain intrusive. As with a lot of life, the devil is in the detail and in tailoring things according to people and context.

The meaning challenge does, however, change what is required of leaders. Suddenly qualities like reflection, the ability to frame and contextualize and an interest in history and wider social trends become important. The ability to tell stories, to use one's intellect to simplify the world, and to put oneself in the shoes of others also become key. The meaning challenge also forces leaders to understand what drives themselves at a deep level and to create the conditions for other leaders to flourish. Before looking at the practical steps that businesses can take, let's first look at the challenges that creating meaning gives rise to for leaders.

4. Meaning Inc. leadership

"It's hard to lead a cavalry charge if you think you look funny on a horse."

Adlai Ewing Stevenson II, American politician and statesman

Think of the challenges facing the business world that we have examined. Think of the shifts in what people want from their work, the increasing difficulty of achieving results and traction, the speed with which business performance can rise and fall, demanding consumers, aggressive and fast-moving competitors and the lack of trust in corporations – created in part by the extraordinary and in some cases obscene temptations of wealth available to business leaders. Clearly, it would seem we need superheroes rather than mere leaders.

Yet leadership is, of course, a well-trodden path. There are countless models circulating in the business world that claim to provide the blueprint for success for those at the helm. Over the years, more and more has been added to the bucket of what is required for greatness. Yet nobody has bothered to take much out of the bucket, so it has just got heavier and heavier. Indeed, leaders are now weighed down by a profusion of frequently contradictory advice and expectations in a plethora of areas. Many sit uncomfortably and leadenly on their leadership horses, pretending to be something they are not.

We admit that we are not altogether blameless. YSC has not always been innocent in adding to the leadership burden. A while back when we researched and presented a leadership model for Guinness, John Dunn, management and organizational director exclaimed: "This is an extremely rich and comprehensive model. Are our leaders expected to walk on water as well?"

In fact, Steve Jobs did turn up to a Christmas party, during his first ascendancy at Apple, dressed as Jesus Christ. Jobs is a talented man whose distinctiveness is embedded in his ultimate goal of "making a dent in the universe", but he is by no means a water walker. If the many accounts circulating about his style at that time are to be believed, he was a highly controlling individual, who badgered people and was incredibly critical. He could destabilize the organization and had a reputation for erupting in anger if he didn't like the answers people gave him. According to the authors of *iCon*, people stopped going into lifts at Apple in case they met him because of his reputation for putting people on the spot.[1] Employees didn't know if they were going to emerge from the lift with or without a job.

In short, if a multi-dimensional leadership capability framework were applied to Jobs he would flunk miserably. This is because he is a leader who possesses incredible and distinctive strengths and, correspondingly, some incredible and distinctive limitations. This is central to the notion of "spike" – towering areas of strength applied in an intense way are immeasurably more powerful than scoring reasonably well across a range of leadership dimensions. The catch is that spikes always create downsides for the individuals who possess them and these need to be managed carefully. Like him or loathe him, Jobs's impact is underpinned by the fact that he is always being true to his spikes – he is always being authentically himself and therefore sitting naturally on his leadership horse.

Jobs's spike is his inexorable courage and charisma. He possesses a relentless desire to make an impact, not just to the world, but to the universe. At the heart of this core sense of purpose is his focus on the fundamental question of "Why?" He has the capacity to create intense focus, for himself and others, around the point of it all and the reason why his people are working in the first place. It would be fair to say that Jobs, phase one, was not a Meaning Inc. leader. However, by phase two of his Apple career, the arrogance that dominated his early style had been replaced by a strong emphasis on the team and, overall, a much more humanistic approach. He focused far less on being the leadership Messiah and much more on giving others room to contribute and shine – a key feature of something we call the *Good Enough* mindset. As we have seen, these characteristics have enabled Jobs to create meaning for employees, to revolutionize three different industries and to change people's lives across the globe.

At the core of meaning-led organizations is the question of what type of leader is required to create environments where individuals find a sense of meaning. For us, the attributes of such a leader include their ability to focus on the why of organizational existence, a Good Enough mindset, a distinctive meaning-making spike which they harness in an intense manner, the key qualities of creativity, coherence, compassion and courage, and a deep insight into themselves and others.

In this chapter we elaborate on the approach, mindset and qualities required of Meaning Inc. leaders, discuss how such potential leaders can be developed and share examples of people we have worked with to achieve this. As part of our exploration into what makes for Meaning Inc. leadership, we deliberately identified leaders operating at a variety of levels of seniority to illustrate that meaning can, and should, be created throughout an organization. Indeed, creating meaning is not just the responsibility of the CEO, but of every leader.

Tell me why?

The most powerful distinguishing feature of Meaning Inc. leaders is their focus on the question of why: Why are we here? Why are we doing this? Why should we embrace this project, change initiative or target? Why should we work together in this way or provide service in that way? Why should we be energized by any of it? Looking back at the approach leaders have adopted over the past 40 years in the West, we see three distinct periods:

1 **The What:** During the 1960s and 1970s, the grooming of leaders fundamentally lay in the arena of transferring skills and knowledge. MBA programmes became the focal point for the development of leaders in the Western world, manifested in models such as the Boston Consulting Group's Growth Matrix, Porter's work on competitive advantage and McKinsey's 7S model, to name just a few. Great leadership was about having the answers and steering the organization towards success.

2 **The How:** During the 1980s and early 1990s, the focus of leadership tilted towards people rather than facts. Peter Senge's book, *The Fifth Discipline,* spearheaded the thinking about how leaders could develop their employees' abilities to learn and adapt in a rapidly changing environment.[2] The best business leaders were seen as fantastic coaches, able to define what "great" looked like for their direct reports and coach them towards brilliant performance.

3 **The Why:** From the late 1990s to the present day, the focus on leadership has been on the why. If historically leaders needed to understand the dynamics of the business as well as have the insight and skill to get the best out of people, the leaders of today need to set a context for people that allows them to anchor their activities to something meaningful. Today's leaders need a way of mobilizing people, moving out of the way and letting others get on with it. People don't want to be told what to do, but rather, to be given scope to exercise their own judgement and creativity.

Each of these periods has built on the one preceding it. Today's Meaning Inc. leaders can't neglect the "what" and the "how", but they do need to focus more and more of their energies on defining and redefining the "why". Many leaders think that if they have explained the "why" once, people will remember it. However, experience shows they need to reaffirm the meaning context constantly as events develop. As Viktor Frankl said: "If people know why, then they can endure all sorts of barriers and hardships."[3]

Knowing your song

John Bines, who was group marketing director at insurance broker AXA UK when we first started working with him, is someone whose leadership style aptly reflects this strong "why" orientation. An understated yet challenging approach, coupled with integrity and humility, despite his exceptional intellectual and interpersonal capabilities, were hallmarks of his style. His whole ethos was underpinned by a real eagerness to ensure that time was spent productively and wasted effort was minimized. He worked to ensure that any activity undertaken within his area was anchored in a clear supporting rationale. He would regularly ask his people why they had embarked on a particular direction, why they were calling a meeting or why they were hoping to solve a particular problem. In fact, his own managers were surprised by how often he would insist that they ask this of their people. His approach did create some frustration for his team and colleagues, not least of all because they couldn't always provide a robust and defensible answer for him. Some would exclaim, "What do you mean – why?" However, the marketing function was one of the most productive and focused in the business.

Through his coaching relationship with us, one of the things John began working on was trying to provide a stronger why *context* for others rather than simply asking them the question. He believed that his approach was right, even if it could be disorienting for people, but wanted to facilitate a why orientation in others more effectively. We helped him to frame the "why" case more clearly for others and articulate what they were really hoping to achieve in the first place.

John's focus on the "why" also led him to ask himself quite deeply about the point of it all and what meaning there was for him at work. In fact, after much deliberation, he decided to leave the corporate world and he joined Save the Children as its UK fund manager – a decision he has never regretted, despite the sacrifices he had to make around salary and benefits, on top of the expense that goes with raising a houseful of four children.

If leaders are to effectively provide a strong "why" context, they first need to be absolutely sure they have clarified it for themselves. In the words of Bob Dylan, "But I'll know my song well before I start singin'."[4] The truth is that many leaders do not allow themselves sufficient time and scope to clarify their song and genuinely explore the "why". The easy and obvious answers are there: building wealth, getting promoted, beating the competition, increasing revenues – but these are not the answers that people want or need. They are not the answers that will engage people in their work in a meaningful way.

The "why" approach focuses on the fundamental things that leaders need to do and achieve when they lead. Let's now look at the mindset which is required to enable this:

● The Meaning Inc. mindset – good enough is good enough

Many leaders have an obsessive, disciplinarian mindset oriented around execution. While this can drive results, at least in the short term, it undoubtedly crowds out the meaning agenda. Indeed, the default setting for many leaders when the going gets tough is to grasp the levers themselves and make the decisions. However, this ends up shrinking other people and making them feel less of themselves. The Good Enough mindset, on the other hand, is one of empowerment and facilitation rather than control. Instead of a laissez-faire orientation, Good Enough is about respect and humility. It is a subtle yet powerful concept. Critically, Good Enough is as much an underlying attitude as it is a set of behaviours.

Many managers and organizations struggle with the unhappy results of leadership behaviours that are perfectionist, obsessive and striving. Such behaviours often lead to exhausted and disempowered staff and cultures that discourage freedom of responsibility and personal development. Yet, some people enjoy working with this sort of leader because it means they don't have to think for themselves. Good Enough leadership, on the other hand, both expects and fosters individual responsibility.

One of our consultants recently observed the former CEO of a client sitting in an airport lounge. Like many men used to power but now without it, he seemed somehow shrunken. A man of great integrity and intellect, he had been passionate about the company and run it with a firm, parental hand for many years before being ignominiously sacked as it failed to respond to new market conditions. It emerged, as we started to work with the new CEO, that his predecessor, clearly with the best of intentions, had in many ways failed as a leader. Like an over-anxious, obsessive parent he had insisted on taking responsibility for all decisions. No one knew the company better than him. No one was more committed. It was not good enough for him to be good enough; like a benign dictator he needed to be omniscient and to be seen as the ultimate custodian of the business's values and mission. Publicly, he was the voice of the company. Talented people drifted off or resigned themselves to a lack of any meaningful influence. The company got lazy; people knew they could hide behind their managers. Decisions got endlessly passed upwards into a byzantine maze of procedures and policies which queued patiently for his attention. Meaning was not alive and co-created, but ossified and stale. People had almost lost the capacity for independent thought and action.

A Good Enough mindset doesn't require heroes or water walking. It requires leaders who are very, very human. By which, of course, we mean flawed, awkward, anxious at times, doing their best, capable of great moments of brilliance and compassion but also of stupidity and mean-spiritedness. It requires people who can accept the great strengths as well as the imperfections of the human spirit. Being Good Enough means providing the platform for rather than the answers to the range of meaning needs their people have. It is about creating space for people to grow and develop independently and to create meaning for themselves rather than being told what their meaning should be. This constitutes a shift away from a heroic, egocentric perspective of leadership where the leader achieves success to one which recognizes that all the leader can do is create an environment within which others can connect to things that matter to them.

Good Enough leaders also show a heightened sensitivity to the needs of others. It is this that lies at the heart of their ability to create authentic organizations that meet their people's needs for meaning in a way that is energizing but not overwhelming. A few lucky people have this talent naturally; most of us have to work pretty hard at it.

The Good Enough approach is derived from Donald Winnicott's notion of Good Enough mothering. Winnicott is often considered the most significant British psychoanalyst of the twentieth century. He is admired for the profound, subtle and often poetic insights he has brought to the question of human development and, in particular, the relationship between mother and child.[5] The question of "Whose meaning is it?" was something that Winnicott was particularly interested in exploring in his work with children and mothers. For Winnicott, one of the mother's central skills is her ability to provide a "facilitating environment" for the child's true self to survive and flourish. Indeed, several of his concepts – the "good enough mother", the "true and false self" and the "facilitating environment" – are particularly relevant to anyone who is either a leader or trying to support others' leadership.

Their relevance to the issue of meaning in business is that they help to illustrate and define a kind of fundamental underlying attitude that the very best leaders usually demonstrate. This is revealed in their appreciation of the complexity and messiness of human behaviour, in their recognition of the need to tolerate failure and error, in their acceptance of the peculiar narcissistic burden of leadership – the need to accept others' often unconscious and primitive desire to be led without being corrupted by those desires. It is revealed, above all, in their recognition that leadership, just like parenting, has a strong teaching component; and that good leaders – like parents or teachers – need to gain an accurate understanding of their pupils' psychology if they are to help them achieve their creative potential.

One of Winnicott's key insights was that parents who try too hard to be perfect end up squeezing the life and joy out of their children. Leaders need to recognize this too. Indeed, the corporate landscape is littered with the corpses or walking wounded of organizations that were led forcefully, that possessed supposedly strong and robust cultures, but whose culture and processes have proven hopelessly rigid and unable to adapt to a changed external environment.

As an Edwardian, Winnicott did not have much to say about fathers, but it is reasonable to assume that if he were alive today he would recognize the Good Enough parenting skills of fathers too. It is relatively straightforward to see the link between parenting skills and leadership, as illustrated in Table 4 overleaf.

Not surprisingly, perhaps, given that Winnicott was concentrating on mothering behaviour, the Good Enough characteristics have a strong feminine tone. Many of our clients have recognized this implicitly, if not explicitly, and are investing considerable amounts of money into educating their managers to be less controlling and competitive with each other, and instead more facilitative, self-aware, creative, collaborative, and nurturing. This can be difficult to achieve, but they are doing this because they recognize that these qualities do liberate people to achieve and that without them, the businesses they run may not be sustainable.

When you walk into a business run on Good Enough principles you can instantly tell. People are energized, care about how they can add value and feel trusted to take creative responsibility for their actions. Like well-adapted, well-adjusted children, they are authentically themselves and able therefore to be authentic with each other, their customers and their suppliers. Meaning in these organizations is not locked away in a presentation. It is not a sterile list of financial targets nor is it the private fiefdom of leaders. It is something alive and shared, something that belongs to everyone and that is being continuously brought into being by the thoughts, feeling and actions of everyone engaged in the great task of helping their enterprise succeed.

Table 4 ● Good Enough parents and Good Enough leaders

Characteristics of the Good Enough parent	Characteristics of the Good Enough leader
Willingness and ability to tolerate her child's destructive impulses and his attacks on her	Ability to process multiple conflicting agendas effectively
Ability to hold up a mirror to the child so that he can make sense of his own behaviour and learn from it	Feedback and coaching orientation towards others
Ability to be resilient in a robust but non-retaliatory, non-rejecting way	Firm but fair. Maturity to tolerate others' experimentation and failure without rejecting them
The children of Good Enough parents are more likely to...	The colleagues and organizations of Good Enough leaders are more likely to...
Grow and exist in a playful, spontaneous manner – developing what Winnicott called "creative originality"	Have the confidence and courage to explore possibilities and develop their full potential
Develop an appropriate sense of their own power	Be realistically confident and authoritative – neither meek nor arrogant
Stay in touch with their true selves	Be and feel authentic. Feel their personal lives are in line with their professional lives
Have a more grounded sense of reality	Have the confidence to face up to the real world

For this to happen – like the parents who choose ultimately to put their child's interests before their own – leaders need an attitude of mind that has at its heart an absolute commitment to serving the capacity for creative growth of their colleagues and followers. To achieve this, leaders need to cultivate their own playfulness, mindfulness and humility. The Good Enough leader understands, above all, the complexity of organizational life and the limits of what he or she is able to achieve on his or her own, as well as the importance of creating the conditions in which individuals can flourish and then trusting them to use their freedom wisely.

The Good Enough leader – an example

Archie Norman, ex-CEO of Asda, is a classic example of a Good Enough leader. Norman went to Asda, a leading British food retailer, in the early 1990s when the business was in serious trouble. The challenge was something of a poisoned chalice and Norman showed great courage or foresight, depending on your view, in taking it on. In the following years, through a mixture of strategic realignment, focus on the basics and, most importantly, the implementation of a creative and values-driven leadership and cultural change, Norman and his team not only saved the business but turned it into a roaring success – it was perhaps the biggest turnaround story in British business over the decade.

We got to know Norman well through working with him at Kingfisher, the home improvement retailer, at Asda, and also at the technology-driven communications company Energis. He possesses a forensic intellect, a real capacity to see the world as it is, as well as enormous drive. He is also a highly principled and values-driven individual; straightforward and direct in his approach. With these strengths, which had in the past allowed him to achieve enormous success at McKinsey and Kingfisher, it would have been natural for Norman to take the reins emphatically and drive the changes that Asda needed in a highly controlling manner. However, he resisted this temptation. Knowing that his own core strengths around bringing strategic clarity and imaginative thinking to a business were not necessarily going to be enough to engage a diverse population, he brought in Allan Leighton – a real man of the people. Leighton's approach was much more focused on building strong relationships, energizing, encouraging and mobilizing the Asda people. Together they implemented imaginative plans for focusing and engaging the workforce.

As a Good Enough leader, Norman recognized where he could add value and genuinely allowed space for other leaders to flourish. In fact, many of his senior management team went on to become CEOs in top British businesses – probably a record for a management team: Phil Cox as chairman of Spirit Group, Tony Campbell as chairman of Punch Taverns, Allan Leighton as chairman of the Post Office, Justin King as CEO of Sainsbury's, Richard Baker as CEO of Boots, and Paul Mason as CEO of Matalan, Levi Strauss Europe and Somerfield. What's more, even with the departure of Norman (to pursue a career in politics) and other key executives, the performance of Asda has continued to be strong.

This is a very different story from that of another company outside the retail sector with whom we have worked. This particular company had achieved legendary and iconic success in its market during the 1970s and 1980s, principally through very strong leadership. Through rigorous attention to detail, a passion for excellence and a real deep knowledge of the business, the CEO achieved exceptional things. To this day he is a hero figure within the business. But in our view he was almost too strong, too good. He wasn't just Good Enough. In many ways, he *was* the business and when he left there was a vacuum that nobody could fill. The business quickly unravelled and is only now beginning to find its feet.

The key message of the Good Enough mindset is that creating and leading a Meaning Inc. company is not about perfection, heroism, providing a panacea for all the meaning voids of the organization or telling people what their own meaning should be. Rather, it is about demonstrating the attitude and behaviours that will set a meaning context for people and allow them the space to connect that meaning to what is important to them. It is about having the confidence to allow others the freedom to flourish in their own way.

Spikes and meaning

Exceptional leaders aren't necessarily well-rounded characters, but typically exhibit spike strengths in focused areas. The higher you go in an organization the more "spiky" the individuals tend to be. Embracing these distinctive, individual spikes and honing them to an Olympian standard is a core part of Meaning Inc. leadership. Spike also fits perfectly with the Good Enough mindset – having a Good Enough attitude allows individual spikes to emerge and develop in a way that striving for perfection or roundedness just doesn't.

For too long, leadership development has been focusing on the weaknesses and failings of leaders. The truth is that no one can recall a great leader who got to their particular summit by creating a remedial action plan around an area of uncharacteristic average-ness. Great leaders are not reconstituted, patched-up paragons who, because they raise their game to an acceptable standard in a couple of discrete areas, undergo a magical transformation such that no leadership challenge is beyond them.

Great leaders succeed because they are exceptional at some facet of their performance behind which there are a raft of other areas where they are really not effective at all. Indeed, in some areas they have a dangerous talent void which stands out as much as their spike. Put another way, some of the most memorable and strong leaders are just plain quirky. Quirkiness in leaders is that combination of an amazing leadership strength with a transparent downside, or weakness, which can come over as a stark oddity.

While spikes are important for all leaders, they are especially important for Meaning Inc. leaders because they provide a platform for the leader to authentically engage others. First, people are quick to see through efforts at being something you are not – whether or not you sit comfortably on your particular leadership horse. Nothing destroys meaning more rapidly for people than a sense that they are getting a textbook-driven and fabricated perform-ance straight out of some leadership manual. Meaning Inc. leaders, therefore, need to authentically be themselves by developing spikes which genuinely go with their natural grain.

Second, to achieve the exceptional and distinctive impact which is needed to create a sense of meaning within companies, leaders require distinctive and unique skills. There needs to be something which sets these leaders apart from others and gives people a reason why they should follow them.

Third, the flip side of developing a leadership spike is that it creates room for others to fill in the gaps – to develop their own spikes, exercise judgement and creativity independently; to grow and shine. It allows people to be Good Enough.

It takes two

It is interesting to see how many successful Meaning Inc. companies have been led by a double act: Sergey Brin and Larry Page at Google, Bill Gates and Paul Allen at Microsoft, Steve Jobs and Steve Wozniak at Apple. Of course there are exceptions to this – Virgin has the characteristics of a Meaning Inc. company yet Richard Branson is clearly a one-man show. However, the trend is so pervasive that in Silicon Valley venture capitalists these days positively look for leadership partners, as they have found this is a significant predictor of success.

When we talked to Goldman Sachs, one of the things that they singled out as being distinctive about their culture was the number of co- , tri- or quad-heads they have in many parts of the business. This flies in the face of management orthodoxy but at Goldman Sachs it works. Many companies talk about teamwork. What better way of demonstrating this than to have it right at the top?

The must-have spikes

As part of the research into Meaning Inc. leadership, we looked at our own assessments of leaders over the years and selected a small sample of Meaning Inc. leaders. We applied a rigorous definition of Meaning Inc. leadership and set a high bar for being considered for this category. Leaders were only selected if they met the following three criteria: they had to have been in a senior position long enough for the impact of their style to be visible; they had to have created a meaningful environment below them as assessed by their people's views; finally, their impact on business results had to be strong. Eventually, we identified over 30 people who could be classified as Meaning Inc. leaders under this definition. We looked closely at the characteristics of each of these leaders and collated the themes. As expected, we found they were all quite different. However, when we looked further we found that every one of them had a spike in at least one of four areas: creativity, cohesion, compassion and courage. Pulling these together with the qualities we have talked about so far, we arrive at the following model of Meaning Inc. leadership:

Figure 4 ● Meaning Inc. leadership

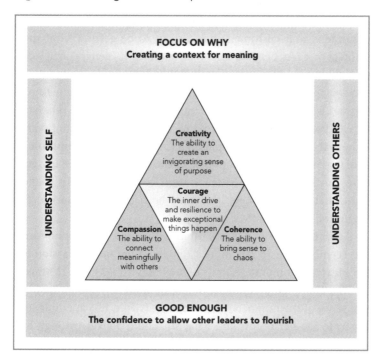

● Creativity: the ability to create an invigorating sense of purpose

Creating meaning requires fresh, innovative thinking and the ability to break away from old ways of framing the world and doing things. It requires an ability to connect with the external realities of the world, to imagine how a business's purpose can be connected to emergent trends, to see how things could be different and to make that happen inside an organization.

A decade ago, the Royal Bank of Scotland (RBS) was a successful Scottish financial institution that decided to take over National Westminster Bank. This was widely regarded as a case of a fish swallowing a whale. RBS has gone on to become the world's fifth largest bank. Jayne-Anne Gadhia joined RBS in 1998 as head of the Virgin One account and is now head of consumer finance. From her early days, she felt that something at RBS was wrong – that people didn't seem to believe that they could actually help customers, that customers didn't seem to be getting what they wanted or even needed, and that banking in general needed a real shake-up. Although a strong-minded person, Jayne-Anne showed real guts to challenge the ways things were and to put forward a vision for how they could be different in the relatively stiff and sceptical world of banking. With unswerving confidence in her view, she set her people on a total crusade to revolutionize banking and to break the mould. In short, she set out an invigorating purpose – one based on "a fresh challenge". If this sounds somewhat Branson-esque, that may be because she worked for Virgin for eight years.

As with all spikes, there is often a downside, and Jayne-Anne was seen by some to rely more strongly on her innate passion for her ideas than on pure analysis of how they could work. However, she is a chartered accountant by background and has an instinctive sense of the numbers. Her stock rose within RBS as employees began to see her results and what she could deliver through her team. People began to flock to her banner. This is where her ability to create meaning added enormous value. People work for the ideal

– to shake up banking – as well as for her personally. She creates great loyalty and an inspiring sense of purpose that banking can genuinely help people.

Looking more closely, the qualities that underpin **CREATIVITY** include:

- **External connection:** A deep understanding of where the world is going – economically, politically, technologically, demographically and socially – and the capacity to spot the opportunities these realities present to create meaning.

- **Flair:** The imagination to translate opportunities into invigorating and meaningful goals that gel with the ongoing nature of the business.

- **Organizational mould-breaking:** The capacity to create new organizational ways of operating that fit with a ground-breaking purpose.

In the external world, great examples of creativity in leaders include: Richard Branson and his capacity to create a bold platform to challenge monopoly industries and provide customers with greater choice – something which has helped turn Virgin into an $11 billion business and one of the most respected and recognizable brands in the world; Steve Jobs, who has succeeded in igniting the fortunes of businesses across three industries through his desire to dent the universe; and Jamsetji Tata, who had the creative insight to set the Tata business the purpose of giving India the benefits of becoming an industrial nation. All these leaders share the incredible gift of creativity – of seeing the world how it could be.

Coherence: the ability to bring sense to chaos

One of the biggest issues around meaning is the sense of chaos and uncertainty people feel in fast-changing organizations. The complexity which leaders face is unrivalled and creating a strong sense of coherence and clarity for people is, therefore, critical if they are to feel engaged in a meaningful way. Meaning Inc. leaders who play to this spike anchor things for their people.

Let's take the example of John Condron, CEO of Yell. As described on page 162, this was a business historically rooted in the Yellow Pages directories which has transformed itself into becoming an international business with a strong footprint in the US and which has also successfully moved into the digital age. What's more, the business has managed this change while continuing to deliver robust performance.

When you meet John Condron, he comes across as an individual with an independent-minded take on the business world. He does not believe in selling himself or his achievements publicly and is dismissive of leaders who make a lot of noise not backed up by substance. On the surface, you would say he was conservative. Except, of course, that he has driven an enormous amount of change in his business with hardly anyone noticing. One thing is obvious, he has kept the business clearly focused on what it is and is not. He has driven a quality programme through the business relentlessly and with focus over many years. He has resisted short-term fads and, once embarked on a course of action, drives forward consistently. At Yell, people are clear on what is important and what they need to do. Things are contextualized and staff are focused. Remits are clear. Yell's business environment is fast moving but inside the business feels steady and anchored.

The qualities that underpin **COHERENCE** are:

- **Contextualization:** The ability to frame and reframe issues for people in a way that links the external (opportunities and expressed organizational purpose) with the internal (organizational history/DNA, individual contributions and efforts).

- **Clarity:** Strong insight into how different internal elements of the business fit together. It is about being able to clarify for others how the various activities of the organization inter-relate and depend on each other in a way that fosters understanding and cooperation.

- **Focus:** The capacity to sustain crystal-clear focus on specific goals over time. The ability to say no to things and resist distraction.

The nature of coherence qualities means they are particularly relevant for leaders operating within attention deficit organizations (see page 32). The chaos and confusion that characterize these organizations has to be resolved if any sort of meaningful focus is to be achieved. Jack Welch was a superb example of a coherent leader during his time at General Electric. He gave the people of GE a crystal-clear picture of what the organization was about, where it was headed, what the challenges were, what was expected of people and how their performance would be measured and rewarded. Everyone just knew what was expected of them. Archie Norman is another example of someone who creates coherence and clarity for people in a world of change.

Compassion: the ability to connect meaningfully with others

A large proportion – over 50 per cent – of our Meaning Inc. leaders were strong on creating meaning through their ability to connect with people. In particular, they were able to position things in a way that played to people's deeper drives and needs. In short, they were able to give people a sense of "what's in it for me" if we do this. Through this, they were able to mobilize the energies of others.

Take, as an example, David Gardner, formerly European CEO of EA (a gaming company) and now operating in a group role with the same organization. His spike is his human and spiritual values combined with his exceptional ability to connect with people. David was virtually worshipped by his people. "DG is a God," we were once told. He connected to absolutely everyone and really cared about them. Similarly, he cared deeply about the social impact of the products the company was producing and EA led the way in non-violent games. He also worked with the noted architect Norman Foster on designing the head office so it would connect with the people and what they did in it. An early workshop had the theme "Why I love EA", in which we discussed how to break the £0.5 billion European turnover barrier while retaining values. Gardner was very aware of the life stages of the staff, and understood that as the business matured and the people in it got older, their needs would change. EA was committed to attending to those changes. Following our coaching relationship with him, he went on to work with someone who specialized in spiritual leadership.

The qualities that underpin **COMPASSION** include:

- **Environmental radar:** vigilantly tuning into the interpersonal and political dynamics around you; being able to identify the subtle undercurrents and understand the unsaid and unnoticed.

- **Mobilization:** the ability to engage and mobilize others around a course of action by understanding their deeper needs.

- **Generosity:** putting yourself in others' shoes and being committed to their financial, emotional, social and practical needs.

Tata's leadership was a great example of compassion in action. They showed an unprecedented level of care and generosity to their people though difficult times. At Genentech, also, the level of attention to the needs of people, through initiatives like near-site child care and a generous maternity policy, shows a strong compassionate culture.

Courage: the inner drive and resilience to make exceptional things happen

At the heart of Meaning Inc. leadership is a quality most people would recognize as courage – not only great belief in one's convictions and the ability to envisage new realities but also the sheer drive to bring these possibilities to fruition. In the end, only tangible delivery and impact create meaning, and just about all our

Meaning Inc. leaders have shown this quality in one way or another. This requires incredible resilience, a capacity to stay positive in the most difficult of times and to have the gumption to resist the easy short-term options. In today's world, managing ferocious pressure for results without sacrificing long-term objectives or one's sense of purpose or values requires leaders who can cope with pain and pressure in the short-term without buckling. All the Meaning Inc. leaders described so far show such courage.

The qualities that underpin **COURAGE** are:

- **Ambition to make a difference:** The drive to make an impact as opposed to being driven by recognition, status or the trappings of success.

- **Positive belief:** Seeing possibilities and solutions rather than problems; having the discipline and focus to keep plugging away in the face of adversity to ensure goals are actually achieved.

- **Long termism:** The courage to think long term and to hold off against the temptations of short-term prizes.

Jamsetji Tata's resilience in the face of British opposition; Richard Branson's capacity to court bankruptcy in the pursuit of his vision when advisers and banks were telling him to consolidate; Masaru Ibuka's willingness to pay people's salaries out of his own savings in the early days of Sony. These are all examples of courage.

Understanding yourself and others

In order to develop these Meaning Inc. leadership qualities, to identify and effectively utilize a meaning-making spike and to shape a Good Enough mindset, leaders must have a deep understanding of themselves and those around them. The process of developing self-insight begins at the tangible level of learning about one's impact on others, extends to having a deeper understanding of personal spikes, strengths and limitations, and how to leverage and compensate for these respectively, and culminates in a deep and profound sense of what an individual stands for and values. This is a difficult process for anyone, but without self-knowledge, no leader can hope to use his or her inherent talents to their full potential.

Strong self-insight also incorporates being aware of the blind spots that typically accompany any towering area of strength. Great leaders understand and live with their weaknesses. The ones who sustain themselves over time have ways of making sure their weaknesses don't matter. They not only understand how to use their spikes to greatest effect, but are able to identify the people and support they need around them to complement those spikes – which is where insight into others comes in. In recognizing the importance of tuning in to the needs and perspectives of others, Tata sends all its people out to do community work, in a concerted effort to develop their sense of compassion for others.

Having a real understanding of others is critical for Meaning Inc. leaders because it allows them to tune in to and appreciate people's different meaning needs. For some, their meaning needs may be about self-actualization and fulfilling their true potential as human beings, for others it may be about taking home a decent salary to their families. Whatever those meaning needs may be, understanding and responding to them could be the best chance leaders have of attracting and retaining talent in the future.

Developing Meaning Inc. leaders

A significant proportion of our work with organizations is focused on the development of meaning-making leaders. Our intention here is to give an overview of the elements of a typical Meaning Inc. leadership development programme and the impact it can have on individuals and the businesses that they lead.

Our guiding principle is always that leadership development is a journey rather than a one-off silver bullet dispensed from a guru in a context far removed from the pressures of work. The programmes are therefore strongly linked to the business context and have multiple components stretching over about 12–18 months, each reinforcing and building on the one before and giving leaders opportunities to actively work on their leadership back in the workplace over that time.

Reflection and feedback are core features throughout the programme. For example, leaders produce a personal lifeline of their success, happiness and performance at both work and home from their early school days up until the present. They produce video diaries to track their development journey and how they perceive their effectiveness. This is calibrated with feedback from work colleagues, family and friends.

Support and challenge are key themes. YSC coaches spend four hours in a one-to-one development discussion with each leader – exploring their backgrounds, drives and reviewing the feedback on their insight into themselves and others from the survey data. From the outset, the focus is on creating an environment of shared learning, trust and supportive challenge.

The core elements of the Meaning Inc. leadership model are covered and brought to life though case studies, guest speakers and a variety of challenging exercises designed to take leaders outside their comfort zones and stimulate fresh thinking about how they lead. Practical sessions focus on storytelling, contextualization techniques and the Good Enough approach.

Leaders leave the programme with a clear action plan to take their development forward as well as a modus operandi for the group, to ensure the leaders keep supporting and challenging each other back at work. Before they leave, they produce another video diary as a record of the commitments they have made to change and of how they will work with others to track their progress.

A number of follow-up activities help to embed change and sustain learning beyond the actual programme. A one-day event brings the leaders together to review their progress, learn from each other's successes and failures and use techniques to clarify and consolidate the direction of their leadership journey. One exercise uses visualization techniques which enable leaders to develop a motivating vision of their leadership in the future and help them to map out the steps required on their journey towards becoming that leader. In another exercise, they identify an object to act as a metaphor for their leadership journey. They take away with them a set of key questions specific to their own development goals which will be tested with a small group of stakeholders every four months for a year using Pulse Feedback™. Examples include a book to signify one leader's journey to develop their story-telling skills, a shoe to remind another leader to "walk a mile in other's shoes and understand other's perspectives", and a brick as a counterbalancing reminder to another leader to be open and transparent with others. The testing is done three times a year. Pulse Feedback™ is a trademark product run by YSC's Psymmetry business – it electronically collects and collates feedback on a small number of questions designed and agreed with the individual concerned.

The impact of Meaning Inc. leadership development

Feedback from leaders of companies that have implemented meaning-making leadership development programmes and the evaluations given by their stakeholders suggest that such programmes help leaders to make powerful personal changes. This is both to their leadership – in terms of the way they engage followers – and with respect to their own personal and life goals. There are also clear signs that the principle of linking development to delivery has an impact. One operations leader commented on how his increased efforts to get out and paint the bigger "why" picture for both his team and interdependent teams had led to a 37 per cent uplift in his revenue stream, most of which could not be put down to market conditions or other factors. "It might sound simple but if I had stayed stuck at my desk trying to work out a better strategy or technical solution rather that getting out and really talking to people about how what they are doing matters and fits in with the bigger picture, I would have missed my budget again like last year." So, Meaning Inc. principles look like they can do wonders for the bottom line.

In summary, the challenges for leaders in creating a Meaning Inc. company are significant. The following are required:

- A focus on "why" – the most powerful, distinctive feature of Meaning Inc. leaders is their relentless attention to the fundamental question of "why". This is about moving from the "what" and the "how" of leadership to mobilizing people through clarifying why their activities are worthwhile and meaningful.

- A Good Enough mindset – this is a leadership attitude that has at its heart an absolute commitment to serving the capacity for creative growth of one's colleagues and followers. It requires a depth of confidence to let others flourish rather than taking all of the responsibility, burden and glory of leadership. To achieve this, leaders need to cultivate their own mindfulness and humility – the Good Enough leader understands, above all, the complexity of organizational life and the limits of what he is able to do and achieve on his own.

- A distinctive meaning-making spike – this is a towering area of strength which, when developed and applied in an intense manner, can allow leaders to have a unique and special impact in any situation they engage. A spike emerges from the Good Enough mindset since it requires leaders to understand and compensate for the downsides associated with all spikes by making room for others to grow and excel. Meaning Inc. leaders tend to have spikes in at least one of the following four areas – Creativity: the ability to create an invigorating sense of purpose; Coherence: the ability to bring sense to chaos; Compassion: the ability to connect meaningfully with others, and Courage: the inner drive and resilience to make exceptional things happen.

● Underpinning all of the above is insight into themselves and others – this includes a finely tuned awareness of their own capabilities and limitations, a deep understanding of the context in which they operate and the uniqueness of others, including their different meaning needs and how these may change over time. Developing such insight requires leaders to delve deep into themselves and to honestly, vigilantly and critically evaluate themselves and others.

Developing leaders who can envisage, build and sustain Meaning Inc. companies is therefore no mean feat. It is one that, for many, requires a fundamental shift in perspective – from control to trust, from "what" to "why" and from the heroic to the Good Enough mindset. Through this, and the behaviours and skills that flow from it, there is a greater chance of freeing organizations from the exhausting tyranny of joyless and meaningless tasks that sadly still oppress many people in their working lives.

Having looked at the qualities required to lead in a Meaning Inc. world, let us now look at what businesses can actually do to build such cultures.

5. The power of an invigorating purpose

"He who has a why to live for can bear almost any how."
Friedrich Nietzsche

The film *The World's Fastest Indian* tells the story of Burt Munro, a New Zealander, who at the age of 63 decided to attempt to break the world speed record on his Indian Scout motorbike at the Bonneville Flats in Utah. Munro, a loner, toiled away in his makeshift shed for over forty years adapting his bike, using anything he could lay his hands on. He kept himself going day and night through his single-minded sense of purpose.

This determination drew others to his cause. A group of young tearaways, who had had an acrimonious relationship with Munro's motorcycle club, helped him on his way, once he had put together the money to travel to the US in 1962. Then disaster: when he arrived at the Bonneville Flats, he discovered that he had missed the deadline for registering for his record attempt, not by days, but by months. The apparently strict rules administered by enthusiastic bureaucrats were quietly bent to allow him to proceed. When it came to the attempt itself, those responsible for monitoring the safety of the bikes were aghast at the corners that Munro had cut in modifying his Indian Scout. They, too, decided to look the other way. Munro was allowed to ride. He succeeded in hitting a world record speed of 179 miles an hour for a bike below

1000cc. Subsequently in 1967, at the age of 68, Munro set a new record of 206 miles an hour, a record that amazingly still stands for his class of bike.

The Munro story illustrates three things about an invigorating sense of purpose. It keeps people going and gives them enormous energy and resilience. It forces people to be creative and to bend the rules. Lastly, it magnetically draws others, even one's enemies, to a cause.

A sense of purpose with high goals flowing through an organization is a distinctive attribute of many Meaning Inc. companies. Tata in India; Orange, The Body Shop and Virgin in the UK; Apple, Hewlett-Packard and Google in the US – around the world, companies flourish when they have a magnetically unifying sense of what they are about.

Yet what was a novel idea has become a garden overgrown; the corporate world is awash with statements of purpose, mission, vision, and values. Only a handful of companies manage to create true meaning through these initiatives. In many organizations, purpose and mission statements actually seem more of an empty ritual. What, then, does it take to create a company from which the bulk of the managers and employees truly derive meaning through purpose?

The purpose and mission bandwagon

The findings of books like *Built to Last* by Jim Collins and Jerry Porras have impressed on executives the need to have a clear sense of core purpose in their businesses. This advice was very much pushing at an open door. For a long time, senior executives have been searching for something more than bottom-line results. When asked in a workshop what he wanted on his gravestone, one executive told us emphatically that he did not want it to state that he doubled profitability over a five-year period or increased the share price – or even that he made millions for his family. "What I'd like," he said, "is that I was of service to my people, to my customers, to my family and to society at large." This yearning to make a positive contribution is much more typical of managers than the stereotypical portrayal of them as avaricious drivers of limitless profit. Here are some examples of the kinds of purpose statements that companies have produced:

- **GlaxoSmithKline:** To improve the quality of human life and enable people to do more, feel better and live longer

- **Walt Disney:** To make people happy

- **The John Lewis Partnership:** The happiness of its members (all staff are shareholders) through worthwhile and satisfying employment

- **Microsoft:** To enable people and business throughout the world to realize their full potential

- **Google:** To organize the world's information, making it universally accessible and useful

Real life

While such statements are easy to make, they are harder to bring to life. Fewer people now find such aspirations sufficiently motivating. For example, one senior executive, when asked his expectations of a board off-site, said to me, "They'll probably come up with a new purpose and mission statement – we haven't had one of those for at least six months."

There are many ways to miss the mark when it comes to the effective use of purpose and mission statements. Walt Disney's "To make people happy" can apply to just about every facet of life, leaving people wondering how distinctive a proposition it is. Nike has experimented with a range of aspirational sounding statements at various times. These include: "To experience the emotion of competition, winning and crushing competitors" as well as "To keep the magic of sport alive" and most recently, "To bring inspiration and innovation to every athlete in the world [everyone is an athlete]".

All these formulations smack of overstretch. Similarly, Microsoft's statement quoted above seems to cover just about every facet of life. If people feel that a purpose statement isn't truly grounded in reality and taken seriously by the senior leadership to the point where it affects decision-making, then a lot of activity around purpose and mission can be rendered meaningless.

Another problem occurs when a new CEO joins a company and has no sense of its historical traditions. Thus he or she imposes a new sense of purpose without any regard as to why people joined and stayed with the company over many years. A novel sense of purpose mechanically distributed throughout a company does not "a great enterprise make". This is doubly true when the CEO ignores the necessity for a fundamental transformation of the people and their ways of working. The result is a moving statement hitting an immovable organization, in which case the statement and the CEO usually fall first, and fast.

As a consequence of all this, purpose statements pinned up on the noticeboards and staff canteen walls of most organizations often lack traction. There's a strong feeling among many employees that, in actuality, the real emphasis of the leaders is the hard stuff: financial performance against budgets, investment decisions, divestments, target markets to be in, and so forth. The lofty purpose statements appear more as afterthoughts than the platform for the business's strategy. At best, they are considered a waste of time or bland truisms. At worst, they generate deep cynicism.

As one senior executive of a financial institution remarked: "I know our expressed purpose is to offer exemplary customer service, but the dark secret at the heart of banking is that we make money by stitching people up and hoping that they won't notice or shift banks."

● Purpose in action: Apple and Steve Jobs

To appreciate how purpose can and should be enacted in a company, let's take the case of Apple Computers. The history of Apple and Steve Jobs has been extensively documented in a series of articles and most notably in Jeffrey Young and William Simon's book *iCon*[1] and in Alan Deutschman's *The Second Coming of Steve Jobs*.[2] People have come up with a variety of explanations of Apple's success. Our own take is that the corporation's success is substantially to do with the authentic sense of purpose that Steve Jobs embodies and which finds expression in all his business ventures.

The first thing to say is that Apple's official statement of purpose – "To make a contribution to the world by making tools for the mind that advance humankind" – isn't all that remarkable or even precise. Neither is it the real driving force of the company. This is better captured by Steve Jobs's phrase of "making a dent in the universe" through technological innovation.

Right from the time the company was founded by Steve Jobs and Steve Wozniak in 1976, it held a passion for breaking new ground at its core. The relentless pursuit of elegant customer-oriented solutions at a time when computers were complicated machines only accessible to nerds required a passion for doing things differently. Jobs and Wozniak looked for this in the people they recruited, as well as a core belief in what computers could be in the world. People were prepared to work all hours and often for limited benefits because they believed in this purpose. The Apple II, the first truly integrated machine that you could use right away rather than having to assemble, was the first fruit of this passion and propelled the company to its initial success.

Apple rapidly became a large concern – and that's when the problems started. People had not joined Apple to derive commercial benefit from existing ideas; they were there to shake things up. This is after all what had driven Jobs. Dutifully, the company began to hire people who had experience of running a business. Jobs himself persuaded the president of Pepsi, John Sculley, to join Apple with the famous question: "Are you going to sell sugar water all of your life when you could be doing something really important?"

However, as the company became more orthodox, Jobs himself started to feel marginalized. He collected a small team around him to work on the Apple Mac. Ironically, given that he was chairman of the company, this team flew a pirate's flag above their HQ to show how they were different. They succeeded in alienating large sections of Apple. Despite being badly paid by Jobs and often poorly treated, a remarkable number of people put huge amounts of energy into the Apple Mac. Jobs's passion for the project and refusal to accept blockages – he came to be called "the reality distortion field" – helped bring it to fruition. But, after the initial euphoria of the launch, early sales failed to match expectations (subsequently it was a big success) and the writing was on the wall for Jobs. He departed from the company he had founded.

Apple subsequently went through a series of talented CEOs who failed to drive the company forward. None of these executives, it should be noted, questioned what Apple was about. In fact they accepted the original formulation. The trouble was, they did not embody it in the visceral and total way that Jobs had. In 1993 John Sculley was forced out after Apple's market share fell from 20 per cent to 8 per cent. Two other CEOs followed. Both found it difficult to come to terms with Apple's maverick culture as moulded by Jobs. Decisions just did not get implemented, there was lack of discipline, with infighting and frequent leaks. In 1997 Apple lost over $1 billion. The magic had gone.

Meanwhile, Jobs had put his reality distortion skills into two new ventures – NeXT, a business-oriented hardware and software company, and Pixar, a fledgling computer animation company trying to prove to a sceptical world that computers could one day produce an animated film. These ventures drained Jobs of virtually all the money he had made when cashing in his Apple shares. But the passion for denting the universe kept him and others going. A key early success was to get the then Disney animator, John Lasseter, to join Pixar. This Jobs did by pointing out to him that at "Disney you can make great films, but here you can make history." Remarkably, both Pixar and NeXT eventually succeeded. Pixar produced the first computer animated full-length feature – *Toy Story* – and in the week of the launch went public in a move that made Jobs a billionaire. Apple itself bought NeXT for close to $400 million and 1.5 million Apple shares.

The sale of NeXT brought Jobs back to Apple and, in 1997, largely the same board that had engineered Jobs's initial departure made him "Interim CEO" of the company while they looked for a permanent head. But almost magically Apple's performance started to turn around. To be fair to the CEOs who had preceded him, Jobs built on what they had started. He made some tough decisions, but this time people fell into line because he told them that the core purpose, "to dent the universe", remained. Dutifully, once the financial performance of the company had stabilized, they started working on the next big idea. The iMac, iTunes and the iPod were born. In three years under Jobs Mark II, Apple's market capitalization went from $2 billion to $16 billion. Today it stands at over $60 billion.

What does all this illustrate? Anyone who doubts the power of a passionately held sense of purpose authentically pursued need only look at how, in the hands of Jobs, it has served to transform three industries – computers, film and music. The story illustrates a number of other things. First, it's not the purpose you have on the walls or what comes out of your mouth that matters. It's what you believe. Second, the unreasonable pursuit of a dream can produce much better business results than the focused pursuit of profits by applying conventional business values. Third, your purpose has to gel with the people you have recruited or things fall apart in internal battles and strife.

Purpose lost and found

The subtlety of purpose in action can also be illustrated by looking at some examples of where companies have stalled or gone wrong. All companies have an implicit sense of purpose which governs their choices. Frequently, this is different from the stated purpose. Companies are much more prone to purpose-drift than they realize. They shift away from what has historically driven them without being aware that they are doing so.

Take the case of Sony. Created in war-torn Japan in 1945 by Masaru Ibuka, who explicitly tasked employees with the goal of restoring Japan's national pride through technological innovation, the group began life with no equipment and battled severe energy and material shortages. Salaries were paid out of Ibuka's personal savings. Slowly but surely, the energy and creativity of its workers began to pay off. The business became a going concern in Japan before storming the international stage in the 1970s.

However, by the mid-1990s Sony had started to stall, and its share price in the five years to 2005 has declined by over a third. Widespread accounts began to circulate of the fiefdoms that had grown up within the company and the lack of cooperation between departments. Sony increasingly suffered adverse customer reactions. A web site was even created by its critics to circulate negative stories. In 2004, this quintessentially Japanese company appointed Howard Stringer, a Welshman living in the US, to tackle some of these problems.

While a variety of factors explain Sony's recent problems, one of the issues dogging the company has been a loss of fundamental purpose. Although Sony always emphasized innovation and the restoration of Japanese national pride as its twin drivers, the latter was the chief factor which kept the business aligned and which focused and bounded the creativity. Once its aim of restoring pride had been achieved, and the business became global, and therefore much less of a Japanese enterprise, it was left with innovation as its core purpose. But in the absence of the other pillar, the unifying glue was lost and the company became less tightly disciplined. Sony, in other words, has to learn to adapt to a situation where one of its driving principles is no longer relevant. This will take time and will necessitate a reconfiguring of the deepest instincts of the business.

Sony's situation in some way applies more generally to Japan and Germany. A catch-up drive has been a key feature of these countries' motivations throughout the twentieth century. In fact, it is possible to see World War I, as far as Germany was concerned, and World War II, with respect to both Germany and

Japan, as arising from a desire to emulate the imperial success of other Western powers which Germany and Japan had historically missed out on. After World War II, this catch-up was played out in a different way through economics rather than tanks and planes. However, having achieved their goal, the core sense of purpose for both countries has evaporated and it is this which could lie behind the stagnation experienced in more recent times. Both have gone – with virtually no interim period – from vastly over-performing to lagging significantly behind other developed countries in terms of GDP growth. One might argue that this plateauing is inevitable once you reach a certain economic threshold. Yet to date this has not held the US, for one, back.

Other businesses, too, have suffered from purpose-drift. Disney's purpose – "To make people happy" – was always too general a statement to be their true corporate driver. Rather this could more accurately be described as "a deep-seated drive to innovate in providing family entertainment". It is this radical spirit that led Walt Disney to create the first full-length feature film cartoons and the innovative attractions of the Disney theme parks. Roy Disney and others have complained that the company's recent performance problems have arisen because the original sense of purpose has been replaced by a more machine-like drive for commercial success, as well as a preoccupation with rewards for key executives. A consequence of this has been that Disney allowed Pixar to become the innovator, in the digital age, for family entertainment; an oversight that the company had to correct eventually through an expensive acquisition of Pixar. Similarly, James Burke of Johnson & Johnson, CEO of the company during the Tylenol crisis, when the discovery of cyanide in some Tylenol capsules created a nationwide panic, says that getting back to the organization's Credo, drafted by General Robert Woods Johnson II in the 1940s, just might have been what saved them in the crisis.

What the above examples illustrate is that core purpose often operates in an unseen way and that things can change for the better or worse without people being aware of it. All too often, executives do not know what the true purpose driving a company has been or is. Purpose-drift is common and even subtle shifts can lead to a dramatic impact on performance.

Purpose in Meaning Inc. companies

In meaning-driven companies, we see the sense of purpose flowing through the whole organization – being part of its history and framed in such a way as to engage the energies of the most forward-looking and aspirational employees. Let's look at how this is done.

First, these companies create a meaningful purpose, one so powerful that it becomes the chief corporate propellant. Second, these companies convert that purpose into a source of managerial and employee energy by making it live and by creating strong linkages between the purpose and key activities. Neither of these is easy to do, so let's see how it works.

The way in which purpose is framed is critical in terms of the extent to which it is motivating and energizing. It is not enough to have a core sense of purpose; it needs to be one that inspires. Words are not the issue here. Boards frequently torture themselves to find a set of words that cover who they are – and usually end up creating an elephant by committee in the process. What's more important is identifying the core concept that can energize a company going forward. In the words of Lord Browne of BP, it is important that this also "gives people a sense that the best is yet to come".[3]

Purpose statements can be classified into one of three categories, or levels. The least powerful is a *metrics purpose*, typically focused on financial or other targets. The next level is purpose that is, in essence, an *existence rationale*. Ultimately, what leaders need to strive for is an *invigorating purpose*.

When the purpose of an organization is at the metrics level (such as sales or other financial goals), there is almost no benefit to the company. Consider this statement from Coca-Cola in 1994: "We exist to create value for our shareholders on a long-term basis by building a business that enhances the Coca-Cola trademark."

How motivated would you feel by that? People find purpose least interesting when it is framed in terms of benchmarking targets, competitive aspirations, or narrow financial criteria. While at a lower level, such goals can be useful in focusing the efforts of a business, such aspirations are frequently seen as inappropriate and far from compelling definitions of a company's true sense of purpose.

A second issue with such a narrow sense of purpose is that it is seen to play more to the interests and motivations of the senior leadership. Making a company the biggest in its sector or beating a rival on some arcane set of metrics might serve to puff up the ego of the CEO, but it has less attraction for people on the frontline. At worst, such goals can be seen as solely driving the compensation interests of senior executives. Lastly, it is increasingly the case that beating another company at a certain criterion has much less attractiveness in a world where people are sceptical (or indeed, cynical) about over-identification with their organizations and really cannot see a valid reason why their company is (or should be) any different from any other in the sector. In short, coming to work every day just to punch up the numbers on an arbitrary, and remote, scorecard is not something that can motivate anyone for very long.

More meaningful, though not fully energizing, is the purpose statement that centres on an *existence rationale*. These framings of purpose dominate today's corporate landscape. They tend to centre on service provision, customer focus, or need satisfaction. They help sharpen people's understanding of why a business exists and the needs that it serves in the world, and are helpful in terms of guiding key strategic decisions around product development as well as informing day-to-day behaviour.

However, framing purpose in this way is less compelling and meaningful than it could be because it does not place employees as players in a wider social narrative, which is what they increasingly desire today. Second, many customer or service needs that companies talk about satisfying can seem prosaic, somewhat low-level, or plain boring. It may be important for people, for example, to have easy access to a rental car, but is this goal likely to inspire anyone? Third, such statements of purpose frequently fail the distinctiveness test. Frequently, they embody aspirations that any company in a particular sector might legitimately aspire to. As a result, while companies derive some benefit from an existence rationale purpose in this way, it doesn't really create a distinctive and positive advantage for the company's people.

The power of a purpose comes to life only when a company employs an *invigorating purpose*, the highest level of purpose framing. Invigorating purpose is focused on changing rather than servicing society. We have established six types of purpose that truly inspire others. Let's consider each of these six ways to frame an invigorating purpose in turn (see Table 5).

Universalization

A purpose based on universalization is essentially a set of aspirations around bringing things enjoyed by some to all people or to particular sections of the world community that have missed out. This is what has driven companies like Tata through their entire history: to bring the benefits of industrialization to the people of India. Wal-Mart's purpose – "To allow ordinary folk to experience the same things as rich people" – is also an example of universalization. Despite failing some other Meaning Inc. criteria, on this dimension Wal-Mart is successful. Arguably, it is precisely this sense of universal purpose that has allowed the company to flourish and persuade communities to support its growth. The key driving force for Henry Ford was to make the motor car accessible to everyone. Similarly, Larry Page and Sergey Brin at Google wanted everyone to have free access to searching the web – they only thought about making money from the venture at a much later stage.

Framing purpose in terms of universalization is helpful for businesses for a variety of reasons. First, it allows employees to feel that they are part of a wider narrative, that they are playing a role in a bigger historical process. Second, they are fighting for

Table 5 ● Types of invigorating purpose

Sub-type	Definition	Companies	Values	Dangers / Issues
Universalization	To allow everyone to experience what the few have	Tata Wal-Mart Google	Fairness Equality	What do you do when you achieve your aim?
Innovation	To go where no one has gone before	Apple Sony	Pioneering spirit	How to keep innovation engine going while making discoveries
Fresh challenge	To challenge complacency and the "big guys"	Virgin Orange	Underdog empathy	What happens when you become big yourself?
Excellence	To strive for perfection in one's art	Toyota BMW	Achievement Drive	Does not inspire everyone because of narrowness
Global responsibility	To do business in a way that is sustainable and ethical	BP Interface	Community spirit	People can question authenticity and realism
Human values	To do business in a way which recognizes the humanity of employees, suppliers and customers	John Lewis Starbucks GAP	Human concern	Potential conflict with profitability
METRICS PURPOSE – limited motivational value			"To achieve XYZ financial or other goal"	
EXISTENCE RATIONALE – moderate motivational value			"To provide XYZ service / product in XYZ a manner"	

the underprivileged of the world to have the advantages enjoyed by others. Third, a universalization purpose frequently allows companies to co-opt the political authorities and the public at large to their agenda. Lastly, and most importantly, a universalization purpose enables business to make the tough decisions in order to survive and prosper. These decisions are much more palatable when seen in the context of a broader agenda and shared sense of positive intent. People at all levels come to believe that the organization must survive because its existence has implications far beyond one company's payroll or stock price.

Innovation

Being cutting-edge, breaking new ground and developing things that nobody has developed before play significantly to people's motivation. Without specifically saying so, it is what drives much of the intense activity in the myriad of IT and biotech start-up companies across the globe. The reason that purpose framed around innovation is energizing is that it plays to people's desire for distinctiveness and excitement.

Global responsibility

A purpose based on global issues has also been embraced by some companies to give their activities greater meaning. Environmentalism and the needs of disadvantaged sections of the world are two key aspects of this. Both are at the heart of BP's redefinition of itself as "Beyond Petroleum" and in its desire to seek mutual advantage in dealings with producer countries. Companies operating in industries that are suspect in terms of environmental impact have sometimes gained competitive edge by seeking to do business in a more environmentally conscious manner. The business newsletter *Green Business Letter* tells the story of Ray Anderson, of Interface, a floor covering company in the southeast US.[4]

In 1994, he felt a "spear in the chest" when he realized that his company's operating policies were, in effect, unsustainable, because they were not friendly to the environment. Anderson and his team reversed those policies in almost every major way. When asked by the newsletter to comment on how he viewed the 10-year period spent in his help-the-planet quest, he commented: "It's been the most exciting in my life. We feel like we're reinventing the system and that's fun. We've been through the toughest business cycle in our history and we've survived, thanks to sustainability and the commitment we've made in this direction. I don't think we would have made it otherwise." Interface is now the largest global provider of modular carpets and while its share price has had a rollercoaster ride, it has shown solid performance.

One danger for companies that go down this route is that the sense of responsibility can appear to be just tacked on. You have to be serious about operating in a certain way to avoid the inevitable concerns about hypocrisy and skin-deep values.

Excellence

As mentioned before, Ronald Blythe, in his book on the rural poor, *Akenfield*, talks about the meaning and satisfaction rural workers obtained from "the field ploughed to perfection".[5] For companies like Toyota and BMW, this drive for perfection is what they are about. Being truly brilliant at one's craft propels people at all levels within these companies.

Toyota frames its purpose as "to contribute to society through the practice of manufacturing high-quality goods and services". This seemingly innocuous statement, when taken to its logical conclusion, leads to a culture that is obsessive about quality and continuous improvement. Companies trying to copy Toyota's production processes and systems invariably fail because they don't catch the fundamental core purpose and values that are needed to make them work.[6]

While this framing of purpose is highly motivational for some, it can leave those who want to have a broader impact on society considerably less satisfied.

● Fresh challenge

A framing purpose based on being the underdog company that brings fresh challenges can be equally compelling. When a company is fighting the forces of arrogance, complacency and anti-competitive tendencies displayed by larger, more established players, it can whet the work appetite of all employees.

Fresh challenge is the key driver at Virgin. David Silverberg captured the essence of Richard Branson and his Virgin group of companies in an article for *Digital Journal*, [7] Silverberg noted that when Branson compiled evidence that the much-larger British Airways was "smearing" Virgin Airlines, he "defended his company like he was protecting his child from a pack of bullies". Branson and Virgin ultimately won a settlement of $1.5 million, which, Silverberg notes, was divided up by Branson as a "windfall to his staff, giving each employee a BA Bonus of $400".

But note one of the most important points made by Silverberg: "This story shows the two different sides of Branson the billionaire: There's the bombastic underdog, a man determined to fight the industry with as much passion as he can muster, even if this means using a publicity stunt or two. Then there's the man who will funnel a court settlement to his employees, a boss who remembers how he got where he is today. This is the charmer, the smiling everyman, the favourite uncle. Over the years, he's expanded the Virgin brand into 236 different companies, encompassing everything from cell phones to airlines to colas. Together, they are worth more than $11 billion (CDN). With so many businesses under his thumb, Branson has branded Virgin as a David fighting corporate Goliaths."

The last point does illustrate a potential problem with this approach: what do you do when you become one of the big players yourself, and how do you react to others trying to do the same thing to you?

● Human values

A framing purpose based on treating employees and other human stakeholders well also finds increasing resonance with people today. This was at the centre of the Body Shop's mission in its early years. Similar in approach is Starbucks, which not only talks about the primacy of its employees but also how well it looks after its suppliers. As evidence of its values, Starbucks even provides benefits to its part-time workers. These people values were illustrated in a discussion we had with senior Starbucks executives about another senior colleague who had seemingly done a good job in terms of turning the results of a particular market around, but who was not so great on some employee-related values. After being given an opportunity to fix the issue, a few instances of the old behaviour reappeared. As we were trying to give balanced feedback on this, we were abruptly stopped by Starbucks. "You don't understand, just one instance is enough for us."

A purpose framed with respect to the interests of particular groups of people is compelling because it gives any business a sense of direction with a human face. This is particularly so if the suppliers involved are a distressed group in need of protection, for example Third World farmers or segments of society who need to be taken care of.

Many companies try to focus and energize their employees by short-term numerical targets. Many more try to rationalize the value of the business by virtue of whom it serves. Yet only a relatively small number of companies have created (and adhere to) core purpose statements that are at the highest level of potency – an invigorating purpose.

● Creating an invigorating but realistic purpose

You might be thinking all the above is well enough for companies starting out but wondering what you can do in an organization or part of it where the culture is already well established? The answer is – a lot more than you think. Nevertheless, much care and effort are needed if this is not to be a more mechanical exercise.

No company is forced by the nature of its business to go for purpose defined by metrics or an existence rationale. This happens because leaders have not given enough time or creative energy to thinking deeply about what their business is about.

The shift in the tectonic plates of the global economy, for example, creates significant opportunities for international companies to frame their purpose with respect to the universalization themes. The annual income of the world's four billion poor people is US\$14 trillion, larger than the US economy. Individually they are poor, but in aggregate they represent a huge, under-served consumer market. C. K. Prahalad, the business scholar and writer, talks of the fortune that can be made by companies operating at "the bottom of the pyramid".[8] He argues that this is a new competitive space for businesses and that organizations that are best placed rapidly to design and deliver the products and services that poor people need are likely to be the world's next true multinationals.

This is a space in which Tata has operated and one of its latest ideas is to produce a \$2000 car for the mass market in India. This is a natural yet bold step for them. Banks also have huge opportunities to provide for the financial needs of those that they have been reluctant to touch in the past. ICIC, an Indian bank, has carved out a space for itself through new and creative products – such as \$2 accident insurance and a mutual fund that costs only \$2 to join, delivered through a network of kiosks. Wal-Mart has been lobbying India intensely to gain access to one of the world's fastest-growing retail markets – an ideal place for Wal-Mart to realize its core purpose to "allow ordinary folk to experience the same things as rich people". Just about every multinational has the opportunity, in short, to frame their purpose, at least in part, in terms of universalization.

However, in order to do this effectively, businesses will need to stop thinking of the poor nations of the world as victims or as a burden and start recognizing them as resilient and creative entrepreneurs and value-conscious consumers. Imagination, and the courage to refocus the efforts of companies on this sector of the global population, will be necessary for businesses to embrace the possibilities that this creates. If you are going to sell toothpaste to an Indian mother, you need to know that she may not have access to running water, that she can't afford to pay for and throw away the packaging and that the main competitive products aren't other toothpastes but the twigs of the neem tree. Poor consumers, often living hand to mouth, and with limited living space, shop every day, but not for much. Already in India 30 per cent of consumables such as shampoo, cosmetics and cold medicines are sold in single-serve packages.

If companies can show the imagination and courage to get this right there is a real opportunity to create a virtuous circle, unlike the well-documented vicious circle of aid-supported dependency. Corporations can help build viable markets out of the world's poorest people, and step beyond corporate philanthropy.

Businesses could also think much more deeply about other emergent global issues – such as environmentalism, sustainability or the rise of crime and anti-social tendencies. Regardless of which sector a business is in, it can endeavour to be more environmentally conscious and socially responsible. This is essentially the position taken by BP and Interface. While embracing purpose in these terms might require businesses to put up with some short-term financial hits, the medium-term payoffs in terms of external PR, customer attitudes and employee commitment can be considerable. Any company that breaks out of the pack in its industry sector in this way is likely to enjoy competitive advantage – but only if the effort is genuine.

For companies that find it hard to frame their core purpose with reference to a broader social agenda, there is still the opportunity to position oneself with respect to innovation or breaking new ground, which allows people to feel that they are part of a wider human narrative of breaking down boundaries and barriers. Peter Drucker, one of the world's first management gurus, once said that most businesses which exist today do so because "at some point someone made a courageous decision". Building creativity by reconnecting with history is therefore open to many more businesses than one might first imagine. The spirit of innovation, in particular, can be lost in the mists of time when a business becomes more stable. Yet, a little historical digging can unearth a multitude of possibilities.

Finally, all businesses have the opportunity to at least frame an aspect of their purpose with respect to the excellence theme or the way they treat their employees or handle suppliers. Simply making explicit what the true craft of a business is, and what it has the opportunity to excel in, can be valuable. In addition, while people want good products and services delivered at a cheap price, they do not want this to be at the expense of employee mistreatment or driving suppliers into the ground. Businesses have a real opportunity to educate their customers and will lose less than they think in the medium term by taking the moral high ground.

A model for building purpose

Building a realistic but invigorating purpose requires the integration of three areas, and answers to the questions posed by each area (see Figure 5).

- **The person:** one must identify the personal values of the key people in the company. Members of the senior team need to look within themselves, peel back the layers and explore what they truly value in their lives at a deep level. Unless the leadership is personally aligned with the organization's purpose, it will fail to resonate in an authentic way with the rest of the company. It is also likely that leadership behaviour will not fully support the espoused purpose statement if it is not embraced at a deep, personal level by them.

- **The organization:** it is critical to understand the key sense of purpose that drove the business early on and that sits within

Figure 5 ● Developing purpose – some questions

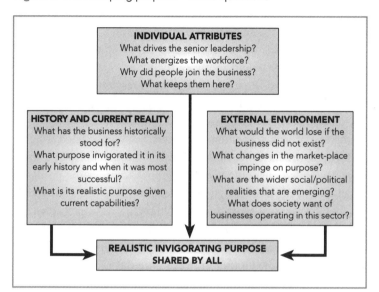

its DNA. In addition, it is important to understand what purpose can realistically be supported by the business's core capabilities.

● **The environment:** leaders also need to understand the opportunities presented by changes in the wider social and political environment, changes in consumer expectations and where the business environment is heading in general but also in their sector.

To illustrate how this model can be applied, let's take the case of Burger King (BK). At one point its defined purpose was "to be the best quick-service restaurant in the sector by quality of service and profitability". A few years ago, and before BK was sold by its then owners Diageo to a consortium of investors, we performed an exercise with its board. To start, the board members all agreed that the sense of purpose implied by the statement was not particularly motivating and that it failed to provide much traction with either employees or managers. We asked them to look at the history of the company in order to identify what truly drove it, as well as to think about external perceptions and the way the market-place and competitors were evolving. We also did an exercise to find out what the board members thought would motivate them.

Some way into the exercise, the vice-president of operations, who had been with the business for over 25 years, commented that BK had always been successful when it had focused on trying to be the best at its key business of burgers, but had suffered when it had tried to broaden into tangential areas of food or other business lines. He pulled out some historical graphs to prove the point. At which point, the marketing vice-president pulled out some of her data which showed that, despite being negatively perceived on many dimensions, the company's reputation for burgers was still exceptionally strong with consumers. Competitor research was also produced showing that BK was losing out to gourmet burger outfits. Finally, another board member said: "Well, isn't that it? Isn't that what we are about; being the best place for burgers?" Somebody else said: "Yes! It's in our name, and it's what drove the original founders of the company."

"Being the best place for burgers" was something that was deeply rooted in the history of the company and that people at all levels could relate to. It was invigorating because it played to the excellence theme. This formulation was eventually chosen as a much better statement of purpose than the original metrics iteration. The purpose statement was also translated into a more medium-term mission: to fight back against the up-and-coming companies that were eating BK's lunch – or more literally who were having BK's customers eat their lunch with them. BK had been so busy chasing McDonald's, it had forgotten who it was and neglected its own backyard.

An invigorating purpose for Britain

To illustrate the usefulness of the above model, let's apply it to a country – Britain. When considering history, it is clear that Britain's most successful period in world affairs was when it had a strong external orientation. This was a time when Britain sent its explorers and settlers to far and distant reaches of the world and which eventually led, albeit for a brief period, to the creation of the largest and most extensive empire the world has seen. The industrial revolution, widely seen as the source of Britain's rise to global prominence in the eighteenth century, was a consequence rather than a cause of this extensive global reach. Because of this breadth, Britain has some unusual attributes. As a state it sits on the UN Security Council, has close ties with the US and is also part of the Commonwealth of Nations. It also has a prominent role in the EC. No other country begins to match this level of engagement with the world. In addition, English is the *lingua franca* of the world community.

Now let's look at what's happening externally to Britain in the world. The most obvious trend here is the rise of globalization. Vast tracts of the world are coming into play in global business in a manner that was unthinkable before. This is already putting strains and pressures on world institutions and relationships between governments. New multi-lateral institutions will need to be formed and old ones re-formed to respond to these changes. The sharp increases in global trading will also create huge opportunities for middle-men and countries that are able to connect different parts of the world through trade.

Does not all this create enormous opportunities for a country with the attributes and instincts of Britain? Quite simply, could not Britain's unique and invigorating purpose in the new world be to "play the role of a constructive and positive midwife to the new global order"? A kind of Venice of the 21st century. Playing to this theme has huge potential upside, both economically and in terms of political influence, for Britain. This theme also plays to some of the core attributes of Britain's population. London is one of the most cosmopolitan cities in the world. The population travels more extensively than most and is more open to external cultural influences than almost any of its European neighbours.

All three elements of the purpose model – history and current reality, external environment and individual attributes – are, therefore, consistent with such a formulation of purpose for Britain. To some extent

Britain's leaders do at times play out this role, but explicit recognition of it would have a profound impact on policies and practices across the board. For example, to truly play such a mediating role Britain would have to ensure that it preserved appropriate balance in its relationships with all major blocs in the world rather than getting too close to any one. Britain's educational policies and language training could also be targeted towards the different blocs with which the country needs to connect. Its trading policy could also be more explicitly focused on emergent business themes that are likely to be required in an interconnected world. Finally, Britain could take a lead role in actively driving change in significant world institutions such as the UN and the IMF and acting as an honest broker of what the changing world requires of these institutions.

● Making purpose live

Meaning Inc. companies do not simply draft a compelling statement, they act upon its declared purpose. There are two major ways of doing this. First, converting the purpose into a source of managerial and employee energy by creating strong linkages to key business decision-making. Second, by developing short- and medium-term goals that link core purpose to more immediate objectives.

The central truth is that, in Meaning Inc. companies, purpose affects and informs all decisions. The unspoken, underlying assumption in average businesses is that day-to-day behaviour is principally driven by the pursuit of results and profits. Senior leaders need this for their survival and to reward themselves appropriately. However, core purpose statements only start to have real resonance in a business when decisions are taken that are clearly driven by these aspirations at the expense of other priorities. Inevitably, in Meaning Inc. companies significant decisions and actions are taken that are unambiguously driven by their company's core purpose and which typically conflict with the raw pursuit of profitable gain.

Let's take the case of Diageo, the world's largest drinks company. Aware that it is the industry leader, the company has decided that it needs to play a significant role in managing the potential positive and negative public reactions to its products. This has led Diageo to take a strong stance on responsible drinking, which is now one of the key priorities for the CEO, Paul Walsh. Walsh says he is focused on this area, "not just because it is the right thing to do but because self-regulation now is better for all of Diageo's stakeholders in the long run". He is emphatic about the sense of possibility here. "In this company, we are masters at marketing. That is about changing people's attitudes and, ultimately, behaviour. We need to put those skills to use not just in promoting our products but in ensuring that we promote the right social behaviours in our communities. We can make a significant contribution to society by getting this right."

At first, Walsh says that people felt Diageo was paying lip-service to responsible drinking, so it worked hard to drive home the message that it was serious. The company communicated a strong and clear marketing code to all its businesses that prevents them from promoting alcohol using sex, health arguments or images which appeal to young drinkers. Each market is required to have strategies around responsible drinking that fit in with their wider plans for the business. This, argues Walsh, is essential, as every market faces different issues in this area. Some developed markets face the problem of binge drinking while in other markets, the main issues are around drinking and driving. Painstakingly, a little at a time, the company is driving the message home.

Walsh is equally clear on another point: "In this area, it's best to nail some achievements first rather than just talking about your aspirations. Only then do people take you seriously." The company's efforts have won over many detractors. NGOs that would have been suspicious of Diageo now regularly sit around the same table to discuss issues. The company has also made a strong effort to involve its competitors as, in the words of Walsh, "collectively the industry is only as strong as its weakest link".

The Diageo example illustrates that there are no short-cuts if a particular reformulation of purpose is to be taken seriously. You have to work patiently inside and outside the business to make the change real.

Another extremely important way of bringing purpose to life is to explicitly use it to recruit people. A purpose only lives if it is in the hearts of employees. While companies do need to recruit people with diverse backgrounds and skills, to make this diversity work there needs to be a unifying set of core drivers. Tim Hoeksema, CEO of Midwest Express the US airline, says: "My advice is: be sure that there is a common vision that is felt by all your employees. As you bring people on board, choose people whose values are consistent with the values you have ... if you get the best people you can, all heading in the same direction, all focused on the same important things, you've gone a long way towards accomplishing what you want to accomplish."

Linking purpose to other goals

Are there tested and proven ways to take corporate purpose and link it throughout the company? Emphatically, Yes! While purpose sits at the top of the hierarchy of goals of an organization, it is also important for leaders to recognize the hierarchy of other objectives and goals. In particular, leaders must consistently portray how the achievement of sub-goals (or more prosaic aspirations) actually allows a company to achieve its long-term sense of purpose. In many companies, there is a pointless debate between what constitutes purpose, vision, mission, goals or strategic intent. In Meaning Inc. companies, leaders strive to demonstrate how different goals all fit together.

An invigorating purpose needs to be backed up by a more concrete and tangible set of objectives. Jim Collins and Jerry Porras talk about the importance of having a mission as well.[9] By this they mean a clear and compelling goal, often with time frames that focus people's efforts. They identify three types of mission statement that are particularly valuable:

- **Target setting:** setting an audacious but clear future goal. John F. Kennedy's mission of a man on the moon by the end of the decade is an example.

- **Common enemy:** identifying a company to overhaul or beat. Sony, for example, supplemented its purpose at one point by a mission to kill Matsushita.

- **Role modelling:** identifying a company in another field that you want to emulate. An example of this would be "becoming the Google of your industry".

Not many companies, however, tend to articulate goals at a variety of levels and show how they interconnect. Although it seems obvious, many executives fail to point out that driving the company's long-term sense of purpose will require a short-term drive for profitability. In the absence of making these linkages clear, with trade-offs openly acknowledged and conflicts discussed, it's all too easy for people to feel that the purpose statements have no relevance. All too often leaders will hold these pressures inside their minds without articulating them to the rest of the people who operate the business. Yet, sharing these issues can help strip away confusion and increase employees' motivation.

In sum, a Meaning Inc. leader in the pursuit of the benefits of having an invigorating purpose needs to do the following:

- **Understand the business's real core purpose.** All businesses have an underlying purpose that drives their actions. Often this is different from the espoused purpose. The starting point for moving forward is to know where you stand in the first place. Dig into history to find out what drove the business in its infancy and during periods when it has been at its best.

- **Frame a core purpose that is invigorating.** Crafting a business's core purpose at an invigorating level is more feasible than people might think but requires deep thought and a willingness and capacity on the part of the leadership to think hard about external social trends and pressures. It also requires a level of conceptual capability and imagination that is not always in plentiful supply, even at the top of organizations. It is not enough to wish for an empowering purpose. If you and your team cannot draft this on your own, employ someone who will probe, push, and test the group until a leadership vision emerges from the exercise.

- **Build core purpose on solid foundations.** It is counterproductive and unrealistic to craft a core purpose that does not resonate with the underlying DNA of the business or the people who are a part of it. Core purpose statements, therefore, need to be tested orally within the business in authentic conversations about their realism and relevance. Time and effort are also required to explain them, to explore the implications of truly living by them. Create your core purpose – then lead the challenge to make it authentic.

- **Demonstrate that core purpose is taken seriously.** This can only be done by making decisions that would not be made if the core purpose didn't exist. Passing up on opportunities, doing something that goes against the delivery of higher short-term results, and being prepared to take a stand on issues are all necessary if people throughout the organization are to feel that leadership is serious about what it says. In the absence of this, there's likely to be a sense of detachment and cynicism.

- **Develop missions and goals to provide more immediate focus.** Invigorating core purpose statements can be incredibly motivating. They do, however, represent a long-term view of what a business can contribute. Galvanizing action and change in the short term frequently requires the development of a set of goals which are instrumental to the achievement of the core purpose but which have a more concrete and tangible feel.

- **Map out the hierarchy of purpose, mission and short-term goals.** Leaders in a business can help to juggle a series of competing priorities and make trade-offs. Articulating long-term goals (and then the intermediate steps needed to achieve them) – as well as noting any short-term pressures that may need to be negotiated – will be necessary if people are to understand the challenge of pursuing an ennobling purpose without lapsing into cynicism. Employees can accept tough decisions provided they can see how they support a purpose that is worthy and in which they believe. And people who believe in the purpose of an organization are likely to find meaning in the work required to sustain it.

6. Meaning through history, values and continuity

"Continuity does not rule out fresh approaches to fresh situations."

Dean Rusk, US Secretary of State 1961–1969

Imagine, just for a second, that you're the CEO of a major American airline. Competition is fierce, you've got record levels of debt and, with declining passenger numbers, profits are under pressure. Now imagine that it's the morning of September 11, 2001. What goes through your mind as you watch the day unravel? And beyond the shock, grief and anger at that day's events, what goes through your mind later, when you discover that the business is endangered as transatlantic ticket sales plunge a further 40 per cent? What do you do? What do you say to your people?

The American Airlines CEO, Don Carty, while recognizing that the attacks had precipitated "the worst financial crisis in the history of the industry", also called upon the business's "long and proud history" and talked of how this would give American Airlines "a solid base for ... resolving our financial challenges". Indeed, American Airlines has an illustrious history going back to the days of Charles Lindberg, whose original aviation company formed one of the constituent companies of the group. In World War II, to help the Allied efforts, the airline gave half its fleet over to the military. Inside the business, the call to history resonated with people's feelings about the company and was seen by insiders as "incredibly galvanizing".

Contrast this with the action of the United Airlines chairman and CEO, James Goodwin. He sent a letter to all employees a few weeks after the attacks warning that United was "literally haemorrhaging money. Clearly this bleeding has to be stopped – and soon – or United will perish sometime next year." The letter helped to send both staff morale and United's shares plunging to a level even lower than they fell in the immediate aftermath of the attacks. In the space of a few weeks, the stock plummeted by over 25 per cent. The same kinds of workers who had rallied to save American Airlines revolted against United. Two weeks later, under pressure from the unions that owned a significant part of United's stock, Goodwin paid the price for his comments and was replaced.

This story, however, has a sting in its tail which illustrates both the importance of meaning and how easily it can be destroyed. Following 9/11, Don Carty won many plaudits for keeping American Airlines viable – the only major US airline not to disappear or file for bankruptcy. But, in 2003, Carty and his associates tried to pass through a controversial compensation plan for senior executives. The unions, who had done so much over this period, dug their heels in. They were able to accept sacrifices to keep a proud and venerable national company going, but were not prepared to bankroll "unfair packages" for those at the top. The call to history worked when it was perceived to be genuine but not when other, more questionable, motivations appeared. The unions withdrew their support and Carty departed.

How leaders frame decisions and make connections between current challenges and the past is therefore crucial if people are to understand and back their agenda. Just look at Winston Churchill's or F. D. R. Roosevelt's wartime speeches. When describing their cause, they repeatedly called upon their country's history and values. They did so, because they understood that providing people with a solid sense of identity in a time of crisis – a sense of "this is what we are about" – gives people a context, a bigger picture, which they can draw on to make sense of what is happening. Used in this way, a sense of identity can locate current events within a broader story, a grander narrative, which says, "It may be tough today, but this is part of something bigger and more enduring and while this day shall pass, we will remain."

Of course, providing people with a sense of identity is not only important in times of crisis, but in day-to-day business as well. This is because the sacrifice that human beings make by going the extra mile needs to be rewarded by an understanding of how they fit into a bigger picture. This need is fundamental to humans: religious belief, philosophy, and scientific endeavour are all manifestations of it. And when this need is not met, when people lose sight of how they fit into a business and how the business fits in with the wider world, they become disconnected from it. They become as much observers of the business as participants, as it gradually loses meaning for them and sinks into being little more than a source of income and an unfortunate necessity.

To feel truly connected to a business, then, employees need a context that makes sense for them. The previous chapter explored how businesses could help people connect to the bigger picture that is the business's positive societal purpose and future goal. A lack of such a compelling connection is one of the main issues in the soulless organization. In this chapter, we will explore how businesses can help people connect to the bigger picture that is the business's identity – its history, values and fundamental essence – even in times of change. This is one of the main challenges in today's attention-deficit organizations.

The continuity challenge

Change, adaptability, flexibility and opportunism have become the mantras of most modern-day businesses. Vast proportions of leaders' business education centres on the disciplines of change management. In many large consultancies, the change divisions are the biggest contributors to income. As the tenure of senior executives shortens, the scenario of the new CEO sweeping away what has gone before and outlining a bold new plan is not just increasingly common, it is frequently the only reality that a business knows.

Paradoxically, in spite of all the above, one often sees less and less true change on the ground. An increasing number of these change initiatives are either not having the impact they should have or are simply failing. More and more, leaders are grasping the handle of change only to see it come off in their hands. Many create the illusion of change with lots of activity, the launch of new initiatives, and endless restructurings, without much actually happening where it matters – at the grass roots.

Increasingly, it's not just those at the lower levels who are bemused, but also those purportedly leading the charge, however enthusiastic they may appear. Listen to what one HR director had to say when asked what she felt about a new initiative from the third CEO in five years: "We've all got our tin hats on and are keeping our heads down until it all passes, which, judging by past events, shouldn't be too long." In this increasingly common situation, businesses breed better spin-doctors than change agents, commitment becomes just a buzzword – a mask you wear in public – and change risks being stillborn.

Somewhere in all this, businesses seem to have forgotten the power of a grand narrative and the basic need that people have for a sense of continuity and identity. Just look at any merger for an example of the role of continuity in evoking commitment, and the dangers of discontinuity. No matter what is publicly said there is a winner and a loser, as one culture becomes more dominant than the other. And this creates a tension, as the people who were wedded to the latter lose their sense of continuity and find themselves having to either shift their allegiance or become increasingly disconnected from the business.

Consider what happened when Hewlett-Packard split its telecommunications and measurement businesses from its core computer business.[1] The new company, Agilent Technologies, was keen to differentiate itself and so established a new set of corporate values. Unfortunately, they initially moved too far, too quickly, leaving people feeling disconnected from the HP values that up to then had been a significant part of their corporate identity. The then CEO, Ned Barnholt, has described how he set about trying to instil the new values of speed, focus and accountability, but started to encounter resistance, with people saying, "that's really good, but that isn't why we joined Agilent or HP". In other words, employees began to lose their sense of connection to what the company was about. Realizing this, Ned re-adjusted his message to emphasize how Agilent would be building upon the very best of the core values of HP, while also adding new values that could make them a high-growth company. Had he not created this visible continuity, by locating the new Agilent values in the grand narrative of HP, he would have risked fundamentally undermining the commitment of Agilent's people to the company.

Without continuity, change can seem purposeless, activities can seem disconnected from the whole and cynicism can quickly develop with continual shifts in direction. Continuity enables identity, identity enables connection, and connection enables commitment. And an over-emphasis on achieving short-term competitive advantage, with the increased and continual change that it brings, threatens it all.

Unless businesses can learn how better to provide a sense of context, continuity and meaning for their people, the situation isn't going to improve. In fact, it's going to get a lot worse. Let's look now at what businesses can do in this area.

Understand your organizational DNA

The starting point is to work out what you have got in the first place. This will give you an idea of what to keep, what to change and, most importantly, the barriers you will face in selling change.

The idea of organizational DNA emerged from a biological metaphor of organizations that has been lurking for a long time in the background of management theory, largely because the message of survival of the fittest has provided a seemingly natural model for market competition. Just as in biology DNA is the genetic building-block of life, organizational DNA is an organization's core components – the fundamental building-blocks that make it what it is. Ram Charan and Noel Tichy have thus defined it as "the operating mechanisms, behaviours, attitudes and dialogues so deeply ingrained in the corporate psyche that institutionalize an organization's mindset and strategies".[2] It is akin, therefore, to an organization's personality or soul. The consulting firm Booz Allen Hamilton also refers to DNA as comprising Structure, Decision Rights, Motivators and Information.[3]

But where does this DNA reside? We have a clear and radical view on this, which initially people sometimes reject, but which over time many come to agree with. The DNA literally sits within the employees of an organization. Over many years, the people in any business undergo natural selection, just as do the genes in an organism. Only certain types are attracted to a particular company in the first place. The "inappropriate" types, who do make it through the filters, are often "tissue-rejected" (see page 164) after a while. They leave in frustration or are sacked. More rarely they are acculturated and go native. Through this process of natural selection and adaptation, exactly as in biology, an organization is left with a particular gene pool – not metaphorically, but literally.

A while back we were working with a leading UK advertising agency. In its prime, it had had an outstanding creative reputation but had been plagued with endless internal conflict and tension. Various efforts to end the in-fighting had just not worked. This had induced a sense of helplessness in the CEO who talked of something intangible in the walls – a miasma he called it – which just held the company back. He even wondered whether moving buildings would help get rid of this miasma. It soon became clear that the miasma wasn't in the walls at all but rather went up and down in the lifts. In other words, it was in the people. Quite simply, the edgy, creative reputation of the agency had attracted very particular types into the firm. The leaders had tried to impose an alien way of working which was destroying what gave these employees personal meaning. We helped the CEO work out an organizational strategy that took this into account, which essentially entailed being realistic about how much people could change and developing processes that managed the consequences of certain behaviours rather than seeking to eliminate them.

Consider, by contrast, the case of Yell, a highly successful company that originally produced the Yellow Pages directories in the UK, but which has moved to become a global business providing consumers with information through a range of channels, including digitally. This massive change has been managed in an incremental and unassuming manner by CEO, John Condron, who really knows his business and his organization. While Yell has brought in some new people, it has done so selectively and carefully. When Condron is introducing newcomers to the company, and they ask him about the Yell culture, he says he often just opens the office door, points out the first person who walks past and says, "that's our DNA".

If you want to understand your organizational DNA, the best place to start is to look at the people who have joined and stayed with you. The best way to do this is to:

- Identify a cross-section of people at all levels who have been with the business a while and who seem to fit and bond with the culture.

- Talk in-depth to them, or get outsiders to do so, about what makes them tick, why they joined the business, what keeps them there, what energizes them and what frustrates them. A sharp and incisive light needs to be directed at people in order to get beyond superficial views.

- Pull the themes together to understand the collective DNA and therefore what is or is not possible within your business and how things need to be positioned to gain traction.

Insiders and outsiders

So, if you accept that continuity is important if an organization is to have a robust sense of meaning, who can best provide it? The answer appears obvious: a sense of meaning through continuity is best provided by people who really understand the organization and its culture. Such knowledge is accumulated over time.

This flies in the face of the ongoing fashion for recruiting senior executives from outside the business to bring about change and deliver growth. There is research which backs the case for insiders over outsiders.

Martin L. Martens published an extensive study into the effects of recruiting external CEOs when companies float.[4] He looked at 435 flotations in the technology sector and divided them into: a) those that kept their founders in the CEO role; b) those that removed them; c) those that placed them in another less central role. He then looked at what had happened to the share price of the business over a period of time. His findings are intriguing. In the first instance, companies that removed the founder from the CEO slot and brought in an outsider did better. The average float valuation was $72 million for these companies as opposed to $65 million for those that kept their founders in the CEO position. Investors clearly felt that bringing in a new and often experienced CEO would help take the company to a new place and, since float valuation is significantly affected by sentiments about future prospects, expected the companies with new CEOs to perform slightly better. But when Martens looked at the data over time, things had turned on their heads – not just slightly but massively. Over three years, companies that kept their founders as CEOs had a 12 per cent rate of return annually, while for companies with new CEOs this return was a jaw-dropping minus 27 per cent. Not surprisingly, the rate of failure in these companies was also much higher.

Bringing in outsiders often looks good – and is a relatively easy lever to pull – but it frequently does not produce the goods.

This was neatly illustrated in a study commissioned by an FMCG to find out what kinds of people they should bring into the business. The company had recruited a large number of senior executives at considerable expense to shake the business up. To start, we suggested looking at these new recruits to see how they had done. We thought people needed at least a year to prove themselves and ideally two. The problem was, as we got stuck into the data, it rapidly emerged that not many people had stayed two years. Of the 50 or so senior imported executives, a full 60 per cent had gone by that time. What's more, no one had realized this. The few who had stayed and done well had created a sense that the strategy was working and people had quickly forgotten about those who just hadn't worked out. Outsider recruitment was far more risky when line roles were being filled but was more successful for functional positions.

Despite these sobering statistics, there is a growing trend for businesses to throw external candidates at a perceived need in the organization. Indeed, research indicates that 45 per cent of organizations report that at least one third of senior executive positions are filled by hiring externally.[5] Businesses see individuals who possess qualities that they believe are currently less common in the organization and so introduce them in the hope of breeding-in the desired qualities. Yet, all too often, insufficient attention and assistance is given to embedding the new people into the business. As a result, many of the newcomers leave after a year or two, as they fail to fully understand and gel with the existing organizational culture. In fact, research indicates that a staggering 40 per cent of those hired from outside fail in the first 18 months.[6] Borrowing a metaphor from biology, we call this phenomenon "tissue rejection".

People often underestimate the difficulty of grafting something new on to something old because they fail to appreciate the importance of continuity for performance. Companies, of course, need to find ways to get something old to stretch and evolve into something new, but frequently the ingredients are simply thrown together and the grafting or stretching process is left to itself. All too often, then, the new team members fail to gain traction and the old team members end up feeling unvalued and less motivated.

What is lacking for both parties is a clear and shared understanding of continuity and identity around what the team is doing and where it is going. Without this, it can be difficult for people to see how they fit in and, without that, commitment to the team and the company can falter.

All this is not to say that the injection of outsiders is always a bad thing, but the following observations can be made:

- The injection of small numbers of outsiders to stimulate and provide fresh thinking is valuable and frequently works.

- The injection of outsiders to fundamentally change a culture is fraught with dangers and generally ends up in disappointment all round.

- If you want to use outsiders to change a culture, move fast and bring in a substantial, critical mass of people, otherwise your efforts will fail.

Leveraging history

For most individuals their identity – who they are – is inextricably linked with their past: where they've been and what they've done. Organizations are no different and a business's history is thus fundamental to its sense of identity. Realizing this, BMW has an official history and has set up a museum dedicated to keeping this story alive. "BMW does not just stand by its history, but deliberately preserves it as a vital element of its identity," says the company's web site.

One of the best examples of a business that consistently tries to make the most of its history is American Airlines. As mentioned earlier, the company has its roots in the earliest days of air flight and can trace its history back over 80 years. The company has an official history that is laid out in its own museum and, as we saw earlier with Don Carty's post-9/11 speech, it continually and deliberately refers back to its history as an aviation pioneer as a way of trying to create a sense of identity and meaning for its people.

Or consider Tata, which has produced numerous publications on the heritage of the group and which continually and proudly refers back to the company's history when making statements about future direction. In 2004, for example, the company launched a series of events across India under the badge "A Century of Trust", with the aim of informing employees and customers of its history. People joining Tata receive lessons in the history of the company. With both American Airlines and Tata the message is, "you're part of something historical and significant here".

Goldman Sachs is another organization which takes its history extremely seriously. In fact the company recently employed some anthropologists to dig into its history and culture and to unearth key themes. They also attach a high level of importance to telling and re-telling stories that bring these cultural values to life. The same emphasis is placed on embedding these stories throughout the firm's learning and professional development efforts.

Yet creating and referring back to an official history is only half the story. There are also unofficial histories within businesses – the histories that are created around the informality of the coffee machine – that can also inform a business's sense of identity. For people in the canteen talk about what has been happening to them, out of which ideas and perceptions about the organization arise.

The above examples illustrate the importance of story-telling in organizations. For years, evolutionary psychologists have been arguing that the human mind is uniquely adapted to gossip and to the telling and remembering of stories. This is how through the ages cultures have passed on their truths and core values. How effective would *The Iliad* or *The Mahabharata* be as a Powerpoint presentation? Yet the slick deck of slides has become in many companies the only means of communication and discourse.

The value of values

At the core of a company's identity lie the implicit values and ground rules that govern its day-to-day behaviours. Values are the building-blocks that create the culture of a business.

As an example of the importance of values, let's look at Toyota's production system. Many observers have tried to understand its success, but failed because they focused on Toyota's visible activities and structures rather than the unwritten values around quality that underpinned these activities and structures.[7] Businesses wishing to replicate Toyota's success would have been better served by trying to replicate these values than trying to reproduce the precise structure and procedures of the production system.

The problem with identifying and defining an organization's values, however, is that the majority of organizations have tended to be shockingly poor at it themselves. The business world is littered with appallingly bland and crass examples of values statements that have little impact on the people within the business. Many values statements, for instance, have tended to focus on ethical guidelines that involve overly general statements, such as "Respect for the diversity and individuality of all people" or "Commitment to integrity", which lack any immediate obvious relevance to day-to-day activities. As a result, they have tended to be meaningless for the majority of employees, leaving the values at best ignored, and at worst generating cynicism.

The use of generic-sounding values statements is thankfully in decline and businesses are instead developing values statements that articulate more precisely the behaviour they believe is core to the culture and will make for a successful working environment. As an example of this, consider these values statements from Siemens: "I am a good colleague", "I am a team-player – I feel responsible", and "I keep my promises – I only promise what I can keep". These are very different from generic values statements because they are more specific and are grounded in the reality of what people do, day-in, day-out.

At Ritz Carlton hotels, all staff carry around a copy of a credo card, which is a constant reminder of what the company is all about. On one side, in large type, is the corporate motto, "We are ladies and gentlemen serving ladies and gentlemen." To some, this may sound clichéd, but you only need to read it once and you know what the organization is all about. On the other side of the credo there is a list of 20 basic rules, which are a suggestion as to how the credo can be translated into real behaviour. These rules include statements like "smile – we're on a stage", "escort guest rather than pointing out directions" or "be an ambassador of your hotel in and outside of the workplace". This is useful because it gives a clear indication to employees of what is expected of them at a very simple behavioural level. As a result, they enable the espoused values to feel authentic, real and relevant to the individuals who are expected to live them out.

Levi Strauss and Mars both explicitly refer back to their organizational history in their values statements and thus embed them in real events. Levis Strauss's values of Empathy, Originality, Integrity and Courage don't, on the face of things, sound any more encouraging than any other values statement. But they have cleverly woven these values into a story about the company, showing how they have been lived up to throughout its history, in a way that makes them feel authentic and gives them substance. Likewise, Mars has its "Five Principles" and declares that, "In one form or another, the Five Principles of Mars have guided our company since its very beginning … More than a statement of values, they are a set of fundamental beliefs that help to define Mars as a company … They express our vision not only of who we are, but where – and what – we want to be."

● A model for creating values that live

Businesses, however, cannot just be guided purely by the past when crafting their values. Over the years, we have evolved a set of considerations that need to be taken into account for companies to develop a viable and meaningful set of values that build on past

Figure 6 ● Developing effective organizational values

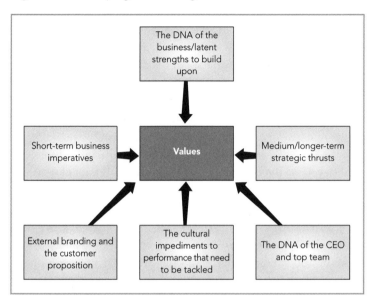

history but which also help the organization adapt and face the future.

Each of the areas in Figure 5 needs to be taken into account if the job of developing values is to be done well. If you don't understand the values of the CEO and the top team, the words and the music just won't match. The company will say one thing but senior executives will drive other priorities in their day-to-day behaviour. If you don't take into account the history and DNA of the organization your values will just be alien aspirations that lack meaning for your people. However, you can't just be internally focused, you also need to look externally and ask what your customers want of you and what other leaders in your industry are doing. Finally, it is critical to factor in the business's future strategic goals and the organizational changes needed to deliver these or your values will appear stuck in time. Doing this helps future-proof the values.

As an example, consider J. Sainsbury, which we talked about briefly on page 89. When he took over as CEO in 2004, Justin King was keen to identify a set of values that provided organizational glue for the business. He had seen the power of this in effecting the turnaround at Asda, where he had previously worked. Internally, some were surprised that King should focus on this, given the serious position of the business. But for him it was a key building-block of the cultural transformation he wanted to achieve.

A group led by the largely new Operating Board, supported by YSC and a team of senior – mainly long-standing – executives, was set up. As a first step, this group worked with other colleagues to get into the DNA of the business. They set about talking to employees at all levels of the business to delve into people's memories and experiences. It was important to understand Sainsbury's history and what made people inside the business tick. The marketing department was asked to provide a consumer perspective on what customers valued in Sainsbury's and what they wanted going forward, and the board went through a similar process with an external consultancy to identify and resolve some key strategic dilemmas. Finally, they looked at what was happening globally in food retailing, from a culture and values point of view, particularly in the US, where some innovative firms had emerged.

The board then met to develop an initial view of Sainsbury's purpose and values. As a starting point, at a dinner before the event each board member, including Justin King, talked about their own personal values and what they could and could not live with. The DNA team then held an interactive session on Sainsbury's history and cultural "DNA" – plastered on the walls were adverts, statements and products from Sainsbury's glory days. They played back the interviews with employees about memories and past experiences. This was at times an emotional session, particularly when people talked about the values the business had lost sight of.

Finally, the board got to work to define both Sainsbury's purpose and its values. It wasn't easy work. People came at things differently. There was a lot of input that needed to be digested and interpreted. The DNA and project team were in the room next door and as the board produced views, they were passed through to the other teams for comment and challenge. At one point, the project team felt the board was missing what people in the business wanted. At another time, the board felt the project team didn't understand what they were getting at. When, after two days, the goal and value statements were produced, the DNA team took them into the business for testing.

Eventually, the values read as follows: Getting better every day, Great service drives sales, Individual responsibility – team delivery, Keep it simple, Respect for the individual, Treat every £ as your own.

They were written up as a story and received an extremely positive reception from the business. Store managers, in particular, felt the reworked values represented a return to fundamental retailing instincts and helped focus the business on what mattered. The process of identifying them had also produced some significant evangelists for the values, as well as strong ownership from the top team. It may be coincidence (and a whole host of other initiatives were also relevant) but after the values were launched, Sainsbury's started to post month-on-month increases in its market share after years of decline.

Embedding values

Producing the right kind of values is, however, only half the story. You then have to make them live. This is not a process that can be ignored or short-circuited if a business is to get any value out of values. Most organizations, however, tend to launch their values as glossy leaflets or as one big communication exercise. What is needed is a more concerted, personalized form of engagement.

Take the case of a leading, Scotland-based global insurance company. Our task was to help drive and embed a new set of values throughout the organization. It was clear to us, from our in-depth interviews with senior leadership, that the organization's culture, while appropriate to business-as-usual conditions, was in many areas unsuited to its environment. The new CEO's predecessor had been typical of the leadership attitudes that characterized the business – paternalistic, controlling and detail-obsessed. And the result? A disempowered, obsessively cautious and internally focused workforce – and a senior leadership that found itself inadvertently cast on the horns of a dilemma: embracing driving and controlling behaviours that reinforced the culture of disempowerment it despaired of, but when it took its foot off the gas, being faced with passivity and an unacceptably slow pace of change.

We worked closely with the senior team and management group to create a set of organizational values and behaviours that could be used to stimulate new ways of being and acting in the company. It was clear that we needed to appeal to what was true and strong in the organization – its traditions of loyalty, integrity and service – while capturing the shift to a new model of leadership and "followship" behaviours.

The values were designed through a series of large- and small-scale meetings, led by an internal Involvement Team consisting of people from across the business.

This was followed by a series of two-day workshops. Participants attended in their work teams with two other teams and were taken through a series of exercises and feedback sessions to both give them an intellectual and emotional insight into the business's change agenda and to see how these linked to the values. Specifically, the workshops aimed to help them understand the following:

- How they individually and as teams measured up to the values.

- How they could prioritize their activities to make sure they were focusing on areas that would have the highest business and cultural pay-off.

- How they could work more creatively across the business in order to unlock creative and collaborative potential so that new opportunities could be identified and exploited.

Additionally, the workshops introduced people to new ways of working which emphasized open dialogue, creativity, working across boundaries and that rare commodity in the frequently dour and dry world of Edinburgh financial services – fun.

Harnessing values to drive change

To illustrate the power of an understanding of values for driving change, let's take a national example – change in India. One of the dominant values in Indian civilization could best be described as an intellectual/spiritual orientation. There are, of course, many other values, some contradictory, that run through Indian culture, but few would contest the importance of the intellectual/spiritual dimension. This value finds expression in the earliest manifestations of Indian culture. The *Bhagavad Gita*, one of the most important texts of Hinduism, opens with Arjuna refusing to fight because those on the other side are just like him. "I would not do it for all three worlds much less for the pleasures of this one", he says. The emperor Ashoka, whose chariot motif adorns the Indian flag, laid down his arms and converted to Buddhism because he could not countenance any more war. The highest caste in Indian society is not the merchant or warrior caste but the Brahmins, who concern themselves with intellectual and spiritual matters. India's is the only major civilization where vegetarianism is the norm, driven by respect for all living things.

Through the ages, this value has conditioned what India has been good at. Chinese civilization, much more practical in its orientation, has a host of inventions to boast of including printing, gunpowder and the compass. Indian civilization invented the zero, chess, algebra and the Arabic number system now used throughout the world. This was taken from India by the Arabs, whose word for mathematics at the time translated as "the art of the Hindus". All these developments were the product of intellectual play and concern with matters sublime. Even today China beats India hands down at manufacturing, but in the more esoteric world of IT or biotechnology, India has a clear lead.

Many business leaders desperately want to instigate cultural change but become frustrated because people just won't embrace the themes they want to drive. The early fighters for Indian independence faced similar obstacles. Despite the justice of their cause, they just could not get people behind them. Gandhi, when he returned from exile in South Africa in 1915, quickly saw the problem. The independence movement had not understood the roots of Indian culture. Immediately he advocated going out to talk to the people. Not the middle classes but those who lived in the villages. He and his followers listened, talked and built a picture. In his "There is no salvation for India" speech Gandhi insisted that the independence struggle be conducted in a language ordinary Indians could understand, both metaphorically and literally: "Our languages are the reflection of ourselves and if you tell me that our languages are too poor to express the best thought, then say the sooner we are wiped out of existence the better." The *satyagraha* (steadfastness in truth) movement, with its spiritual tones and principles of non-violence, that Gandhi and his Congress then launched, firmly played to a core value in Indian civilization. It was like a lighted match being thrown into a parched field.

Today, there is another opportunity to play to this value. Despite India's recent economic success, virtually every commentator bemoans the terrible bureaucracy and corruption that afflicts the country. Businesses succeed in spite rather than because of the institutions of modern India. Despite countless initiatives, the problem seems intractable. The first point to make here is that this problem is the dark side of the intellectual/spiritual values mentioned above. The highest intellectual/spiritual castes in India have always expected others to bankroll them and their pen-pushing activities through donations. Historically, these castes have controlled the other castes, including the commercial ones, and have expected to be given a proportion of commercial wealth for their dubious input. Although there are many other reasons for corruption, this peculiarly Indian aspect makes it especially pernicious and intractable in that country.

Yet there is a solution – by appealing to intellectual/spiritual values, some of the elite might just play ball. The coin needs to be flipped so that the positive rather than the negative side of this value is accentuated. One possibility is to develop for India a grander purpose in the world that plays to this core intellectual/spiritual value and which makes its local negative and individual expression less likely.

This is exactly what Nehru did in India after independence. Appalled by the dynamics of the Cold War, Nehru set up the non-aligned movement to prevent the world from falling into two antagonistic camps. India led this movement and it was a clear expression of a core Indian orientation. The dominant castes in India fell into line and in the 1950s the Indian political and bureaucratic system had a reputation for being efficient and much cleaner than it is today. Interestingly, despite the reliance on state planning, the Indian economy in this period did extremely well relative to others, posting upwards of 5 per cent economic growth a year. This matched or exceeded many of the countries that later surpassed India. The India–China war of 1962 effectively put an end to India's non-aligned alternative, as well as its high-profile role in world affairs. Nehru, his ideals shattered, died soon after. Corruption escalated and the Indian economy stagnated, achieving growth rates of barely 3 per cent, while many of its competitors pulled away.

Today, while the economy is doing much better, the lack of a global sense of purpose for India, which is in tune with its values, is arguably the missing ingredient needed to remove a core blockage to future success. Catch-up motivation, which works in other countries, is not enough to engage the Indian elite and pull them back from their pen-pushing or parasitic instincts. A theme for India, somewhere along the lines of what Nehru originally envisaged, but updated and made relevant to the current world situation, is a possibility. The essential point here is, if you are going to change intractable behaviour, recognize the need to play to or reverse some core values.

In summary, when harnessing values to drive change you must:

● Understand your history, values and DNA. But do it right or don't do it at all. Going through the motions when trying to define or describe your organization's history, values or DNA is usually worse than not doing it at all. People aren't fools and they know when something feels real or not. So take your time to look at all the areas that need to be considered to make your values realistic, relevant and future-proofed.

● Involve people. Any process of defining organizational DNA *must* be inclusive and involve a thorough understanding of your people at all levels. Otherwise, it will feel imposed and you increase the risk of the output feeling inauthentic. Don't tell, ask. Organizations, like individuals, tend to assume they know what they're about, what they're good at and what they're not good at. As a result, many – if not most – tend not to proactively seek out their employees' opinions about this. Experience has shown, though, that when leaders do take the time to ask, they are frequently surprised and almost always develop a more sophisticated understanding as a result.

● Be clear about your purpose. Before embarking on a process of defining organizational DNA, make sure you are clear about what you want to use the information for and what you hope to accomplish with it. Those organizations that clearly articulate for their people what the process is about and – importantly – how it will be useful, tend to receive far more open and enthusiastic involvement. If an organization facing a period of difficult change states upfront that it sees an assessment of its identity as an essential foundation for understanding how various characteristics of the business might help or hinder it in meeting the challenges, this will provide a clear rationale for involvement and help diffuse any confusion or cynicism about the project.

● Give change a context. When you inject change into your business, launch it with a story that embeds the change in what has gone before, so as to create a sense of continuity for people. Look into the history of how previous changes have been managed and don't assume that what you are trying to do has not been attempted before. Likewise, don't assume that fresh blood will know how to translate their different skills and qualities into real change within the business. Help embed new people within the business, for example, by creating a story around their recruitment and pairing them with experienced hands who understand the extant DNA and know how to make things happen within it.

- Treat identity as a resource. Organizational history and internal identity should be considered as a corporate resource in the same way that external branding is, and be managed at the same level. Particular individuals should therefore be assigned responsibility for identity management. When evaluating the impact of change initiatives, consider the effect on identity and the price of the ensuing loss of meaning.

- Create alignment. Align your business with its values and make sure that nurturing organizational history and values is seen as one of the basics, rather than just as a "nice-to-have". Make sure that there is a clear alignment between leadership and management practices and the dominant value themes. Make your leaders accountable for how they and their teams contribute to the organization's values. Examples of this are systematic feedback that focuses on how individuals contribute to core business values, or making leaders financially accountable for their legacy to the corporate values (for instance, through using a balanced scorecard system or generating a leadership capability framework that incorporates the desired behaviours).

- Recruit outsiders carefully. Try to achieve as much as possible with people who know your business and understand your DNA. If you need to go outside, be aware of the risks and give people help to engage and become effective within the organization. Monitor the results of external recruitment and be prepared to admit mistakes and learn.

Organizational history, DNA and values are a powerful mechanism through which you can come to understand both the core characteristics and the cultural and psychological nuances that form the bedrock of your business's identity as a platform for driving true and lasting change effectively. They are a mechanism through which you can create a sense of meaning, connection and commitment in your people by enabling them to remember, recognize and understand the context of current events. And, most crucially, they provide a means for you to counter-balance the short-term pressures on your business that threaten to undermine its long-term ability to change and develop. Indeed, it is increasingly not just a case of businesses being able to provide a context for change, but of needing to.

Rarely do leaders within business find much time to consider such things – the demanding realities of everyday work tend to intrude. But if business is to succeed in fully engaging people in change and evoking real commitment, it must make the time, because life won't get any easier. In an increasingly challenging and turbulent market-place, nurturing your organization's history and values is fast becoming one of the basics.

7. Inside-Out branding

> "It's not slickness, polish, uniqueness or cleverness that makes a brand a brand, it is truth."
>
> Harry Beckwith, author on advertising and marketing[1]

Returning from a business trip on Virgin Airlines, I got talking to the driver of the limousine that picks up Virgin customers who are using their Upper Class service. I was somewhat critical about Virgin trains as I had experienced a number of delays travelling with them. The driver instantly leapt to Virgin's defence with a number of explanations as to why the problems on the trains were not Virgin's fault, and then launched into a broader defence of the company. He talked about how proud he and other employees felt to be associated with the Virgin brand. He also talked of an experience he had when collecting Richard Branson from his home. He had arrived early at the Branson household and rather than letting him wait outside in the car, Branson had invited him in for a drink and a bite to eat with the family. I was impressed by the driver's loyalty to Virgin, even more so a few days later, when I found out that the limousine company is not part of the Virgin Group at all, but an outsourced entity.

Clearly, this driver, along with many thousands of employees, felt proud of the Virgin brand, wanted to be associated with it and was keen to protect it from any efforts to diminish it. When you engage with any Virgin business, it is clear that the brand finds life in the behaviour of the people – there is a distinct friendliness, vitality, creativity, customer responsiveness and sense of fun that are all core elements of the external Virgin brand. Virgin is also one of the most trusted brands in the UK, as evidenced by its ability to successfully expand into diverse business areas and geographies with only the brand values staying constant; that consumers will follow such leaps is testament to their faith in the brand.[2] Virgin is an example of "Inside-Out" branding – the utter alignment with how the brand is lived and communicated, both internally and externally.

By Inside-Out branding we mean:

- Bringing the same insights, care and attention towards understanding the impact of a brand on employees, as on researching the impact on customers.

- Building brand identity internally rather than outsourcing it to external agencies.

- Only going public with a brand identity once it is clear that what it promises is being lived internally.

The Virgin brand is a reflection of its creator, Richard Branson – a quirky, risk-taking man with a zest for life. The people Virgin hire and the businesses they go into are also a complete reflection of the brand. However, it is the fact that the brand is lived internally which creates the initial trust. Inside-Out branding creates trust, meaning and authenticity for both employees and consumers.

Richard Branson says that one of the key drivers of Virgin's success is the power of the brand. He also says: "For nearly 250 days of the year I travel around the world, trying to make Virgin the most respected brand in the world; not necessarily the biggest, but the best."

The previous chapters on purpose and organizational values have explored the internal drivers which, when used properly, give businesses a sense of purpose which goes beyond the rational and frames the broader meaning or mission it is trying to achieve. Connecting with history, values and core skills helps to ground this purpose in the fibre of the organization – by codifying its personality and soul. This chapter looks at the third point of the triangle – the interface a company has between its inner workings and the outside world – namely its externally focused consumer and corporate brands.

The brand is Orange

External branding is a lens through which companies, and by extension the people who work in them, are viewed. A survey showed that people working for one of the UK's 83 superbrands have significantly higher levels of commitment, loyalty, trust and pride than their peers at lesser-known companies.[3]

Take the case of Orange, a highly successful international mobile phone company, with roots in the UK. Most observers would agree that a key driver of Orange's success with customers has been the fresh and responsive brand image the company has cultivated, in part, through its highly innovative marketing and advertising. But what about the impact on employees? Madeleine Bunting of the *Guardian* newspaper visited one of Orange's call centres and was surprised at the sheer buzz and commitment she found in people engaged in work that was frankly tedious, emotionally demanding and relatively poorly paid.[4] After listening to a few calls being answered, she quickly found herself getting irritated by the tone, attitude and repetitive whining of customers. But in call after call she did not see the Orange people falter once. They went on doing this for the whole day with only a half-hour break for lunch and two 15-minute breaks for coffee. Even after all this she found that the workers were full of a "near implausible enthusiasm". A number wore branded T-shirts by choice. Newcomers who had been sceptical at first had virtually all been turned around.

The commitment Bunting had witnessed was almost certainly the sense of meaning and pride instilled by the brand. The psychological reward of being associated with a positive brand and an internal culture that lived the brand values was the key distinctive feature. Orange's people have no doubts about this. To quote Nicole Louis, at that time Orange's head of brand communication: "They fall in love with the brand. It's like a relationship." It is easy to describe the Orange experience and see and feel the power of the brand in action. It is much harder to achieve and we have only seen a few businesses get it right. It is also not always easy to sustain. Subsequently, as Orange was taken over, Madeleine Bunting felt that the motivational effect of the brand had diminished.

Branding as a topic excites strong feelings. For the pro-lobby, brands are the external showcase for a company. They are an avenue for a business to state its purpose and values – to its customers, stakeholders and employees. By making these explicit, brands force businesses to behave in ways which are true to these principles. In short, they keep businesses honest, responsible and responsive. More than this, they represent freedom of choice, and are a mirror of societal values.

For those who are anti, branding goes hand in hand with globalization and capitalism as corporate evils. Brands encourage us to consume more than we need, have aspirations that are unrealistic and they make promises that they cannot keep. Rather than empower and inform us, they are manipulative entities which are the acceptable, cuddly face of capitalism.

As consumers we are bombarded by brands which compete for our attention and loyalty. We are encouraged to form relationships with brands, and to see them as conveying something about our personal choices and values. Sometimes we choose to support a brand because of the celebrity who endorses it – identifying with that celebrity in doing so. Strong brands invoke emotional reactions in us, and represent values and purpose that go way beyond the concrete properties of the goods on offer. They become shorthand for the personality and ethos of the business, and the people, that produce them. Most of us have strong affiliations (or relationships) with certain brands – and feel equally strong feelings against others. Branding influences our personal choices by posing the question – "Do I want to be associated with this?" But before we look at what today's consumers want from brands, let's turn the focus on what brands do for employees.

Branding and the employee experience

When Freud wrote that *lieben und arbeit* (love and work) are the keys to happiness, he also said that a key function of work was to connect us to reality and the society of which we are a part. Work positions us in the scheme of things and shapes our social identity.

What we feel about the identity it gives us is crucially dependent on how others view the organization for which we work. This, in turn, is influenced by branding. The importance of this point is often missed and cannot be overemphasized – branding influences psychologically the most important non-tangible aspect we get out of work: our sense of social identity.

"Social Identity Theory" considers our numerous "social identities", which correspond with our membership of different groups. For example, at any time we might be employees of a business, a player in a sports team and one of a group of friends. Once we have identified ourselves as part of a group, we seek to use that membership to enhance our self-esteem by positively differentiating our group through comparisons with other groups along some meaningful dimension.

Furthermore, as the social psychologist George Herbert Mead observed, our sense of ourselves is, to a substantial extent, driven by how others see us. Through a subtle set of mechanisms we start to behave and feel in the way people expect. So branding does not just influence our social identity, it also shapes what we think of ourselves and how we behave. Put another way, an airline stewardess who works for Virgin gets a strong sense of social identity out of it but also probably at some level starts to become the person others expect of her.

As employees, the impact of external branding of the products, services or company we work for on our pride, sense of meaning and personal identity is extremely strong. As with all consumers, we have our personal likes and dislikes. But more than that: the external branding of a business can help to create meaning, purpose and belonging for its employees, who can:

● Share the success and feel proud to be part of an admired external brand. The Superbrands survey (see page 181) repeatedly demonstrates the pride that comes with being associated with a success story.

● Identify with the external brand values. These, by extension say something meaningful and congruent about their personal values. Successful brands such as Virgin and Nike actively encourage pride in their brand and are overt in nailing their brand values to the mast and using these as guiding principles which all are expected to identify with.

- Experience a virtuous circle between the external brand values and the internal culture. This is the power of Inside-Out branding. The external branding sends a message about how employees can expect to be treated, which is reinforced by the day-to-day experience of working within the business. Inside-Out brands practise what they preach.

- Choose to work for businesses whose values and principles align with theirs. According to a UK study by the Chartered Institute of Personnel and Development, 85 per cent of employers are experiencing difficulties recruiting the right calibre and fit of people, with many now focusing on using their external brands as a showcase for their businesses and hence attracting the type of people who will gel with the business.[5]

The businesses which create a positive brand in the minds of their employees will be the ones which embrace our notion of Inside-Out branding. Doing so will not only have a positive impact on employees, but, because of profound changes in what consumers want and their attitudes towards brands, Inside-Out branding is also the only option for creating brands that are experienced as meaningful and authentic by the outside world. Let's therefore turn to the pressures coming from consumers before looking at how to make all this happen.

The consumer revolt against brands

"The conscious and intelligent manipulation of the organized habits and opinions of the masses is an important element in democratic society."

Edward Bernays, nephew of Sigmund Freud and a pioneer of PR and marketing

From its inception, marketing via external brand positions has represented more than the tangible properties of the goods promoted. In the 1920s, Bernays promoted Lucky Strike cigarettes to American women as a symbol of liberation and independence – captured by the slogan "Torches of Freedom" and backed up by imagery of emancipated, empowered women inhaling enthusiastically on the cigarettes. Smoking became a symbol of female autonomy and, ironically, given Bernays's views on the use of marketing, freedom of thought.

This neatly illustrates the power of brands – they unavoidably form associations at an emotional, unconscious level. From Freud onwards, the power of the unconscious to influence our behaviour has been recognized and exploited. Associating products (cigarettes) with emotional needs (independence) produces a tie that goes beyond rational choice and strays into unconscious attachment and loyalty between consumer and product. When it goes well, argues Kevin Roberts in *LoveMarks*, it can create ties which fulfil genuine needs and lead to a relationship between customer and brand.[6] By extension, employees bask in the good reputation of the brand.

The nature of the relationship between consumer and brand, and particularly the balance of power in the relationship, has shifted dramatically over the course of the twentieth and into the 21st centuries. Consumers, from a position of passivity and acceptance of brands and their messages, have become much more discerning, savvy, informed choosers of brands. The rise of the mass media and the availability of information has promoted far more astute end users who are more aware of their buying power and its ability to influence. In parallel, the ability of businesses to control their brands and get to their consumers has been diluted.

One of the reasons for this is that the traditional media has fragmented. Today's consumer is used to on-demand, opt-in media channels, and can avoid messages or adverts they don't want to see. They want to consume those products which are meaningful and resonant with their values – and not to be troubled by those which don't. They want "their" brands to be consistent through each point of contact with them, while also being responsive to their needs. Essentially, the relationship has evolved into one where the consumer has more power, and the brands which are going to succeed are those which can captivate and intrigue consumers, forming powerful connections which breed "loyalty beyond reason".[7]

Brands are now undeniably big business, and can be a significant asset on a company's balance sheet. For example, the Coca-Cola brand has an estimated brand value of US$67.5 billion.[8] For a brand to maintain its value it needs to perform a delicate balancing act between the needs of different stakeholders – its consumers, employees and financial backers. Some survey results illustrate the difficulties in walking this tightrope.

The emotional power of branding gives rise to tremendous opportunities to generate loyalty, belonging and a sense of relationship between brand and individual. According to Kevin Roberts, CEO of Saatchi & Saatchi, and the author of *Lovemarks*, this will be done by building respect and establishing love. However, the dark side of this is the potential to breed suspicion and mistrust, and a perception of being manipulated and becoming the victim of spin rather than experiencing a responsive two-way relationship. Brands that will have the edge in the 21st century need to behave in ways which will build lasting relationships and bonds between themselves, consumers and employees. To do this, brands need to adhere to some basic principles of good behaviour within relationships.

For example, brands need to demonstrate their authenticity by promoting a set of brand values that say something legitimate and accurate about their business. Virgin can stretch its brand as its core values (value for money, quality, innovation, fun and a sense of fresh challenge) are as applicable to travel as they are to banking or entertainment. The central idea is elastic and not constrained by particular products or geographies.[9] Conversely, McDonald's can authentically claim to be a leading purveyor of hot, convenient take-away food at a competitive price. Its brand has huge recognition for these qualities. However, attempts by McDonald's to move into the healthy food take-away market were perceived to lack authenticity and were widely derided. Take, for example, what the *Guardian* newspaper had to say: "The new salad, with six different sorts of lettuce in it, is made with croutons and a dressing so rich that one helping contains nearly twice the calories and more than three times as much fat as a standard hamburger."[10]

In the eyes of many, the McDonald's brand simply could not authentically move into the healthy food space – especially when the reality was found to fall short of the brand promise.

Only connect

This leads on to the next challenge faced by the much scrutinized 21st-century brand – that of demonstrating coherence and consistency. Through personal experience, reading media coverage or observing business performance, the words and music must match. Otherwise, this is an easy breeding ground for cynicism, distrust and the destruction of meaning. Unprecedented access to information, consumer sensitivity to mismarriages between spin and substance and, increasingly, a vocal, active anti-corporate lobby, all point to the need for large-scale brands to consistently and repeatedly be genuine, truthful and loyal to their brand values.

Local and global

Starbucks has a brand position which emphasizes community and a home from home – the experience one has of drinking in a Starbucks is only partly about the coffee. Indeed, this position is consistent with Starbucks' origins as a single-site coffee house in Seattle in 1971. Belonging to the Starbucks community, which offers a certain ambiance and the reassurance of the known, is all part of the brand experience.

However, Starbucks' expansion into 36 countries has brought it under fire for the perceived inconsistencies between its community brand values and the impact it has on those communities it touches. It has been accused of destroying local businesses by "clustering": a term which describes the phenomenon of an area being saturated with a company's branches and so forcing local competitors to close down.[11] Starbucks' relationship with coffee growers and the effect of its pricing on their communities has been similarly criticized.[12] Far from promoting the idea of community more broadly, Starbucks stood accused of undermining both local and distal communities where it traded.

For Starbucks to continue to expand its brand, these inconsistencies have needed to be challenged, and in a way that has credibility. So, while the company's web site can showcase the corporate social responsibility policy, and portray the face that Starbucks would like the world to see, perhaps the more compelling evidence for its probity as a good corporate citizen comes from third-party commendations for its behaviour. For example, Starbucks works with Oxfam to develop fairer trading practices with its coffee farmers (in the process leveraging its reputation by association with Oxfam's strong brand). Its success in defending its brand under fire is shown by the external accolades it has received from its peers. It was *Fortune*'s Most Admired Food Services Company to Work For in 2006, and was top ranked for its social responsibility. It was also 29th in the *Fortune* 100 Best Companies to Work For in 2006.[13]

Starbucks neatly illustrates key points of brand consistency. First, if you don't walk the talk then there are too many avenues, protest groups, interested media and general sceptics who will shine a light on your inconsistencies, to the detriment of both the relationship between consumer and brand, and employee and brand. Who, after all, would want to work for a third-world-exploiting, local-business-destroying multinational? Second, those companies which are truly brand-led will expose their core values and purpose – and hence run the risk of being found out but equally, reap the reward of being seen to practise what they preach. Increasingly, consumers in developed, industrialized societies are classified as "inner directed" – they want real, authentic experiences and connections with their worlds, and are increasingly rejecting the over-hyped, unattainable world promoted through much advertising and large corporate activity.[14] So, rather than experiencing the community promoted by a chain of coffee shops which offer the same experience worldwide, they seek out the genuinely local café. Large, monolithic consumer brands have to work harder to manage the personal, close touch that their smaller, more quirky rivals manage with relative ease.

A global brand which achieves this consistently is Apple, a company admired for its innovation, product and service development and ability to attract and retain the right talent. What distinguishes Apple from other global brands is its attempts to forge close, personal relationships with its consumers. Apple is so loved by its customers, that they are often the ones to bring innovation and concerns to the company, which welcomes and acts on this responsiveness and communication.[15] This creates intimacy and responsiveness, regardless of scale.

Living the brand promise

As the share of national wealth taken up by service industries increases and manufacturing continues to go the same way as agriculture – requiring fewer and fewer people to deliver what society requires – the people on the brand frontline are the people who matter. Many external brands are centred on delivering a consistent experience: this is mediated as much by contact with employees as it is with the actual products. Therefore, where service is the key differentiator between brands, having employees who behave in a way which is consistent with the brand proposition is the secret to delivering a consistent relationship between customer and brand. If we look at the most valuable global brands, those which are adapting most rapidly and successfully are those which have the knack of delivering a consistent brand experience through each contact point. They understand that the product (the "what") should be as consistent as the experience wrapped around it (the "how"). By extension, employees need to behave in ways which are congruent with brand values. Applying the same logic to the relationship between brand and employee implies alignment between the values that your external brand conveys and those which your employees experience internally. This means turning brand values into coherent and meaningful internal processes, procedures and behaviours is central to creating meaning for employees, thereby attracting those who are naturally congruent with your brand, and retaining them.

In conclusion, the relationship between consumer and brand has shifted to one where consumers have (and realize they have) considerably more power than previously enjoyed. They want brands which say something meaningful and that they choose to be associated with. They demand a better quality of relationship between them and the brands they choose. These relationships are characterized by trust and respect. Brands which can build these relationships are those which behave in ways which are authentic and resonate with their values. They are consistent and trustworthy. Finally, they are responsive and create channels for communication. Successful brands are those which recognize this and work to understand their consumers' needs and build lasting bonds with them.

● What is the opportunity?

A key to building a powerful brand is to put Inside-Out branding at the heart of your consumer proposition. Quite simply, in order for consumers to experience a brand as authentic, consistent, responsive to their needs and meaningful, it has to resonate with and be delivered by people who live and breathe it. Before we turn to how to achieve this, let's just look at what a good Inside-Out brand looks like:

● It has a strong sense of identify which differentiates it from the competition, and which is grounded in the business's history and unique purpose. These values are authentically translated into employee values and behaviours which, in turn, define the character and personality of the brand. Inside-Out brands are not afraid to boldly state what they will – and won't – do. In this regard, authenticity is the new brand benchmark, which goes beyond bland logos, false promises or radical, ungrounded changes in direction.

● Coherence between espoused and actual values is key. Gaps between what a brand promises and what it delivers are easily exposed. People feel conned, leading to cynicism and damaged trust. In a connected, media-rich environment, where we have unprecedented access to information, simple spin and manipulation will not wash. This is certainly the truth for jaded consumers who increasingly turn to those brands whose promises match reality. It is also increasingly true for employees who experience the brand in action day to day.

● People are the new products. The paradigm has moved away from manufacturing to service. Brands are increasingly more about the human face of the company than what a company makes. This interaction has to be managed to make the brand work and feel consistent and authentic. Creating alignment between how employees live the brand values and how they experience working within the company is the key to making this work. Increasingly, from a consumer perspective, the brand experience is mediated by contact with another person: it is the quality of the interaction which contains the brand essence and meaning.

● According to Saatchi's Kevin Roberts, only brands, not blands, can create meaning.[16] The brand values must feel more like life-chosen principles which are well defined and differentiated. Employees are less likely to emotionally engage in a meaningful way with bland, undifferentiated brand positions. Getting this right is crucial to success in a weightless, non-goods economy.

To build the relationship between employee and brand, the brand values need to be reinforced at every contact point. Further, the development of the brand needs to harness the insights of those who experience it daily – the employees. Practically, this means:

● The external brand should act as a showcase to pull in people whose values resonate with the brand. It should convey a message about the type of people who will fit with the culture and enjoy a positive relationship with the brand. The external brand should give a clear signal of organizational intent – to employees, operations, customers and the market.

   The Swiss wealth management group, UBS, is one of the five fastest climbers in the Interbrand Best Global Brands survey.[17] Despite having grown through acquisitions and mergers, it manages its external face in each of the countries in which it operates consistently. The strapline "You and Us" is designed to convey the experience one should have of interacting with the brand. The advertising speaks to concepts of both scale (adverts feature large, imposing spaces and buildings) and intimacy (for example, two people deep in conversation). These images together give a feeling of size and might, juxtaposed with understanding and communication.

   To employees, the external branding conveys both messages of the customer experience, but also states how they can expect to be treated by the company. According to Jestyn Thirkell-White, UBS's head of brand strategy, UBS makes a point of informing its employees about its external communication campaigns. However, advertising is not what drives the brand: "The advertising reflects the kind of experience that all our training and our processes are designed to deliver."

This, therefore, is how external branding can democratize corporate life, by providing a clear expectation of the type of relationship its employees can expect with the business. For a company that expands rapidly into new areas, having a strong, consistent brand presence conveys a powerful message about the UBS way of doing things. The challenge, of course, is to deliver and maintain the high standards once they are set. By publicly committing to a set of values and behaviours, those supporting the brand will have to work consistently to ensure its delivery – both from employees to customers, but also from the business to its employees.

- Recruitment processes should explicitly recognize and assess the fit between employee and brand. Everything, from the look and feel of the job advertisement, the experience of the assessment process to the final communication should be consistent with the brand values.

Take the luxury car firm, Audi.[18] Its brand is portrayed as a force that releases and directs human energy. This positioning emerged from an exercise to differentiate itself from key competitors such as BMW in the 1990s. A key part of the exercise was to research what differentiated Audi customers from BMW customers. The research revealed that Audi customers liked to build relationships with the dealers and mechanics they interacted with, in order to talk about their cars. BMW customers, on the other hand, were more concerned with efficiency and service than building a relationship. Thus, Audi designed its recruitment process to target people with the right psychological characteristics to match the profile liked by its customers. By canvassing the views of Audi dealers, themes were pulled together to capture the characteristics of the dealers who translate the Audi brand into everyday life. Those which specifically related to the emotional and personal needs of customers – such as being empathic and interested in finding out about the customer and their needs – were then used to recruit Audi employees.

Dealerships with brand-sympathetic staff (those whose personal values align with those of the brand) have boosted net profits by 8 per cent on average.

- In a poorly differentiated market-place brands which codify clearly what makes them unique differentiate themselves, and so allow employees to create meaning through their relationship with the brand. Too many brands shy away from defining boldly what differentiates them from the pack. The result is too many similar, poorly differentiated brands competing for attention and allegiance in a limited, crowded space. Many brands do not identify what they won't do, and what markets they won't compete in.

Pret a Manger is an international brand which has been successful in growing within a crowded market-place.[19] Its differentiator is its passion about the high quality of its food. This illustrates the potential power of having an external brand position which is both authentic and passionate. Pret sells hand-made, natural food through its network of 150 stores. Its simple star logo and "Passionate about Food" strapline are familiar sites on British high streets, with a growing presence in the US and Far East. The business grew out of founders' Sinclair Beecham and Julian Metcalfe's frustration at being unable to buy decent food at lunchtime. Convinced they could do better, they set up the first Pret in 1986. Pret, now 33.5 per cent owned by McDonald's, continues to trade as an independent and strong brand.

Pret's core strategy has always been explicitly about providing freshly prepared, natural food. As far as possible, they have always avoided GM and non-organic produce. The external branding makes this explicit – conveyed snappily in its strapline and reinforced by stories and Pret facts printed on cards, posters, sandwich boxes and napkins in its stores. Pret is proud to innovate to meet its customers' changing tastes (for example, the no-bread sandwich was developed to suit those on the Atkins Diet). When sandwiches are discontinued, they will be brought back by popular demand if customers request them.

This passion for food is key to the Pret experience. In order to demonstrate this passion consistently and with flair they start with getting the right people in. Pret's recruitment strategy means attracting people with a real passion for food – in all roles, from team member to director. Pret wants people who care about the food they eat. Being explicit about this – through its external branding – helps it attract and employ the right type of people. Employees take pride in being associated with a brand that wears its heart on its sleeve.

Pret encourages its people to exercise their interest in food, by thinking constantly about how they can innovate to keep the Pret experience fresh and exciting. Central to Pret's approach is to explicitly value the customer insights that their employees gain through day-to-day contact, and harvest these to tailor its products to identify and meet changing customer tastes and preferences. Stores are in constant communication with head office to give feedback on what's working well with customers and what could be improved. Innovative ideas are rewarded and, if successful, adopted across the network of stores – with the employee responsible publicly acknowledged in Pret publications (so emphasizing the importance of Pret's people to their brand). The employee with the best idea of the quarter (as voted by all shop managers and head office) wins £1,000.

The simple, consistent external branding is mirrored by the communication strategy internally that keeps employees up-to-date with the latest developments in-house. Professionally produced, *The Daily Pret*, *Weekly Pret* and *Pret Express* cover (respectively) short-term issues, broader messages from the directors and general issues about the business.

- When rebranding, use the insights of the people who are closest to the brand to help define how it should be presented. Businesses that use their employees' insights into their purpose can create meaningful, differentiated internal and external brand propositions, which are coherent and values-driven. Using these insights is a powerful lever to build credibility and buy in to your external brand, and also to increase connectivity and enhance the relationship between employee and brand.

Barclaycard is the leading provider of credit cards in the UK. In a market of 50 million cards, it has around 20 per cent. In 2001, however, future market trends began to look ominous. There had been many new entrants to the credit-card business, who were seen as more innovative and better value than Barclaycard. While Barclaycard led the way on reliability, and retained its existing customers well, it was falling behind in terms of signing up new card-holders.

Something had to be done. Barclaycard needed to sort out the current state of play of its product in comparison with competitors, and also to work out how it could be positioned more effectively. To do so, it went down the conventional route of gathering market perceptions – through consumer focus groups and data mining – but also from its own people. Barclaycard hosted voluntary forums to gather its people's perceptions of the company's financial products, and to see how they compared to others in their market-place. The aim was to get help from people who knew the business best – those who worked within it, had contact with customers and, in many cases, were customers themselves. Different groups were asked for their views, including those who chose to use other credit cards. The research went to the frontline, into call centres, to talk to those who had daily contact with customers.

These collected views were pulled together to give a credible, purposeful statement of what the Barclaycard brand could stand for. The brand, it concluded, is an enabler, something that allowed immediate "here and now" access to meet needs. Rather than being a way of buying cinema tickets, it is a way to enjoy a night out with friends. What Barclaycard stood for is "The key to unlocking life's experiences".

This process helped to identify whether external and internal perceptions of the brand aligned or not. For example, Barclaycard is perceived to be reliable and trustworthy – these qualities are recognized by customers and employees alike. Internally, employees felt that Barclaycard's innovation was a strength, but this perception was not captured by its external brand. Externally, Barclaycard was widely held to be uncompetitive on price. This misperception was both damaging in terms of acquiring new customers and de-motivating for employees.

Exploring these qualities helped to define Barclaycard's brand values, which in turn governed how Barclaycard was going to deliver on its promises – both to its customers and to its employees:

- Supportive – being there for customers and knowing what they needed, which was conveyed in the strapline "in my shoes, speak my language". To reflect this value, all the Barclaycard standard letters and statements were reworded to be simple, transparent and clear to customers. Employees were engaged in forums to determine how to explain new products or services to customers – the "in my shoes, speak my language" principle guided how employees were treated in exactly the same way as it would determine how they related to customers.

- Expertise – Barclaycard is the expert, aspiring to be the most admired card and lending business in the world. Expertise also builds on the reliability that customers and employees endorsed as a core, credible part of the Barclaycard brand.

- Cosmopolitan – there wherever you are, there where you need us to be.

- Innovative – brought back as a core value which had been overlooked – after all, Barclaycard had been the first credit card in the UK!

This brand position was then checked back with Barclay-card employees through constant communication and feedback. At every stage in the process of translating the values into new communication materials, designs, logos and so on, employees were consulted and their views incorporated.

The result was a resoundingly successful rebrand which had the support of all the employees who had been part of it – from call-centre staff who volunteered to work extra shifts as the sign-up rate for new customers exceeded all expectations, to the front desk staff who took personal pride in making sure that the external brand logos were kept in good order.

Engaging with employees to define the customer proposition enabled Barclaycard to develop a central brand message "the key to unlocking life's experiences". It is credible, yet emotive without being overly, unattainably aspirational and inauthentic.

Taking the inside out

External brands are powerful, valuable assets which have the potential to form dynamic, meaningful bonds with employees. The brand position flows from an understanding of the organizational DNA and business strategy, and is the public face which represents these to customers and employees. Twenty-first century businesses which truly harness the power of their brands are the ones which live their brands Inside Out – by translating brand values into the experiences that reinforce at each touch point the character of the brand.

Companies which successfully achieve this differentiated, consistent and authentic experience of the brand for both customer and employee will need to do the following things:

- Build their brand identities by putting as much emphasis on employees as consumers. This requires understanding your people, asking them how they would like to be seen and involving them in branding or rebranding exercises. Some of the most authentically lived brands take their values from actual personalities, who in a very real sense live the brand – Richard Branson as the very public face of Virgin is a good example of this. Although Julian Metcalfe is not well known externally, the Pret brand image strongly reflects his persona and passions. In all these cases the Inside-Out principle is applied from the top down.

● Constantly reinforce the external brand identity internally. This needs to be done through communication, training and, in particular, recruiting. Using the brand identity to attract and retain the people who gel with the promises you are making externally is essential. UBS are explicit in using their external brand to send a clear message of intent about how they operate, internally and externally. The brand values are explicitly used in recruiting the right people. Similarly, Audi successfully recruit people based on personality traits, and have seen improved business performance as a result. The external brand proposition is consistently translated into the employee brand, and defines the internal processes, procedures and modus operandi that employees experience day to day. Virgin, again, is notable for its ability to maintain its down-to-earth, challenging and irreverent brand across a range of territories and industries.

● Do not be afraid to be aspirational. The companies that get most internal motivational value are unafraid to define their brands, going beyond physical properties to embrace the aspirational, emotional qualities they are striving to achieve. Crucially, though, these remain attainable and plausible. Thus Barclaycard can credibly claim to be "the key to unlocking life's experiences".

● Take action when the brand is under fire. Openly address the concerns of stakeholders – be they consumers or employees. Take, for example, Starbucks' attempts to address its impact on communities of coffee growers, or Barclaycard's garnering of its employees' insights in order to reframe its external brand proposition.

Powerful brands are those which promote values and meaning, internally and externally. To truly harness this potential means investing in two-way relationships, which respond and develop over time. Brands which do so, and authentically live their values inside and out, will be cherished and nurtured by those who care for them most – the people whose work goes into building them. In this way, they will break free of the controlling, manipulative paradigms which characterize poor branding. Inside-Out brands have the potential to offer genuine choice, promote coherent values and build a lucid sense of purpose for employees and an authentic experience for customers.

8. Having impact

"I cut my finger opening a lever arch file today. It was the shock of being invited to a meeting to discuss stationery use. It hurt."

Entry in a blog kept by a call-centre manager, quoted in the *Independent*, London, November 2004

The need to make a difference – to have an impact – is a powerful motivator. Stuart Rose, a highly successful British manager, is a good example of someone who feels the need to have an impact. Rose built a reputation in the 1990s as a successful transformer of businesses and made himself rich in the process. When, in early 2004, Philip Green made an approach to buy the British retailer Marks & Spencer, which was then experiencing difficulties, Rose accepted the job of CEO and successfully fought off Green's approach. Some were puzzled that he didn't join forces with Green or negotiate the sale of the business to Green and make himself even more rich. The simple explanation is that, having already achieved a lot financially, Rose had at Marks & Spencer – a firm he had worked for when it was much admired – the opportunity to demonstrate his ability and to have major personal impact on reinvigorating the business. He has subsequently displayed a highly focused and determined attitude to creating a sustainable level of success at M&S.

Why impact is important for meaning

YSC's research into the qualities associated with the achievement of success reveals that the desire to demonstrate their own distinctive qualities by altering, changing or otherwise leaving a mark on the environment – to have an impact – is what drives people with potential. Those who strive for success feel a need to prove themselves. This may stem from a feeling of insecurity and uncertainty about how they "fit" with other people and how they are perceived and valued by them.

Those who are most likely to succeed also maintain a degree of independence from their environment. They are motivated to find ways of improving what happens around them. This reinforces their distinctness and self-esteem. They demonstrate a high level of initiative and a readiness to question and challenge. This helps them to harness their strengths and develop their abilities. With this independence of spirit comes a need to "fit" with the environment and to connect with it in a manner that allows challenge to be appropriately received. There is, however, a tension. The underlying insecurities that generate the wish to succeed sometimes fight with the desire to be valued and accepted. Getting the balance right between allowing individuals to challenge while also providing them with recognition and acceptance is an important dynamic if organizations are to maintain flexibility as they grow. Organizations that do not provide individuals with scope to work out how to have their own distinct impact will tend to drive behaviour which is purely about achieving status and recognition. People will learn to "conform" to valued ways of doing things rather than looking to initiate. This will reduce their experience of personal meaning.

An American literary critic, Harold Bloom,[1] developed a theory of the evolution of poetry which he calls the "Anxiety of Influence". Bloom argued that each generation of poets is faced with a personal challenge: how to create a space for themselves in which they can express their own distinct voice. Interestingly, Bloom argued that one way of achieving this was to undermine what had gone before through a deliberate "misinterpretation" of what had been written. Individuals seeking to make an impact within an organization are faced with a similar dilemma: how to be part of the organization without being immersed and lost in it? This balancing act involves another tension: how to develop a sense of self-confidence within the organization rather than a dependence on it? Individuals operating at the height of their capabilities have gradually acquired the level of belief and self-understanding that both allows them to appreciate the limits of what they can do and gives them the confidence to take risks.

The economist J. K. Galbraith[2] wrote a monograph in 2004 that sought to identify a series of what he described as "minor economic frauds" that occur in market economies. One of the frauds he identified relates to the belief that CEOs of big companies should be rewarded highly on the basis that they have a significant impact on their organizations. Galbraith argued that this was fraudulent because big modern companies are in effect large bureaucracies where success depends upon the collaboration of many talented individuals – who all need to feel that they have an impact. Yet as companies focus more and more on consistency and predictability it is harder for individuals to feel they can have impact on the environment around them. The emphasis tends to be on the creation of processes which support the business. The individual's role is then to be custodian of such processes and they are judged to be successful according to their ability to manage process and activity.

The challenge for organizations

The past twenty years has seen a proliferation of activities within organizations aimed at reducing uncertainty. The rapid pace of change in markets, the drive for globalization and fiercer competition have all increased the uncertainties faced by businesses. Organizations have responded by trying to find ways of creating consistency. Performance management systems have become ever more dominant; managers are measured with increasing levels of discrimination. Organizational and strategic changes are frequent, often failing to take account of the organization's embedded culture and values. These phenomena bring with them a cost for employees. What is important to focus on? How do I make a difference? How do I know if I'm doing a good job? All of these pressures will reduce the sense of impact an individual can have.

Organizations tend to use three broad levers in an attempt to create consistency: structure, measurement and change.

The use of structure

Bartlett and Ghoshal,[3] writing in the *Harvard Business Review*, identified two traps that organizations fall into when seeking to create consistency: "Implementing simple, strategic solutions to complex dynamic problems" and, when these failed, "concluding that the best response to increasing complex strategic requirements was increasingly complex organizational structures". They noted that companies which fall into this organizational trap assume that changing the formal structure will force changes in psychology and behaviour. However, this underestimates the amount of time it can take for change and structure to translate into embedded changes in attitude. In the short term, such changes lead to confusion, an increasing sense of helplessness, and inertia. The old ways of creating impact no longer work.

Organizations often look to changes in structure as a response to the increased complexity of global business. Microsoft is an example of a company where structure and process have been used to address in a logical way the need to improve efficiency and collaboration. Even though it continues to be a highly successful business however, these changes have had a number of unintended consequences, notably people feeling mired in endless meetings, with increasing uncertainty about their autonomy.

The "attention deficit organization" typically shows a pattern of frequent shifts in approach to organization of structure. Attempts to deal with these issues are usually driven by a relentless logic. This is why matrix organizational structures are so popular and common.

Most global organizations will at some point have visited them as a solution. However, Bartlett and Ghoshal's research suggests that such structures will tend to increase confusion about impact and so compound the problem. This research indicates that, in order to work, it is critical for people operating in a matrix to be given a very clear sense of the impact they can have by the communication of the values most important to the business's success. Furthermore, the setting of clear expectations, while trusting that people will manage processes, and providing them with clear feedback, all make a matrix structure more likely to work. They will be effective because they generate a sense of meaning by clarifying how people can have impact within the matrix.

Measurement gone too far

The invention of scientific management at the beginning of the last century was a major driver of growth in the twentieth-century corporation. At its core was the idea of measurement of work as a critical lever to achieve efficiency. Such measurement, used wisely, served a dual function: It provided the organization with reassurance about behaviour, but it also gave individuals a "line of sight" between their actions and outcomes. A feature of Meaning Inc. organizations is that they provide clear feedback to people about how they have performed.

Scientific management had a fillip in the 1980s with the development of Management By Objectives (MBO), which became a mantra. However MBO often goes too far and paradoxically results in employees losing their clear line of sight. Instead, there is a proliferation of different kinds of measures which individuals increasingly find difficult to relate to in a personal manner.

The attention deficit organization typically attempts to over-measure. This creates an illusion of control, illusion because what actually results from all this measurement is not control but confusion about what is really important. It will also undermine an individual's ability to operate with initiative.

Such over-measurement often occurs within organizations which feel they have intractable levels of complexity. A critical issue for the current UK government is how to manage the public sector more efficiently. The belief is that there are issues of accountability at the core of the public sector's difficulties. When we worked within the NHS in the mid 1980s, providing coaching to senior managers, one of the most notable things was that individuals frequently had difficulty seeing clearly how they could have traction and achieve a sense of impact because of over-complexity. Interestingly, they tended to react to this by gaining their sense of impact by shifting attention away from the organization they were running, and focusing instead on the public platforms that their roles provided. Instead of relentlessly focusing on how to achieve results, they often looked to become, in the language of one individual, a national figure. By contrast, managers in the NHS today have a very clear range of targets and goals. The government's attempts to instil a sense of accountability have resulted in a large number of mechanisms designed to track adherence to objectives. However, reaction from the workforce suggests that rather than engendering a sense of impact and therefore meaning, these mechanisms are instead creating a sense of helplessness and confusion. What is missing in this over-measurement is the space in which an individual feels he or she can act with initiative and imagination. Instead of making a personal contribution, employees are simply reacting to an externally imposed set of demands.

The creeping tyranny of measurement is often a feature of the "soulless organization" (see page 34). The increasing inward-looking nature that is characteristic of these companies, combined with what is often a growing sense of confidence that it knows how to achieve its results, means a loss of perspective on what is critical to performance is common. Marks & Spencer developed performance management systems that measured individuals on 170 factors. This occurred during the early to mid 1990s when the business was highly successful in terms of revenue and profit growth. It resulted, however, in managers effectively having to manage the demands being placed on them from above rather than focusing on what was under their control, i.e. the stores and the customer. In effect, this led to a loss of flexibility at store level and a reduction in focus on the key drivers of success in the business: sales.

Change for change's sake

Meaning Inc. organizations are characterized by having a deeply embedded culture and sense of capability. As we argued earlier, unravelling the DNA of such an organization will typically reveal strengths and capabilities that have sustained it in the past. The strength of this provides a framework within which individuals are able to judge what is expected of them and how they need to act in order to achieve results that are valued. Efforts to change an organization can go awry because, instead of building in a systematic way on this inner core, attempts are made to take it in a completely new direction. Instilling different values and laying out different expectations of performance will create uncertainty about what is expected and how individuals can have an impact – as does failure to follow through consistently on initiatives to make changes in the business.

A related issue we have noticed that makes it hard for people to generate a clear sense of impact is that the organizations they are part of can rapidly change their minds about what is important. Attention deficit organizations find it difficult to set and maintain focus on clear priorities. One strategy for dealing with the complexity generated by attention deficit organizations is to "keep plates spinning". It is a common feature of most organizations that senior individuals feel they have too many priorities. Attempts are made periodically to focus down on the top four priorities. But these soon change again. The confusion that results makes it hard, if not impossible, for the wider organization to have a clear sense of what is expected and, therefore, how it needs to behave.

Optimizing the experience of impact: lessons from Meaning Inc. organizations

Experiencing meaning through impact in an organization requires a number of simple conditions to be met. Firstly, it is critical that individuals have a clear line of sight between their actions and what is expected of them. This needs to be consistent and predictable so that the individual can establish an internal compass by which they can evaluate their actions. In turn, this requires a clear, consistent set of priorities to be established by the leadership of the organization. In order to have a profound sense of the impact that is originating from their own actions, people need space and autonomy to operate with initiative. Finally, it is important that an individual's actions, the broader strategies followed by the organization, and the values and structures which hold the organization together should all be coherent and meaningful.

The use of these criteria provides some clear principles which can guide the use of the three levers discussed above.

Using structure to optimize impact

As mentioned earlier, there can be a risk when organizations seek to deal with increasingly complex strategic challenges by creating increasingly complex organizational structures. Our research suggests that in order for such attempts to work the following key principles must be followed:

Change structure as a last resort

It is critical that an organization is clear about what behaviours are desired as a result of structural change. As a first step, a concerted effort should be made to embed these behaviours using other levers. For example, if the desired goal is to increase the level of collaboration that happens within the organization, attempts should be made to directly encourage this by embedding activities which reinforce how collaboration is valued. This can be done by signalling this as a desired behaviour in the model of leadership used in the organization. It can also be reinforced by activities such as selecting people for roles who have strong collaborative tendencies. A structural solution, such as a matrix organization, can undoubtedly help but it will only work if other actions are taken to embed the behaviours at the same time.

Give a new structure time to work

Even the most complex organizational structures will work if time is given to properly embed them. It is critical that success and problems are both measured and addressed. Quite often, a change in structure is put in place without any subsequent attention being given to monitoring its success. Even worse, initial difficulty with the structure results in an attempt to create a different structure altogether.

"Stay small while being big"

As organizations grow in size and complexity, the sense of meaning is invariably reduced for individuals because it is harder for them to discern a clear sense of impact. An important guiding principle in building Meaning Inc. organizations, therefore, is to find a way of staying small while being big. One successful example of how to do this is that of BP. In the early 1990s, John Browne became CEO of what was a business in some difficulty. It was extremely large and complex as an organization. One of the first things he did was to disaggregate the business into a smaller number of relatively autonomous units. This step provided individuals with a clearer sense of ownership and accountability. This structural change has subsequently been seen as one of the most important factors behind the success of BP.

The amount of information and knowledge that is now available within organizations has reduced the pressure to organize in a hierarchical way. This has tended to drive a move to flatter structures. In turn, this frequently means that the team becomes bigger and individuals find it harder to establish a sense of personal engagement. Flatter structures can also undermine a sense of career progression. The challenge for organizations is to create tighter, more autonomous units which provide a sense of social engagement but also give individuals discrete and meaningful challenges. The flatter structure therefore often requires the creation of "bigger" jobs. Tesco is an example of a business which has sought to create such large roles. This has resulted in a relatively flat organizational structure. Tesco has been highly successful in both building talent from within and importing it from outside. As a result, it has had to actively manage the challenge of ensuring it maintains the development and motivation of key individuals. It has done this by working actively to ensure the creation of large and meaningful roles. This has required a degree of flexibility and adroitness on its part.

Measuring performance in a meaningful way

The following principles should be followed when looking at how to achieve rigorous measurement in an organization without falling into the traps described on pages 205–206:

Be clear about what is important

In the early 1990s, Asda was a failing British grocer. Weeks away from bankruptcy, a new management team, led by Archie Norman and Allan Leighton, took over. One of the things they quickly identified was a sense of helplessness among those working in the business. People had very little sense of how to achieve impact. This led to a noticeable lack of morale and confidence.

Norman and Leighton drew up a series of initiatives which had at their core a sharpening of the company's focus combined with an opening up of communication channels. "Tell Archie" was one such example – people were encouraged to communicate directly with their new chairman. Managers were held to account if they did not respond in a positive way to new ideas coming up from below. Central to the change was the identification of the "Asda way of working". This defined the criteria by which people's performances would be judged. Norman and Leighton made it very clear that what was important was improving sales, whereas previous management had focused on costs. Employees now understood that their behaviour had to connect with the customer in a tangible way.

Give people space by focusing on outcomes and not processes

A common feature of the "soulless organization" is that it seeks to measure people and set objectives around processes rather than outputs. Marks & Spencer, as discussed above, ended up with the individuals being measured on over 170 objectives. By contrast, Tesco has been an enormously successful business, characterized by a very high level of engagement among its employees. As an organization its success has been built on being very responsive to change, anticipating and even driving it at times. Everything that is valued in the organization derives from a simple focus on an output: satisfying the customer. "The Tesco way" is defined as the challenge of doing things in a way that is "better, simpler and cheaper for the customer". This simple mantra is used powerfully around the business to evaluate every action. It makes clear what is expected of each employee and provides a metric by which people can judge their performance. Critically, it focuses people on outcomes and not on processes. It therefore leads to a strong level of consistency in the business while allowing people to take initiative and exercise their own judgement about what "good" looks like. It also encourages them to look outside the business, not least because they have to know what the competition is doing.

Organizations that fail to identify and communicate the core values on which their success depends can end up with employees who value the wrong thing: i.e. doing the thing right (process) rather than doing the right thing (achieving the desired outcome). This has been a feature of traditional banks, where a high level of value is placed on "knowing how the bank works" and not enough on using people's talents.

The challenge for China

The famous Chinese admiral Zheng Zi conducted a series of bold voyages during the years 1405–1433 which took him to South-East Asia, India, Oman and Africa. These voyages were not light matters – at times they involved 300 junks with tens of thousands of sailors – dwarfing anything the West was able to put together at the time. According to some accounts, Zheng may well have got to North America over fifty years before Columbus. Zheng is revered in many parts of Asia. However, in China, Confucian scholars won an internal battle to ensure his voyages were stopped and that Zheng's exploits were expunged from all records. He had become too big and was seen to be a loose cannon. An opportunity for China to storm the world stage and become a global power was lost.

Strong central control, allied with an equally strong propensity for commercial matters, are powerful features of Chinese culture. Communism took hold in China not because of egalitarian impulses but because it was consistent with these centralizing tendencies. It was not, however, consistent with China's commercial instincts. Not surprisingly it didn't take long for what Chinese leaders euphemistically, and not without a hint of humour, called "communism with Chinese characteristics" to arise. This kind of "communism" must have had Marx and Lenin turning in their graves, as it was in many ways more commercially aggressive than capitalism.

A key theme running through Chinese history is the extent to which the extremely high levels of intellectual and entrepreneurial energy of the population should be released or controlled. All too often, Chinese leaders have experimented with loosening control only to draw back from the uncertainty that this entails. As with the example of Admiral Zheng outlined above, this has often led to China undershooting itself. Going forward, while China may well be able to catch up with the West, it could struggle to really thrive unless its leaders embrace the short-term uncertainty that giving people space and room to exercise initiative and true independence of thought inevitably involves.

For organizations, a barrier to this freedom as in countries like China, can be the fear of unintended consequences. Yet too much control and measurement can also result in unexpected behaviours or unanticipated outcomes. The same can and does happen in countries. China's one-child policy, and its tradition of favouring male children, has undoubtedly helped the country in the short term. But now over 40 million Chinese men cannot find partners. Furthermore, there is a real demographic crunch looming, as very soon a small number of emerging adults will have to provide for a vastly larger number of retirees. Resisting the instinct to control can be helped by an awareness of the unintended consequences of even seemingly straightforward measures.

Managing change to optimize impact and meaning

Change itself can both create or destroy meaning depending on how it is managed. Figure 7 (see page 214) outlines a model which describes the steps needed to be taken in order to maintain a sense of meaning during a change process.

Ensure there is a meaningful case for change

A tangible, clear and compelling story is essential if change is to be perceived as meaningful. It is critical that the leadership frames the change process in a way that is coherent and persuasive. In effect, this means meaningful change must be driven by a real and believable pressure to change. The absence of this will inevitably result in a loss of belief and confidence in the whole process.

Engage the whole organization in authentic debate about the change process

In order for people to understand what is expected of them during a change process and to believe in its validity, it is critical that a systematic process of authentic engagement with the organization takes place. This must move beyond the simple communication of the change strategy to a frank discussion of why what is happening is happening.

Leadership must be engaged in a coherent way

During the process of change all the qualities of Meaning Inc. leadership discussed in Chapter 4 are critical. It is vital that the leadership group operates in a coherent and empathetic manner.

Figure 7 ● Maintaining meaning during change

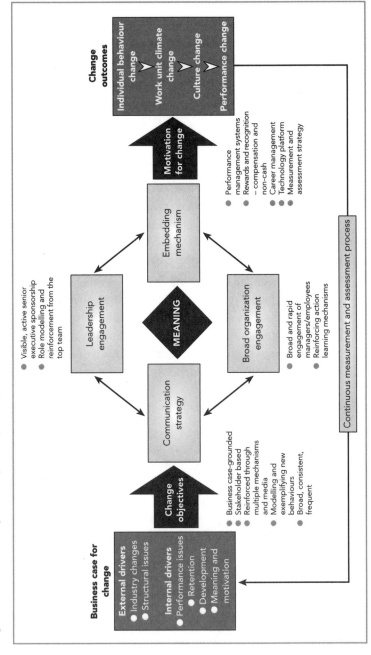

Change must be followed through and embedded

As discussed above, the failure to consistently follow through on change drastically reduces people's sense of impact and engagement. Careful thought is therefore needed about the processes by which people's motivations can be engaged for the long haul. This requires close attention not just to reward systems but also to career management, as well as to how individuals are given rich and helpful feedback about how they are progressing.

To conclude, leadership in a Meaning Inc. organization requires deep sensitivity to the experience of individuals and how they respond to changes in structure, process and culture. As discussed throughout this chapter, Meaning Inc. organizations think hard about how to ensure the sense of impact is maintained and optimized. The challenge outlined at the beginning of the chapter – balancing the tension between creating consistency and giving people space to be distinct – requires just such focused thought. Organizations which relentlessly follow a fixed logic in how they approach the creation of structure, the measurement of behaviour and the creation of change will tend to fail to achieve the appropriate balance.

9. Good to grow

"What lies behind us and what lies before us are tiny matters compared to what lies within us."

Ralph Waldo Emerson

In 1997 ANZ Bank, one of the largest companies in Australia, appointed John McFarlane as CEO to turn around its ailing fortunes. At that time, ANZ was widely regarded as the poorest performer among Australia's banks. McFarlane moved quickly to fix some of the basic operational problems. He brought greater focus, cost discipline and pulled the bank out of unprofitable areas. Financial performance started to improve.

But McFarlane was not satisfied. In his university days he had been the lead singer for the Scottish band The Sekrets and perhaps a certain creative drive led him to want to go further. He was not happy about the way the banks were collectively perceived in Australia. Branch closures and high fees had severely eroded public trust and, even worse, McFarlane found that staff satisfaction levels were poor. Looking back, McFarlane says: "At that time people hated banks ... we needed to change the hearts and minds of people inside the organization." McFarlane and his team formulated a three-pronged strategy called "Perform, Grow and Break Out" to tackle this challenge.

The consulting firm McKinsey was called in to undertake a cultural survey which indicated a big gap between ANZ's values and those of its employees. In 2001, therefore, ANZ launched a cultural transformation programme designed to make it the bank with a human face. Sonia Stojanovic was appointed as Head of Breakout and Cultural Transformation, a role specifically created to drive the new cultural values. A key aspect of the programme was to take virtually all of the company's 30,000 employees through personal development workshops. In addition to changing how people related to each other at work, the workshops led to an overhaul of ANZ's internal practices and inspired the creation of an array of community service programmes in areas such as improving financial literacy.

The results have been dramatic. Previously the least preferred employer in Australian commercial services, ANZ is now an employer of choice; staff satisfaction increased by 35 per cent in the period 2001–04.[1] The bank won "Australian Bank of the Year" three years running and its stock price rose from A$9 to over A$21 between 1997 and 2006.

According to Stojanovic, success comes from tapping into the intrinsic longing for meaning in its employees: "We're giving people hope – the hope to find meaning and not to compartmentalize their lives into home and work and self. We are inviting people to ask the questions: 'Why am I here? What is my contribution?'"

In order to embed the cultural transformation, ANZ also launched a series of "breakout charters" to re-engineer systems and processes in line with the new values. By 2005, this strategy was delivering measurable benefits. Customer satisfaction was at 78.2 per cent, the highest of the top four major Australian banks. Employee engagement was at 63 per cent, one of the best scores amongst large employers in Australia and New Zealand. A significant proportion of the bank's employees were also active in community volunteering and in donating money, with the latter helped by a dollar-for-dollar matching programme offering up to A$1,000 per person.

What ANZ illustrates is that people's feelings about their work can be dramatically changed over a few years. ANZ did many things, but a core part of its programme was to give people the space and the opportunity to identify ways in which their day-to-day existence could be made more meaningful. Insiders are clear, the transformation process focused on "inside-out change". That is, allowing people to think deeply about themselves and what they want. For some, this meant deciding to leave the bank. The programmes didn't teach or push employees in a particular direction. Rather, they helped them think about what was meaningful to them and how this could be harnessed at work. This is light years away from dropping a programme on staff that is designed to develop certain prescribed skills/qualities or that pushes them to display particular behaviours.

Any individual's experience of work is a dynamic interplay between the individual, the organization and the work itself. This chapter looks at how modern companies can give people meaning through allowing them to be themselves and by achieving a sense of personal growth. It looks at what people can do themselves, as well as how organizations can facilitate a sense of meaningful personal development. Let's first consider where the problems are.

● The issues

The CEO of a retail bank confided: "I constantly look for new challenges, learnings and growth – and this is central. I don't tolerate mediocrity – it's challenge, change and growth that serve me – without these my working life lacks fulfilment." At some level, this sentiment is echoed by just about everyone in an organization. People want to grow – both professionally and personally. They will simply not put up with roles that do not give them this sense of development.

While most people want their organizations to help them grow, they no longer want to be told exactly how they should behave or be. They resent being asked to mouth corporate speak or having to embrace without question values or competency frameworks developed by senior leaders. Nor does everyone want to get close and personal with their colleagues. Some just want to be left alone to do their job and then go home. In short, people want development interventions tailored to their needs. For some, this means intense personal activity, for others it means the absence of nonsensical interventions. It is hard for companies to get it right (though easy also to criticize from a distance). Individualistically inclined journalists, in particular, are quick to lambast what they regard as "personally intrusive" development activities in companies and make a joke of them in their columns without realizing that actually many people gain meaning from them.

A crucial question is whether employees are able to bring their full selves into work and whether their job utilizes all of their capabilities. In our interviews, we ask people about characteristics in their private lives that they could bring into play at work. While many people are initially surprised by the question, it usually doesn't take them long to identify many ways in which they are undershooting at work. One fundamental reason is that they "frame" work in a very particular way and conclude that only certain behaviours will be acceptable. Insecurity about their position also leads people to draw back from fully expressing themselves.

Another issue is that in many work environments we are not encouraged to see ourselves in terms of strengths and possibilities. Instead, the predominant bias is towards perceived gaps and weaknesses. This is inherent not just in work but frequently in people's family and educational background. Most organizational cultures term development needs as a euphemism for weaknesses that need to be addressed. While people pay lip-service to concepts such as building on strengths, it actually requires deep thought to embed such a philosophy in a serious way. The consequence of this is that people can withdraw into themselves or spend a corporate lifetime trying to push water uphill, trying to be something they can never be.

The preference for much flatter organizational structures in business also makes it difficult for people to experience a sense of personal growth. Quite simply, it is hard to give people a constant sense of advancement simply by moving them along the corporate hierarchy. Organizations, therefore, need to think creatively about how they develop people in such contexts and in particular about how they ensure people experience fresh challenges which encourage and enable growth. Frustration at not moving ahead quickly enough is one of the main propellants of increased turnover in the job market.

As organizations become more aware of the need to respond to the demand for growth, there is a tendency to develop poorly integrated or poorly focused personal development schemes. It is common for employees to go on personal development workshops which inspire them to embrace new ways of behaving and thinking, only to come down to earth with a thud when they return to the workplace. In addition, for some organizations, personal development can become an indulgent off-line activity of limited benefit to the business. At an extreme, it can shake people up to the extent that they end up leaving the company because of their heightened awareness of the discrepancies between what they can be and what they are allowed to be at work.

Some companies turn to individual coaching. An HR director we worked with, however, has a rather negative experience of this particular approach. When seeking to audit coaching in her business, she found extremely high levels of variability. Even more worryingly, she found that frequently the coach tended to collude with the reality created by the coachee, and that the agenda was often not reality-checked against what others in the organization as a whole might have wanted of the person being coached. Things came to a head when she found out that one person, who had a reputation for being extremely selfish and egocentric, was being encouraged by his coach to stand up more for his needs because of constant conversations with his coach around what was frustrating him at work.

For personal growth to be both meaningful and effective in an organizational context therefore, it has to respond to the very different needs people have around growth, as well as contribute to organizational success. Simply throwing a large amount of developmental cash at the problem without thinking about what it achieves does not work.

Much development activity in companies fails to produce dividends either in terms of impact on business results or in terms of creating meaning for employees. There are three key ways in which companies can drive results and give people a distinctive sense of meaning through personal growth. These are to: a) believe in everyone; b) focus on releasing strengths; and c) create a robust coaching culture. Let's look at each of these.

Releasing potential – believe in everyone

In the late 1960s, the psychologists Robert Rosenthal and Lenore Jacobson conducted an experiment to look at the impact of expectations on educational achievements.[2] They randomly selected a group of children and told teachers that some could be expected to be "growth spurters" because of their results in what was in fact a non-existent test of ability. The children so identified were no different from the ones who were not given the label. Rosenthal and Jacobson then sat back and waited to see what impact, if any, teachers' expectations might have on subsequent achievement. They reported the findings in a seminal book, *Pygmalion in the Classroom*. Slowly but surely, those individuals labelled as having great potential started to pull ahead. The fact that the teachers had greater expectations of them and gave them the opportunity to excel simply helped to make their expectations self-fulfilling.

Since then there have been over 400 studies on self-fulfilling expectancy effects.[3] On average these studies find a positive effect of over 0.6 of a standard deviation – enough to move an average performer close to the top quartile. However, while such effects are well known in the psychological world, they are rarely talked about in business circles, despite the fact that the type of labelling that Rosenthal and Jacobson described is all too common in companies. Most businesses have high-potential programmes where certain selected people are labelled as having the potential to progress far. While sometimes these judgements are based on sound and robust data, it is not uncommon for there to be a certain arbitrariness in the attachment of the label – not quite as bad as in the Rosenthal and Jacobson study, but edging that way. In addition, companies regularly distinguish between their "a", "b" and "c" players, and so on. Furthermore, the mere act of assigning people to roles denotes a certain expectation. Just as in the Rosenthal and Jacobson study, these approaches might work very well for people who get the "good" labels – but, one might ask, what is the impact on others?

The reality, of course, is that individuals do differ in terms of underlying capabilities and talent. But, in seeking to recognize this, many companies lose sight of the untapped potential across their whole range of employees. In addition, they fail to take into account the massive switching-off effect of being told that you're not in a category destined for future stardom. Is getting 25 per cent more out of your top 5 per cent more important than getting an extra 5 per cent out of 95 per cent of your people? It's not rocket science. What would happen if you labelled your entire organization high potential? Would you release energy or would the whole system collapse in a chaotic mess?

Inspired chaos

Some companies have tried this radical approach. Take the unusual case of Semco, a Brazilian manufacturer of ship's parts, that has turned the tables on how things happen in organizations.[4] Ricardo Semler, at the age of 21, took over the business which was created by his father. Previously, Semler had wanted to be a rock star but had given this up because of the competition involved. (Curiously, in our research we have found a number of Meaning Inc. leaders who wanted to be musicians or rock stars.) Since running an industrial business at the age of 21 had not exactly been in his game plan, Semler decided to have fun and make some radical changes. His first act was to sack the majority of the senior leadership because they stood in the way of what he wanted to do. You could hardly blame them; Semler's ideas were not exactly textbook.

Underlying his whole approach was a desire to completely restructure the organization on democratic principles. Job descriptions and business cards were dumped in favour of a philosophy of "do whatever you think will add value". The existence of managers was discouraged and people were organized into self-managed teams. Pay was democratized, with everybody knowing how much everyone else earned, and with most staff determining their own salaries in their teams. Any form of strategic planning was dumped. Semler simply gave people opportunities to prove their worth by allowing them to start up and run a myriad of satellite businesses for which they had energy.

All this has led to an unusual culture. The few people in supervisory roles are evaluated by their staff every six months and the results posted. Employees work at different desks every day. All meetings are voluntary. If people do not have energy for interviewing candidates for a position, the role is eliminated because if people don't care enough to interview for it, then the role is assumed to be unnecessary. A while back, the business held a party to celebrate ten years of Semler not having made a decision!

But what of the business results? Since 1988, the business has increased by close to tenfold with revenues in 2005 approaching $250 million. Today the company manufactures over 2,000 products in a range of sectors and has 3,000 employees. Semler has written about his experience and unorthodox management techniques in *Maverick* and *The Seven-Day Weekend*, in which he reports on how things are evolving. While many might debate the pros and cons of Semler's methods and applicability to other businesses, one thing is clear: he has worked hard to release the energy and talent of his people.

"Organizations rarely believe they're to blame when an employee underperforms," Semler explains. "But if the organization does not provide the opportunity for success then people falter. We accept that every individual wants and needs a worthwhile pursuit in life. It is up to us to provide the environment and opportunity for their gratification. We resort to job rotation, reverse evaluation and self-management to help people tap into their talent. We never assume there are weeds among us." Not surprisingly, there is a queue of people waiting to join the company.

W. L. Gore, the manufacturer of Gore-Tex, has a similarly unconventional approach to utilizing people's talent.[5] Like Semco, W. L. Gore frowns on job descriptions and encourages individuals to contribute in whatever way they can. Leadership positions are discouraged on the basis that people should follow others because of the power of their arguments rather than the position they occupy. To many onlookers, all this would seem to be a recipe for disaster. But it works at W. L. Gore. The company has been turning in stellar performances for years. W. L. Gore also regularly appears at the top of the list of Best Companies to Work For Worldwide.

No one person and no one organization is perfect. On closer examination, neither Semco nor W. L. Gore necessarily implement all their principles in as radical a way as they would like to portray. Statements from Semler can have a contradictory ring, which makes one wonder about the underlying reality. For example, the strong emphasis on reverse feedback suggests that there is a hierarchy and a management structure.

Yet there is a lot which is compelling about these companies. The fact that they thrived rather than collapsed in a mess illustrates the potential value of applying the "believe in everyone" principle. Quite simply, the lessons are: don't let people hide behind labels and positions; give everybody a chance; create sufficient flex in the system to let people contribute in the way that plays to their energy and talent; and don't create elitist development schemes.

When one digs below the surface of cultures like Semco, it is clear that, despite the surface looseness and laissez-faire approach, there are some important and fundamental mechanisms for making sure that people's energies and creativity are channelled in the right direction. At Semco, performance is clinically judged and teams get regular and relentless feedback on how they have performed. The separation of the business into sub-units makes this much easier. Everyone participates in a monthly meeting that analyses the company's performance and people are trained to read balance sheets. While compensation is often decided by teams, the pot available depends on the performance of each business. When team members are making close judgements about your contribution to the bottom line this makes everyone focus and leaves no room for unfairness. Ultimately, Semco is able to keep the show on the road because of these counter-balancing disciplines.

An exasperated Soviet official, trying to fathom the capitalist system, once famously asked his British hosts; "But tell me who controls the bread supply into London?" His hosts were not surprisingly flummoxed by the question. When I visited the Soviet Union in the 1980s, and looked at their empty supermarket shelves, it was rather obvious that whoever was doing the bread control job in London was considerably more effective than his or her Moscow counterpart. The point here, of course, is that a surprising amount of efficiency can emerge from a seemingly chaotic situation, provided the chaos is bounded in some way.

If you are to institute a culture of believing in everyone, then you also have to become laser-sharp in your judgement of performance. You have to create a highly efficient internal market where organizational looseness is channelled by the forces of reward and feedback to ensure focus and discipline. This, of course, is what actually happens in democratic, capitalistic countries. The chaotic free-for-all of the market is given shape by the ruthless survival-of-the-fittest discipline. There is an interesting paradox here. Most of the companies that exist in the West actually exhibit centralist "bread control" tendencies, with all the processes and paraphernalia that come with creating a disciplined system, i.e. tightly defined roles, rules and plans. Places like Semco blow this apart and create, in effect, an internal free-for-all disciplined by ruthless performance feedback.

Judging and rewarding people on results rather than how they do their job has some important knock-on effects. For example, talented executives can often be fast-tracked rapidly through a series of jobs which are supposed to develop them. One executive we worked with had been through four moves lasting less than two years. He ended up in a senior line role, managing a large number of countries but bemoaned the fact that he had not had time to consolidate his skills. When one got underneath the surface it was clear that he lacked confidence in the role that he'd been given –

rightly so, because of the speed with which he had been propelled into it. He didn't know how good he was and neither did anyone else.

The smart move is often to take bigger bets on internal people when thinking about promotions – and then to leave them in roles long enough to enable them to learn about the effects, good or ill, of their actions and for these to be sensibly judged. Simply pulling people quickly upwards, without the discipline of measuring and giving feedback on their performance, creates the illusion of development.

Unique strengths and flow

The renowned psychologist, Mihaly Csikszentmihalyi, has coined the term "flow" to describe the process by which excellence is achieved and engagement maximized.[6] Flow is essentially the controlled and intense deployment of attention. He distinguishes enjoyment from pleasure. Pleasure comes from satisfying our needs for comfort and security, i.e. pleasurable activities relate to returning the body, mind or emotions back to balance and order. The impact of pleasure is to bring one's personal system into homoeostasis, a state of equilibrium. Enjoyment emerges from engaging in activities which enable people to grow through having exposure to novelty and increased challenge. The conditions for achieving enjoyment involve deploying one's inherent skills and attacking goals which are significant and challenging. "A single episode of flow lifts the spirit momentarily – when experienced over time flow helps to make a person unique and indispensable."

A senior executive from an oil company told us: "At sixteen, I'd already fallen in love with mountaineering and everything evolved around it, including my choice of university and the course I undertook. It also determined my career as a geophysicist and an exploration engineer for an oil company. However, I wasn't concerned where it would take me careerwise, I just knew from a very early age I had to follow my passion."[7] This executive had found a sense of flow both at university and in his career by

Figure 8 ● A framework for mobilizing strengths

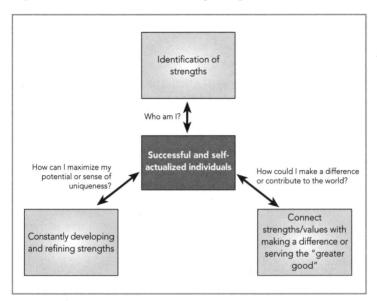

understanding what drove him and by working out the contexts where that passion could be best put to use. In a fundamental sense, his work was always in synch with who he was. This had helped release an underlying passion for his work, taking him far in his career.

Intense and passionate commitment, which comes from deploying one's intrinsic strengths in a way which runs with the grain of one's motivation, is the holy grail of employee engagement within organizations. How can it be achieved? Or, more realistically, how can companies help the majority of people attain it for prolonged periods?

The key is to help people identify their strengths, develop and refine them constantly and, most importantly, deploy them in a way which accords with their own values but which also serves the need of the business.

Identification of strengths

The American business leader Larry Bossidy observed: "I ask people 'what are you good at?' It's remarkable the number of people that don't speak to that question with any degree of self-insight." Understanding your strengths and playing to them is easily understood, but in reality it is difficult to apply. It requires self-awareness and a fundamental commitment to knowing what is unique and inherently valuable in one's nature.

Generally, people need help and prompting to identify their strengths. In our work with executives we endeavour to develop a picture of their spike (key distinguishing strength) through a process of reviewing their life and career in some detail. Identifying the true area of strength which underlies positive performance in a variety of situations is not necessarily easy to do and it is a subtle process. In thinking about your own spike, consider the following questions:

- What made you distinctive when you were a child and at school?

- What have been the consistent underlying passions in your life?

- When people talk about you, what are the consistent patterns around strengths that emerge?

- Describe a situation when you were at your best. What strengths did you access in that context?

- What are your most significant achievements to date?

- What qualities were instrumental in these achievements?

- Overall, looking at the melody of your life, what patterns emerge?

- What are the blind spots associated with your strengths that you have to watch out for?

● What kinds of people do you need around you to compensate and help you?

It is important to describe people's strengths in unique ways which resonate with them rather than to apply a competency framework that narrows the field and looks for strengths only against the aspects covered by the framework. However, it is useful to have some sort of indication of the types of areas in which these spikes lie. On the basis of identifying the spikes for the senior leadership of three multinationals (a total of 262 individuals), we have developed a categorization of spikes. An interesting thing to note is how many different spikes we found (49) in this population of 262. This reinforces the point of looking at people as individuals rather than applying rigid categories. That notwithstanding, we did find that the spikes could be grouped into four broad areas. The percentage of spikes in each category, as well as examples, are illustrated in Table 6 on page 230.

● Intensification of strengths

Having developed a sense of people's spikes, companies then need to push individuals into thinking how they can take them to an Olympian level or, to put it another way, turn a spike into a towering area of distinctiveness? Asking people to think about figures who are exceptional in a particular area either within a company or in the world in general is a good place to start. In addition, it is helpful to think about what the deployment of a strength at a higher level would look like. For example, in this context someone with exceptionally solid project management skills could be encouraged to think about taking this to a higher level in terms of programme management or ultimately orchestration of activities in a whole business. The underlying skill set is the same but it is applied at a higher and higher level. Another area to think about is what challenges would force the individual to take their strengths to a higher level.

Table 6 ● Typology of spikes

Spike area	Frequency	Some examples
Experiential and Technical Spikes	13 per cent	● Uncanny ability to identify and land deals ● Deep organizational understanding and ability to work an internal agenda ● Distinctive, cutting-edge technical skills
Strategic Spikes	35 per cent	● Ability to make the right judgement calls in complex situations. ● Deep desire to understand, learn and improve. ● Powerful intuitive insight into the future needs of customers.
Orchestration Spikes	10 per cent	● Ability to frame issues and bring clarity to complex situations. ● Orchestration of diverse elements into a coherent whole. ● Tight programme management and follow through.
Execution Spikes	22 per cent	● Total personal responsibility and accountability for outcomes. ● Exceptional energy and intensity. ● Determination and resilience in the face of difficulties.
Relational Spikes	13 per cent	● Genuine empathy for, and interest in, others. ● Courage in challenging accepted views. ● Maturity and balance in the face of conflicting agendas.
Mobilization Spikes	12 per cent	● Genuine ability to connect with and inspire others. ● Exceptional story-telling skills. ● Infectiously positive attitude towards others' capabilities

Similarly, getting people to think about the blind spots that come with their strengths, and that need to be managed for their strengths to work to their optimum potential, can be very helpful.

The reframing here is subtle but powerful. For example, telling somebody that they have weak communication skills which they need to develop is much less motivational than saying "you have excellent strategic capability and understanding which we could access much more effectively if you developed your capacity to deliver your thinking in a manner that inspires and persuades others". Now let us look at how you can attack this area.

Putting strengths to work

For individuals and organizations to get real benefit out of the strengths approach it is not enough simply identifying them. They need to be put to work and honed to higher levels through the challenges that are encountered. There are essentially two issues here. The first is to help people connect their strengths with a sense of higher purpose and with the values that they possess. The second is to help people think about how their strengths can actually contribute to the business and how their deployment can be aligned with organizational goals.

Helping people understand what is dear to them and the contribution that they would dream of making is important if they are to experience the sense of flow that comes from deploying your strengths in areas that matter to you. Stephen Covey, the author of *The 7 Habits of Highly Effective People*,[8] followed up with *The 8th Habit*, which centres on the ability to get in touch with what truly drives you and the core values that you hold dear.[9] As we will describe in the next chapter, helping individuals work on this is a key precondition for releasing their leadership potential.

However, the above process can lapse into self-indulgence unless an effort is made to understand how people's personal values and strengths can be deployed in harmony with the goals of an organization. The trick is to establish a dialogue between managers and individuals about how their core strengths can be leveraged most effectively in their current role or other areas of the business. Sometimes, people argue that simply focusing on people's strengths serves to narrow their options within an organization.

On the contrary, we believe that if it is well done, the reverse is the case. The key is to understand that success in most positions can be achieved in a variety of ways, and the help that people need is to understand how their strengths map on to the demands of a role. Approaching the issue in this way allows organizations typically to take higher risks than they might simply on the basis of a narrow consideration of technical skills or functional background.

Take the case of the managing director of a division of a multinational for which we worked. The individual's route to the senior line role had been through a variety of functional roles at the centre which covered strategy, marketing and HR. Finding himself, for the first time, in a significant line role, with a number of country managers reporting to him, was not a comfortable experience. His initial instincts had been to radically adjust his approach and adopt the posture taken by other senior line managers within the business, the majority of whom had grown up through sales or general management positions. The attempted transformation, however, did not ring true and was unsettling for the executive, as well as not particularly plausible for his direct reports. I suggested he go back to thinking about what his distinguishing strengths were and looking to see how these could add value to the role. He quickly identified that strategic formulation and helping country managers develop robust strategic plans, better than any they'd ever done before, was a distinct area in which he could add value. It was like a switch being flicked. Once he had set about adding value in the role in this way, his direct reports became openly enthusiastic about his leadership, which eventually proved to be a storming success. Quite simply, he didn't need to understand the trade better than his people did, or try to be a mobilizing leader of sales forces from a distance. He simply had to be himself and trust that he could deliver value through his capabilities.

Invariably, when people with distinct capabilities are put into virtually any role, they can make a success of it if they play to those qualities and put people around them who complement their skill set.

Putting strengths to work: an example

Having talked about how developing strengths applies to individuals, let us now look at how this approach can be applied at a corporate level, using the example of the brewer, Whitbread.

Whitbread was founded in 1742 by Samuel Whitbread and by 1900 had become one of Britain's largest brewers and pub owners.[9] The company performed well for most of the twentieth century. However, government legislation in the early 1990s put limits on the number of pub outlets that brewers were allowed to own and this acted as a constraint on the company's growth. Its performance at that point started to suffer and the company diversified into other leisure sectors. Eventually, after a failed attempt to acquire assets from fellow drinks multinational Allied Domecq, which was very negatively portrayed by the market, Whitbread decided to sell its beer and pub divisions and concentrate on leisure. By early 2000 it was focused on hotels, pub restaurants, high-street restaurants and sports clubs.

Market perceptions of Whitbread needed to be changed and, having formulated a new sense of what its business was, the company needed to demonstrate that the new model worked and deliver organic growth through its various divisions rather than rely on disposals or acquisitions. The CEO at the time, David Thomas, initiated an ambitious programme to drive the performance of the company forward. This programme has been accelerated and continued under the new CEO, Alan Parker.

In 2002, David Thomas and his key executives decided to take a long, hard look at Whitbread's culture and what the company needed to do in order to deliver much sharper performance. Professor Michael Beer of Harvard University, in association with some of his colleagues, helped drive a thorough examination of the issues that needed to be tackled through a programme called "The Strategic Fitness Process" (SFP).[10] Essentially, this required the top team to explain the purpose and goals of Whitbread to a group of high-potential people who then conducted a series of interviews inside the organization to identify what really needed to change in order to deliver these aspirations. An innovative aspect of the process was that the top executives were required to listen in a fish bowl to the presentation and feedback from this group. The tone of the sessions was to put everything on the table and to then ask the top group to develop responses. The strategies and plans subsequently produced by the executive board were scrutinized by the SFP taskforce. The tone of these meetings was challenging and the board's initial responses were rejected as being way off the mark. Eventually the process produced a pithy 11-point action plan for taking the company forward. This included the restructuring of the organization into brand companies, a focus on developing skills in branding and, critically, developing the leadership culture of the business.

It was clear that Whitbread needed to tackle a leadership culture of institutionalized underperformance. There was a feeling that the company did not address performance issues in key executives and that it was overly tolerant and consensual. There was also a sense that leaders did not know what benchmarks and standards to set, either for themselves or for others.

Angie Risley, the HR director, asked us to help with this challenge. As the first step, working with her team, we spent some time in the business to identify the knowledge, skills and capabilities needed in its leaders within the full range of senior roles. Critical to this was to incorporate data from the external world about the profile of exceptional people in different functions. Having done this, the top 140 or so leaders at Whitbread went through an in-depth "benchmarking for development" process. David Thomas and Angie Risley had already decided who would take part. This was therefore a development exercise, as well as one to ensure that people were put in positions that played to their strengths. Feedback was collected through conversations with key executives against the expectations of leadership that had been set. In addition, directors went through an in-depth review process which covered their life and career to date. Their passions, values and future aspirations were also explored.

One outcome of this was a developmental report which identified an individual's key spike and other strengths, as well as the blind spots and weaknesses that could stand in the way of utilizing these strengths to the full. On the basis of this, each individual, in conjunction with their boss, produced a development plan. One section of the plan looked at the individual's distinctive spike and on how they could best leverage this in order to contribute to Whitbread's success. The individuals were encouraged to think about how to develop the strength further and how to use it in the context of their current role as well as in other positions that might be suitable for them. In addition, they were asked to identify areas of limitation or weakness that stood in the way of their making a full contribution. In tackling these latter areas, they were asked to think about strengths that they possessed and how these could be put to use in overcoming their limitations.

Once the process had been worked through with individuals, key teams in the business met to discuss collectively what had emerged. In the discussions, people got a better understanding of other people's spikes and how the individual wanted these to be accessed and utilized by the team. The teams also gave each other feedback on what people needed to do in order to really contribute maximally. In addition, teams then identified their collective team spikes and development areas.

The spikes and weaknesses of each key team were presented to the top leadership at an organizational level. The critical question here was – do we have the right mix of skills when we think about the team collectively to help drive what we need in that part of the business? This process led to considerable realignment and repositioning of people's roles within the organization.

Despite evoking initial anxiety, the process was received in an overwhelmingly positive manner by individuals, most of whom had never in their lives had the depth and quality of conversation about who they were, their distinguishing strengths and what they could contribute to the business. A key issue was that the strengths-based approach helped a group of people who collectively lacked confidence to regain their sense of self-assurance. To quote Angie

Risley: "Everyone got a much clearer focus on their spike, their blind spot and their development journey. Up until then people mentioned strengths in passing and then focused on weaknesses. It was a real shift and people still talk very much about their spikes."

This leadership intervention, along with the other components of the 11-point plan, had a significant impact on improving the performance of Whitbread. The business started to deliver robust organic growth and its share price more than doubled over a two-year period, achieving gains far in excess of the market average.

Creating a high-performance coaching culture

One of the most effective ways of giving people a sense of growth is to institute a robust coaching culture. As we noted in Chapter 3, high-performing companies, while typically being extremely aggressive around performance, are also equally aggressive with respect to coaching.

When we talk about a coaching culture, we do not mean that everybody in these companies has mentors or external coaches, but rather that all leaders and managers are expected to, on a consistent basis, enhance the performance of their people through robust and honest feedback and a constant dialogue on how things could be improved. People are also expected to develop successors. In some of these companies, for example at Procter and Gamble, managers are expected to devote over a third of their time to coaching, defined in this way. In many, promotion depends upon having ready successors behind one. This is the responsibility for anyone leading a team and they are held accountable for it.

How does a company go about creating a high-performance coaching culture? Let's look at the example of the world's largest drinks company, Diageo.

Diageo was formed as a result of the merger of Grand Metropolitan with Guinness. The group included brands such as Johnny Walker, Smirnoff, Gordon's Gin, Baileys and Guinness. At the time, the business also owned Burger King and Pillsbury's. In terms of the culture of the new company, we felt that a "high-performance coaching culture" should be a key aspect of the new organizational approach at Diageo. We had already introduced the notion to Guinness and the newly merged company embraced what Guinness had already bought into.

Because of a strong belief in getting the people agenda right, Diageo launched an ambitious programme, under the direction of Gareth Williams, the HR director, called "Building Diageo Talent". This had many components. In an initial phase, the top 150 executives went through a personal stock-take to identify key strengths and areas of development in the context of world-class leadership. Individuals worked with their manager to create development plans. This helped build the dialogue for coaching and development within the business.

The next stage was the introduction of a two-day high-performance coaching programme which over time some 5,000 of the top leaders and managers went through. This programme was developed and delivered through a mixture of external support from YSC and internal line and HR managers throughout the global organization. People attended in their teams with the manager present, so that live feedback and coaching on the real things that mattered to the team was practised. Most people attended the programme twice, once as a manager of a team, and then as part of their line manager's team. This helped develop an awareness of issues on both sides of the coaching relationship.

A key aspect of the programme was to go beyond teaching one-off coaching skills for performance reviews to helping participants create a systematic culture with expectation setting, observing performance, understanding performance, giving feedback and identifying mechanisms for change. Key to the programme's success was embedding the notion in people's minds that coaching was not a sideline activity divorced from their "real job" but something that was central to what they needed to do to help them achieve what they wanted. People had not expected that a coaching programme would focus on expectation setting or the robust judgement of performance. However, according to our research, these components are as critical as feedback or practical advice in creating a true coaching culture.

These activities initiated the development of a strong high-performance coaching culture at Diageo. While initially the programme was received in a highly positive manner, it became clear that the intervention needed to be supported by other processes in order to truly embed the cultural shift. In addition, Diageo found that it was as important to focus on performance feedback as on the opportunities for growth and development. Today the journey continues. The business has moved to develop a model of leadership that explicitly encourages authenticity, as well as a leading-edge development programme to help it achieve challenging goals and become an iconic and trusted company. But one thing is clear – virtually everybody at Diageo welcomes the seriousness with which the business has addressed the issue of personal development.

In summary, we would offer the following observations in creating meaning through personal growth:

- Recognize that helping people to grow is not a "nice-to-have" for a business but a fundamental component of what people want and expect from their work.

- Ensure developmental interventions are aimed at helping people find their own sense of meaning. This means adapting interventions to individual need as opposed to dropping programmes of activity on people.

- Take risks and apply the "believe in everyone" principle as far as it can legitimately be applied in your organization. Do not prescribe people's roles rigidly. Allow people to succeed in their own way in positions. Take chances, but leave people in a post long enough to be able to evaluate their performance and for them to learn by seeing the consequences of their efforts. Recognize that applying the principle also requires you to think hard about how you measure performance and the contribution that people make.

- Instil a culture that focuses on people's strengths. Develop processes for honing these to the highest levels. Give individuals help in identifying their latent capabilities and how these could be applied in the context of your business. Look to create teams that have spike strengths in the relevant areas required rather than averaging qualities across the spectrum.

- Give people time to reflect and explore their underlying values and passions. But don't leave it at that. Once this is done, find a way of connecting these passions with what the business needs of them. There needs to be a contract here that works for both parties.

- Recognize that the other side of creating the room for people to contribute in their own way is the need to develop a laser-sharp approach to evaluating people's performance. This is the other side of the coin that keeps a positive philosophy of growth grounded in business reality rather than being a licence for indulgence.

- Instil a high-performance coaching culture. Recognize that this is not the same as assigning everybody a coach. Frequently, a lot of money and time is wasted on external coaching which is poorly connected to the underlying needs of the business.

- Develop the capabilities of your people in terms of setting expectations, giving feedback, observing performance and pulling the best out of others.

- Finally, make growth the agenda of all leaders and managers. It impacts the business most powerfully when fully supported by the CEO and integrated with other initiatives. Do not just delegate to the HR function. Cut all development work that is not supported by key line management as forwarding the aims of the organization. Find methods of measuring the impact of developmental interventions on the bottom line so that commitment and momentum for it can be maintained throughout the business. Recognize that ultimately any development that does not help people perform is experienced as meaningless by both the business and the individual.

10. Belonging

"Successful companies have parties, unsuccessful ones have meetings."

Philip Green, Britain's leading retail entrepreneur

Diageo, the world's biggest premium drinks company, has increasingly recognized the importance of relationships to its success. Gareth Williams, the HR director, says: "One of the things we lost sight of in the past, through the professional, transactional approach to business, is the fact that the quality of relationships both internally and externally is vital to sustained performance. Ultimately it is relationships that allow you to achieve things across our business or influence our key distributors and external stakeholders. Now we are putting enormous effort into this area. Trust is the key to great relationships. Everywhere we get it right, we see breakthroughs in performance."

Diageo's mission is to "Celebrate Life, everyday, everywhere" and it's not only the products that help achieve that. The work environment is informal and conducive to free thinking. The company boasts amazing open-plan offices with numerous breakout areas for people to come together and co-create solutions. Fluidity and spontaneity replace rigidity and form. Consequently, people feel relaxed and at home there – but it also makes them want to work together to build the success of the company. Yet, belonging is, by its nature, a two-way street. Like a demanding family, Diageo requires high participation from its people and judges performance rigorously.

Meaning Inc. companies understand the business value of creating strong relationship cultures. Southwest Airlines is a company that makes an enormous effort to connect with its employees and create an environment where people feel they belong.[1] The corporate culture is highly egalitarian, familial and fun-loving. It actively recruits people from the same family and offers family-type loyalty and job security. Only once, since the company was founded in 1973, has it laid anyone off and, even then, those three people were quickly re-hired. With the knowledge that their jobs are safe and they are being treated like family, Southwest employees have the peace of mind to get on with their jobs and focus their efforts on building business success. It was also the first airline to launch a profit-sharing plan for employees and the only one in the world to provide stock ownership without wage concessions.

Individuality is not just tolerated at Southwest but actively encouraged – particularly when it comes to employees expressing the fun side of their personalities. All employees receive personal birthday cards from the business. What's more, they spend more time planning parties than writing policies! All of this is based on the belief that when people are happy and have the freedom to be themselves, they are more productive and give more of themselves. In turn, when there is a strong sense of belonging within a business, customers want to belong too. Southwest has made a profit for 29 years straight and is the top domestic airline (in terms of passengers carried) in the US, with the best safety record in the country.

So far we have talked about how meaning is created through the way companies behave and understand themselves and how individuals grow and develop within their work. In this chapter we explore how meaning is created for people through relationships and a sense of belonging. We look at why belonging is such an important human need and the detrimental impact of poor belonging on a business. We show how leaders can identify the signs and causes of poor belonging and what they can do to create strong belonging cultures.

What does it mean to belong?

Belonging can be defined along two key dimensions: our relationship with others in the company and how we identify with the company itself. Our belonging needs are met when mutual trust is unquestioned, when we feel liked, accepted and validated by others. They are also met when we feel connected to others through a common cause and shared values, purpose and direction. If you are ultimately aiming for the same thing, whether it be to provide an excellent health service to the community, to push scientific insight or to make the best hamburgers in the world, the sense of belonging this provides is reassuring and highly motivating.

In organizations, the process of belonging begins with a sense of mutual inclusiveness – people liking and wanting to be with others in the organization, but also feeling that others like and want to be with them. University graduates frequently choose their employers, not because of salary or benefits, but because they feel a high degree of personal resonance. There is often a person whom they particularly admired or warmed to during the selection process; perhaps they have a sense that the culture is inclusive or that the values of the organization reflect their own.

Many business leaders recognize these issues and the importance of creating organizations in which people feel they truly belong. Most also understand that fulfilling people's social needs leads to more inspired commitment; if employees really identify with the organization and feel they are an integral part of it, their intrinsic motivation to contribute to its growth and success is inevitably stronger. As a consequence, many well-intentioned attempts have been made to satisfy people's belonging and social needs. However, the challenge facing 21st-century leaders is to create collective belonging that is genuine and meaningful.

Why are relationships important?

Evidence is growing that building robust relationships is a very real factor in driving organizational effectiveness. The growth of annual "best employer" lists around the globe, job advertisements that proudly label their companies as "an employer of choice" and a plethora of consultants focusing their services in this area attest to its importance.

Yet, many people at all levels of organizational life feel a growing sense of disengagement and that they cannot be themselves at work. In fact surveys now routinely report extremely low levels of trust across businesses. The Harris Interactive survey (see page 49) found that only 15 per cent of employees felt they worked in a high-trust environment.[2] In addition, David Guest's surveys since 1996 for the CIPD also report low levels of trust and, even more worryingly, a steep decline over the past few years.[3]

Why should companies be concerned about these trends? In the mid-1990s, a client asked us to analyse the cultural factors that lay behind the most successful companies over a sustained period of time. We had not formulated our Meaning Inc. views at that point. We looked at companies like Mars, P&G and Coca-Cola, and studied their culture closely. As a point of comparison we also looked at companies in their sectors that had been less successful. Three factors tended to be present in the successful companies, whereas the less successful displayed none, one, or more rarely, two, of the factors. First, all successful companies kept their people, recruited mostly from within, and used this consistency to create a clear cultural signature. Second, they tended to have aggressive performance cultures. Lastly, and surprisingly, the emphasis on performance was balanced by an equally aggressive focus on support and coaching.

When we stepped back from these observations, we concluded that all these companies acted in some respect like a demanding family. People felt they were a part of the fabric but recognized that they would be pushed and supported in equal measure to give of their best. Underlying all these factors was the existence of strong interpersonal bonds. The development of robust and close relationships is a strong prerequisite for creating a strong feedback and coaching culture and for driving the cooperation and cross-functional collaboration that is so vital to modern business success. In addition, because relationships were solid, people could be aggressively pushed, sure in the knowledge that this was done with the best of intentions. Increasingly, businesses are aware that strong relationships and trust are the bedrock of effective execution and innovation.

Some fundamental psychological truths underpin this:

People have powerful inclusion needs

Creating environments where people feel they belong is important because people have profound needs for inclusion and social bonding. Redundancies, organizational restructuring and bringing in fresh blood from outside the business is often necessary and done for worthy reasons, but in the broader audit of such change, leaders all too often lose sight of human needs. Attachment Theory in psychology proposes that, from soon after birth, infants have a fundamental need to bond with their caregiver.[4] Indeed, it can be critical for their survival. A study of infants raised in orphanages showed that those who were not handled or raised with loving attention not only didn't thrive but many actually died.[5] The need for attachment in humans is so strong that, even when treated violently by a parent or caregiver, infants and children continue to seek physical contact with them.

Some say the need for food is the primary motivator for attachment behaviour. However, studies on animals found that this does not appear to be the case. Animal learning theorist Harry Harlow tested the development of attachment by removing infant rhesus monkeys from their mother and replacing her with two different surrogate mothers: one made from bale-wire and one wrapped in terry cloth, each fitted with a feeding nipple.[6] They found that infant monkeys became more attached to the substitute terry-cloth mother than the harsher bale-wire mother *even* when the bale-wire mother was the only one supplying food to the baby monkey.

Throughout life, this need for attachment continues to be an important part of our humanness. Having warm and trusting friendships, feeling that you belong and that others care about you is fundamental to us. Likewise, from a meaning perspective, our sense of personal identity and purpose stems largely from our various roles in life and how these roles relate to and depend on others. Feeling and knowing that we *belong* to something beyond ourselves gives us our sense of place in the world and drives us to channel our energies towards that something.

Moreover, the complex goals that organizations are setting themselves rely heavily on human relationships and a level of trust and cooperation that goes far beyond the job specification. Without understanding and satisfying these human needs, the best-laid business plans can fail.

Feeling that you belong and that others care for you is also an important contributor to mental health. In 1978, British psychologists George Brown and Tirril Harris conducted a landmark study of depression in women.[7] They found four vulnerability factors that predisposed women to depression in the presence of an adverse life event. The first and most crucial of these was the lack of a supportive, confiding relationship with their partner. The others were having three or more children under the age of 14 living at home, the loss or prolonged separation from the mother before the woman was eleven years old, and unemployment.

In a 1999 study by the University of Michigan School of Nursing, "a lack of a personal sense of belonging" was found to be a greater predictor of major depression than any other factors, including poor social support, loneliness and being in conflict with others.[8] The study found that even strong social support systems, like having numerous friends or a busy social life, had little impact on how depressed someone was likely to become, unless they felt they belonged to that group of friends. People who felt they didn't belong agreed with statements like, "If I died tomorrow, very few people would come to my funeral" and "I feel like a square peg trying to fit into a round hole"; whereas people with a higher sense of belonging tended to agree or endorse a statement such as "I generally feel that people accept me."

Given that, in America alone, employee depression is estimated to cost the country up to $40 billion each year in lost productivity, mistakes, accidents and absenteeism, the problem of belonging is clearly one that cannot be ignored.[9]

Work is a key provider of our belonging needs

Our fundamental belonging needs have been met historically through our family ties, but also through work and the wider social fabric of our lives. However, the relative decline, particularly in the Western world, of religion, community and close connection with the extended family, means that society is failing to provide for those needs. By default, we are increasingly dependent on satisfying our needs for belonging – attachment and bonding with others – through work. This places significant responsibility at the feet of companies and, as with Southwest, the ones who address these needs will reap the benefits.

Signs and causes of poor belonging

Before we can identify effective ways to create belonging, it is important to be able to detect the signs of poor levels of belonging within a business and the dynamics that destroy belonging. The most apparent signs include high employee turnover, absenteeism and stress-related illness. However, there are also some less obvious behavioural signals that can be equally pernicious, such as poor morale, low energy and efficiency, a lack of innovation, little spontaneous teamwork or cooperation and a reluctance to go the extra mile. All of these can create significant losses in productivity and revenue for companies.

There are two major causes of poor belonging: an erosion of trust between individuals and organizations and, related to this, individuals not being themselves – something we call learned inauthenticity:

Lack of trust

One of the primary reasons why people don't feel they belong in organizations is because trust has been steadily and inevitably eroded. One only has to trace the development of careers to see the immense shift people have experienced in their working lives, from relatively stable and predictable employment tenure to a much more fluid and changeable norm. People can no longer rely on companies to provide them with job security no matter how committed, loyal or skilled they may be. The psychological contract between individual and organization has changed into something mundane and pragmatic. Mihaly Csikszentmihalyi, a noted commentator in this area, concludes: "The absence of loyalty on the part of workers is a perfectly logical response to the absence of loyalty on the part of employers."[10]

In organizations, a lack of trust can have major consequences such as destructive political behaviour, a decline in the efficient execution of the organization's work and even robbery! Gallup found that the item on their questionnaire asking respondents if they have a best friend at work was the single biggest predictor of "shrinkage" – or theft – in the retail industry. "A high level of trust in the team dissuades people from leaving the warehouse door open," Peter Flade, managing partner at Gallup in the UK says.[11] In low-trust environments, information is not shared freely, people are guarded about putting their views and ideas on the table, and cooperation is, at best, mechanical. All this has a significant impact on the speed at which things move forward. It slows the whole cycle of execution and innovation down. And yet, organizations' performance targets tend to be more complicated than they used to be. As a result, to achieve them requires a high level of trust between all members of the organization.

Just as with successful relationships or families, trust is and has to be present in successful companies. If individuals trust each other, and if people trust their organizations and their organizations trust them, the question of give and take becomes redundant because everyone knows automatically that the other side will be fair. In short, if businesses want extraordinary and special commitment and effort from their people they have to make their people feel extraordinarily special. Otherwise, what they get is simply the false impression that people are committed – because they know they have to parrot the expectations – rather than genuinely committed.

Learned inauthenticity

Another major reason why people don't feel a sense of genuine belonging to their organizations is that they have learned to be inauthentic and so have those around them. Take the example of Simon, a senior executive in a media company. He told us: "For so long, I hadn't been bringing *myself* to work. I wasn't really prepared to let others see or know the true me. It wasn't something that had happened consciously – I had just slipped into that way of being. Then I woke up one morning and I realized, I'm living my life with these people, so what's the point of pretending." He then went on to describe how much more fulfilling work had become – rather than superficially going through the motions, he was actively making an effort to connect more naturally with others and to be part of the organizational community and, in doing so, his life felt much more integrated. He felt he *belonged* more.

Like the old Simon, many feel a need to create distance between themselves and others at work. As a result, people are losing both their willingness and their skill to build authentic relationships at work. This is made all the worse since they spend so much of their lives with their work colleagues.

Individuals see the cast of characters constantly changing around them, so it is no wonder they lose the motivation to establish friendships and have authentic interactions with their work colleagues. The uncertainty created by relentless organizational change leads inevitably to a rise in destructive political behaviour. People feel they have to compete harder and smarter in order to get ahead and secure their slice of the cake. This competitive "dog-eat-dog" world over-rides the "we're all in this together" ethos. Many regard work relationships as a zero-sum game where the prize of success is finite: if someone else gains, there is less of the pie for me. For many, therefore, surviving organizational life requires self-protective strategies and wariness in building any real connection with others. Just as in Simon's case, many people have learned to cope with the challenges of modern working life by playing a role and not being themselves. They disengage, sometimes without even realizing it.

Another reason why people have learned to be inauthentic in relating to others is the pressure to conform. As people journey up through an organization, the desire to be accepted by other senior leaders can put limits on the extent to which they are prepared to openly challenge colleagues or say what they truly believe. Stephen Covey concludes from a study of 23,000 US workers by Harris Interactive that "only 17 per cent (of people) feel their organization fosters open communication that is respectful of differing opinions and results in new and better ideas".[12] That leaves a worrying majority of people feeling the opposite way. Such feelings lead to an existence at work that, for many, feels frustrating and ultimately results in disengagement.

Leaders have also mastered the game of inauthenticity. Tough decisions have become the mainstay of their lives. With ever-increasing demands to strip out costs and raise productivity from fewer people, leaders frequently have to decide who stays and who goes – being close to those people makes the process all the more difficult. Some also view business more in terms of numbers or personal ambition than people. For them, the question of engagement or connection may not seem an issue in the first place.

The questions below should help identify whether your company has any belonging issues:

- Do people feel they can be themselves and not play a role?

- Is employee turnover at or above the average for your industry?

- Are there regular occurrences of absenteeism or stress-related illness?

- Are core values shared by everyone in the organization?

- Is there a sense of fun in the day-to-day running of the business?

- Are projects delivered on time?

- Do people cooperate and help each other out without being asked?

- Does the organization host company parties or social gatherings?

- Do people in the organization spontaneously get together socially?

- Is laughter a familiar sound throughout the organization?

- Do people feel that information is available and circulated freely?

- Does the level of communication in the business go beyond the task at hand?

- Do people feel they know and understand each other?

- Do people trust each other?

If the answer to any of these questions is "no" then belonging may well be an issue within the business. Let's now turn to how organizations and leaders can begin to make people feel that they belong.

How to create a strong relationship culture

Organizations intent on providing a sense of belonging should:

Welcome newcomers – not just round pegs in round holes

The most obvious starting point in establishing a sense of belonging is to recruit the right people in the first place – the round pegs, people whose skills will be valued and utilized, who share the corporate ideology and who will like and be liked by others in the business. Business leaders have long recognized this and spend significant amounts on search firms and business psychologists to ensure that round pegs are found for round holes, particularly for the most senior roles. But what about the round holes? Do businesses ask themselves, "Is this person going to feel like they belong here?" and "Do we do everything possible to make people feel welcome?"

Whitbread, the UK's leading hospitality business, has a strong heritage of creating a sense of belongingness. Its mantra is "Welcome with a Smile". People entering the business as new employees invariably talk about what an easy and welcoming place it is to join. They comment, in particular, on the friendliness and warmth of colleagues, the genuine sense of acceptance, invitations to join social and community events and the passion that people share for being part of the team. Despite challenging economic conditions, Whitbread has been a solid business for the last 260 years and enjoys healthy employee tenure.

Develop people's ability to form strong relationships

People receive limited formal training in developing strong, robust relationships. This is curious given that our environment consists virtually entirely of other people. There are significant personal and business benefits that accrue from developing trust and a strong relational culture. These include the creation of alignment, effective execution and the confidence in others to take risks. Such benefits are blocked when people manage relationships as a zero-sum game versus working to create win:win scenarios. However, building strong relationships requires genuine trust, empathy, understanding, honesty and respect for oneself or others.

Be loyal

Retaining the best people is a serious challenge for organizations and the best way of building employee loyalty is to show loyalty to them. We have frequently found ourselves in the position of advising on the merits of internal and external candidates. Bringing in people from outside the organization often carries the promise of fresh thinking and a solution to that ongoing dilemma that no insider has successfully addressed. However, our research shows that the highest-performing companies often grow their own. Outsiders face the learning curve associated with getting to grips with the organization and all its nuances. The speed with which new people can achieve this successfully is often underestimated and the hopes for them to rapidly add value are often unrealistic. Indeed, this is one of the key reasons why CEOs who are parachuted into new businesses fail.[13] The human side of transforming a business – the time it takes to get to know and understand those around you, establish the currency of trust and become in synch with others' values and thinking – is frequently and frustratingly underestimated. Without grasping these human elements, no new blood can be truly effective. Although wielding power and authority can drive immediate results, the true engagement of employees is needed in order to sustain lasting change.

Likewise, it can take time for existing employees to fully embrace incoming people. One business we worked with had a 40 per cent attrition rate because of tissue rejection – when new people are effectively rejected by the organization and end up leaving of their own accord. Therefore, when selecting people for roles, unless there is clear blue water between their skills, go for the internal candidate ahead of the external one.

Loyalty to employees is something the East has typically understood better than the West. Japan, for much of its history, has been notable in operating a job-for-life policy. Take, also, the example of Abdul Latif Jameel (ALJ), a highly successful and innovative Middle East-based international conglomerate. ALJ's philosophy is to establish long-term partnerships founded on genuine trust and respect for their own people as well as for their external contacts and customers. Business meetings are sometimes even conducted at the family home in Saudi Arabia. Watermelon and tea are typically served over relaxed conversations – seamlessly moving across a variety of topics as well as the business at hand. The focus is on building joint understanding and acceptance rather than transacting clinically with people. ALJ is also a Meaning Inc. company on a number of other dimensions. For example, the company strongly believes that profit should not be a goal in itself, but a consequence of sticking to their DNA and values. The Group and its owners are also involved in a range of community projects world-wide, including the Jameel Poverty Action Lab, which acts as a think tank to identify ways of lifting people out of poverty. From selling ten cars in Saudi Arabia over five decades ago, ALJ are now one of the most highly regarded motor distributors in the world.

Make work fun!

Look at the invigorating environments created by Google, Virgin, Genentech and Southwest Airlines. All of these Meaning Inc. companies share a focus on fun without sacrificing professionalism and the delivery of great results. When levels of creativity and inspiration decline, people have less energy for doing new or truly special things for the business – for going that extra mile. In contrast, Virgin's founder Richard Branson says: "More than any other element, fun is the secret of Virgin's success."[14] The experience of flying with Southwest or Virgin is guaranteed to be a shift away from other ordinary airlines. In place of the robotic announcements and mechanical service are jokes, frivolity and a sense that you are part of a party rather than a drill. What better way to counteract the fear of flying!

Look also at the innovation and creativity that readily emerge from these businesses. As we have seen, Google and Genentech give substantial free time to their people to explore their own passions and interests – to dream for a while. This fun time has resulted in an array of new and profitable products for both companies. At Southwest, the space people are given for dialogue and discussion about the company newsletter has helped them to come up with new ways of addressing company challenges – like saving on fuel expenditure.[15]

These are the types of places people really want to work, but sadly it is this focus on fun and belonging that is missing from many post-modern businesses.

Keep work teams together

Strong relationship bonds throughout an organization can be a powerful driver of teamwork. When people know and trust those around them, they are more concerned to help their colleagues and to think about what others expect of them. They are also much more able to exert influence and make things happen quickly. Regardless of someone's level in the organization, being able to pick up the phone to ask a favour of a colleague or having an understanding of who will help you oil the wheels become important determinants of operational effectiveness. When employees are in synch in this way, they can draw on collective effort but also benefit from social bonding and a shared sense of purpose.

There has been an increasing move away from intact teams to creating a head office pool of expert resources, typically based centrally within the organization. With this, individuals have been required to give up much of the traditional notions of teams. While this makes sense from a rational and economical viewpoint, in reality, it creates real dissonance for those people. In particular, individuals often feel that their technical depth and experience are ignored. They can also feel confused about what they are really part of.

The challenge for leaders, therefore, is to recognize the hidden cost of these apparently obvious solutions and to create alternatives that will actually work in the long term.

Make the psychological contract mutual and explicit

While much effort typically goes into documenting an individual's financial package and job expectations, relatively little attention tends to be given to agreeing the psychological contract between the individual and the organization. In many ways, this is much the same as the unwritten psychological contract within families: you do your duty by running nephews to football practice or helping with the wedding arrangements and in return the family will always be there for you when the chips are down. While much of this is implicit with families, more explicit agreement is warranted when it comes to the work environment. Leaders can help to build clarity with regard to the individual-organization psychological contract by knowing their people and getting into the right conversations with staff members.

Levi Strauss Europe is one company that has recognized that the organization can be an ambiguous and challenging one to join. Its matrix structure can create confusion, especially for those who are new to the organization or are used to a more linear and clear-cut way of operating. Consequently, it provides coaching support to line managers so that they not only understand how to operate within the structure, but are also able to help build that understanding in their teams.

Part of this involves discussion about the company's organizational values and what they actually mean in practice. One of its values is collaboration, and thus is intended to drive collective decision-making behaviours across the organization. The matrix structure is designed to capitalize and depend on this form of problem-solving. In the creation of new clothing lines, for example, people from the marketing, merchandising, wholesale, retail and sales functions share their expertise and decide the best way forward. The process means people must influence each other and make compromises in a way that can be frustrating for some. However, the psychological contract requires people to embrace this style of operating and recognize its benefits. In return, the organization gives individuals broad exposure to a number of disciplines and helps to build their insight into what it takes to develop cutting-edge jeans designs.

Encourage individuality

The *Built to Last* companies identified by Jim Collins and Jerry Porras were described as having "cult-like" cultures that create crystal-clear belonging boundaries.[16] However, despite the meaning these strong cultures can create, some people inevitably sign up to the culture more than others and a feeling of going through the motions rather than truly belonging can still exist. This can result in those organizations losing potentially strong talent.

Leaders can help address this problem by modelling openness, directness and diversity. At Cadbury Schweppes, these behaviours have been reinforced and modelled by their leaders throughout its history. Right from its Quaker beginnings, the organization has sought to define itself through a strong community culture, but it also puts great emphasis on accepting people and encouraging individuality. This has helped the business to establish a real sense of belonging coupled with the freedom to be oneself. In the words of one contented employee: "I just can't imagine working anywhere else. It really feels like we're all pushing in the same direction and individual talents are encouraged and idiosyncrasies tolerated. It just works!"

Maximize the value of informal networks

The feeling that you belong in an organization comes largely from a myriad of human interactions which together lead you to feel that you are in the know – that you are an integral link in the information chain. It also comes from knowing that others like you are willing to help and support you. Support networks serve important socialization functions, and these are linked to reassurance. Unfortunately, reference to support networks is not something you're likely to find in the typical induction manual. Indeed, many organizations neither acknowledge nor encourage them.

Nonetheless, leaders can contribute by encouraging more informal space for people to connect. In this way, leadership communities can be formed that are based on identity, communication and respect. On the face of it, this can feel like an unnecessary luxury but in reality the benefits of people sharing ideas, learning from each other and identifying opportunities to cooperate, cross-sell products/services and create more streamlined efficiencies cannot be denied. Leaders can also play an active role in mentoring individuals throughout the organization – particularly by giving people clarity around the unwritten organizational rules and support in understanding and managing organizational dynamics.

People's needs for social belonging and cohesion change over time, depending on their stage of life and what is important to them. In order to create meaning at an individual level, therefore, leaders need to make sufficient allowances for this. Employee engagement decreases the longer people are with an organization. This suggests that initial efforts to socialize and integrate newcomers are more successful than those aimed at long-serving employees or those who have already settled in. There are reports that companionship and socializing with peers after work has become a higher priority for increasing numbers of young people than earning a high salary or progressing up the corporate ladder. The quest for meaning seems to be influencing the nature of people's ambitions and what they seek from their employing organizations. Fun and spontaneity are values which to some extent appear to have replaced the 1980s love of work intensity and obsession with money.

Historically, meetings have been the major forum for managers to have contact with their peers. Unfortunately, formal meetings also bring with them a certain protocol and a business agenda that does not easily enable individuals to truly connect with or understand each other. Even more annoyingly, when not controlled, meetings can dominate your business life – as John Cleese put it in the management training film *Meetings, Bloody Meetings*: "I don't go to work to work, I go to work to have meetings."

By contrast, businesses in the creative arena (advertising and marketing, particularly) are typically skilled at designing and using their work environment in ways which facilitate fluid interaction, teamwork and employee innovation. They show that it is possible to stand back and look for new ways to encourage connection, both in terms of the physical set-up of meeting space and the engagement and friendliness of any senior staff involved. Leadership support and facilitation can also extend to the way in which after-hours activities are encouraged, the chosen formality and informality of different "official" communications and even the stories leaders choose to tell. Each of these actions has the effect of inviting involvement, and each evokes an emotion or an experience within different individuals – be it pride, trust, safety, ownership or a sense of value.

In summary:

- People have profound needs for belonging and social bonding. We spend far too long at work to not have fun doing it or to not really feel a part of it. Relentless organizational change and job insecurity has eroded trust between companies and their people. In response, many individuals have adopted inauthentic and self-protective strategies that ultimately destroy meaning for both parties. However, the po-faced corporate uniform and caricatured observance of protocol that once stood for professionalism is not a feature of Meaning Inc. companies. They work hard to create belonging cultures that allow people to be authentically themselves, and they reap substantial rewards in the process.

Belonging can be created in a number of ways:

- Do not be afraid to create a demanding family company culture. This entails a mutual process of providing people with high levels of loyalty and commitment and expecting the same in return. Newcomers should be welcomed with open arms; people should be given opportunities, with internal promotion preferred to bringing in outsiders wherever possible; and the psychological requirements for belongingness should be agreed in a mutual and explicit way.

- Build strong relationship cultures that emphasise the importance of trust and a genuine win-win mindset. Encourage people to challenge themselves to bring honesty, empathy, understanding and respect for both themselves and others to their relationships.

- People feel they belong in environments where they can genuinely relax and be themselves. Therefore, rather than merely tolerating difference, leaders need to actively encourage expressions of individuality and create enjoyable, invigorating environments.

- Belonging is not the responsibility of leaders alone, but of all company members. Concerted efforts should therefore be made to build and maintain a sense of team unity across the company. Keeping teams together over time enables people to develop a real understanding of how best to work together, utilize each others' strengths and capabilities to an optimum level and to develop the depth of trust and fluid efficiency that is so integral to team and organizational effectiveness.

- People reinforce belonging through overt acts of cooperation and support. Mentoring schemes help new people settle in to a business and circumvent the laborious process of learning the unwritten rules and political dynamics. Similarly, space needs to be provided for people to connect with each other and to share information fluidly through the informal social fabric of the organization. Leaders who have the confidence to give people space for this level of interaction are likely to be richly rewarded with all the special effort and commitment that is in evidence in the very closest families.

11. Rebalancing

> "(The human mind) is like a body that cries out for wine when it needs water and insists it should be dancing when it should in truth be flat on a bed."
>
> Alain de Botton[1]

Work–life balance is not something people typically associate with the entrepreneurial and technological ferment of Silicon Valley in California. However, the companies there have been pioneers in making the time people spend at work fulfilling. Take Google, which has set its creative minds ticking to change people's experience of work. Conscious of the fact that most Googlers are fresh out of university, it has created a campus-style feel with a Google twist. Hence, pool-cue-carrying programmers, jelly-bean-eating assistants and people riding scooters through reception are regular features of Google HQ.[2] The place is filled with palm trees, brightly coloured medicine balls, lava lamps, assorted gadgets and toys, bean bag chairs and even Googlers' pet dogs.

The 10 per cent rule is another notable feature of life at Google-plex. People are given the freedom to spend 10 per cent of their time "dreaming". In order to drive ideas that are truly new, Googlers can explore an interest or idea they are passionate about. It is an unusual policy, but one with a very strong win–win outcome. Googlers get the time and resources to release their entrepreneurial spirits without worrying about whether they will make money for the business or not. Google, in return, gets a happy, motivated workforce and innovative ideas from some of the brightest minds in the industry. The ideas that people are working on in their 10 per cent time are discussed over lunch, communicated internally across the business through intranet bulletin boards and reviewed by peers. If there is enough positive support ideas can turn into full-blown projects.

In this way, Google has been able to launch many ideas that the Google founders, Larry Page and Sergey Brin, would not have been able to come up with themselves. For instance, Krishna Bharat's lifetime passion for news became Google News – a news broking service that ranks news stories from thousands of media outlets according to subject items and organizes information for the user. Rather than just use his 10 per cent, Bharat ended up working full-time on the idea. It was not only the realization of a dream for Bharat, it revolutionized the lives of many journalists and news enthusiasts around the globe.

Googlers are also lavished with fantastic, wholesome, free meals and snacks. There were only 56 employees in the company when Charlie Ayres was hired as the Google chef, to give Googlers healthy, delicious food choices where previously only McDonald's and Krispy Kreme had been available. Charlie ended up setting a standard for Silicon Valley and Googlers often comment on how the food they eat over the weekend is nowhere near as good as at work. The founders were adamant that Googlers deserved all of this. Meaning Inc. companies create balance for people and make them feel special.

This array of delights, is of course, possible for a company as cash-rich as Google. However, the interesting thing is that the founders spent handsomely on creating a special environment and benefits for Googlers right from the start – before it was the superstar business it is today. At the same time, they were frugal with their spending in other areas. For example, rather than bringing in technology from outside, they custom-made their early computers with the use of imitation LEGO blocks and have always relied on word-of-mouth rather than expensive advertising campaigns to create consumer awareness. Similarly, when they floated, they refused to play by the rules and pay exorbitant amounts to Wall Street brokerage firms, but instead offered them less than half their standard fees. They also set a Wall Street precedent by pricing and selling their stock in an on-line Dutch auction in order to eliminate what they felt was the favouritism and unfairness of the usual process. Needless to say, their entirely unconventional way of taking control of the IPO (initial public offering) infuriated the financial world.

Other Meaning Inc. companies also address the work–life balance creatively. Doing so makes people feel distinctive and special – and therefore creates meaning for them. While work demands a lot from people, Meaning Inc. companies are careful to balance this with what they give back and how they signal to employees that they are valued for their unique contribution. For instance, the Tata Group was the first company in India to institute an eight-hour working day – something that went completely against the grain, certainly in India, but also throughout the majority of the working world at that time.

When one looks at lists of the best companies to work for, it is amazing how many are highly demanding and challenging places. International surveys on employee engagement[3] invariably show that people in countries like the US, where people work long hours, are often happier than those in other seemingly more balanced countries like Australia. Many people positively enjoy giving a lot to their work – provided it is meaningful and they get the right rewards. Meaning Inc. companies intuitively recognize this and invest generously in their people because they are confident that it will pay off in the form of loyalty and commitment. Special chefs, 10 per cent dream time and relaxed, fun surroundings are not just empty gestures, but a distinctive way of making the time their people spend at work more fulfilling and productive.

In this chapter, we explore people's perceptions of balance – both with respect to work–life issues but also within work itself. We look into how people are feeling about work inputs and outputs, investigate the key reasons why balance can go wrong and suggest ways in which businesses and individuals can seek to rebalance the scales.

Give and take

Work–life balance is a hot topic. There is a pervasive sense of exhaustion that permeates the organizational ether today – much like the dead hamster on the spinning wheel we talked about earlier. At all levels of a company, people are voicing their concern and frustration with the imbalance between what they are putting into their work and what they are getting out, and between what their work enables them to do versus what they have to forgo in other areas of their lives. Intuitively, people are making this calculation and feeling short-changed. Many wonder: "Do I prioritize my family or my job? Is it more important to play a central role to the few to whom I am closest or to the many whom I lead at work? If I accept a job of such responsibility, must I do whatever it takes to fulfil that role, regardless of the impact on my personal life?" Generally, what's in it for the organization is abundantly clear, but what's in it for the individual often is not.

In the early 1990s, noted evolutionary psychologists Leda Cosmides and John Tooby began interpreting a series of anomalies that research had found in tests of reasoning.[4] Essentially, psychologists had been puzzled by the fact that the same tests of reasoning produced very different results according to how they were presented. Cosmides and Tooby used the Wason selection task, which is a test of conditional reasoning in which people are asked to identify possible violations of a conditional rule expressed in the form "If P, then Q." In general, people perform very poorly on these tests. However, they found that when they reframed the problem around social exchanges instead of logic, and detecting cheaters instead of detecting rule violations (e.g., when the rule becomes: "If you satisfy the requirement, then you take the benefit"), then 65 to 80 per cent of people answered correctly. They went on to reason that people have highly evolved receptors

Figure 9 ● Equity theory of motivation[5]

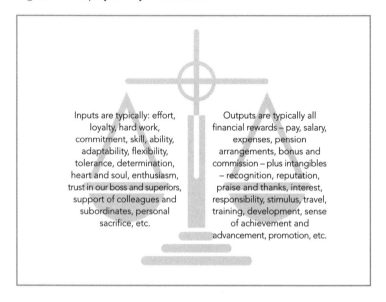

Inputs are typically: effort, loyalty, hard work, commitment, skill, ability, adaptability, flexibility, tolerance, determination, heart and soul, enthusiasm, trust in our boss and superiors, support of colleagues and subordinates, personal sacrifice, etc.

Outputs are typically all financial rewards – pay, salary, expenses, pension arrangements, bonus and commission – plus intangibles – recognition, reputation, praise and thanks, interest, responsibility, stimulus, travel, training, development, sense of achievement and advancement, promotion, etc.

in their minds, laid down through evolution, for social interaction and for detecting cheating, fairness, and rule-breaking.

This ability to detect cheating is supported by the Equity Theory of Motivation proposed by John Stacey Adams in 1963.[6] Equity Theory is based on the notion that people seek a fair and reasonable balance between what they put into work and what they get out of it. Their perceptions of whether or not the balance is correct are formed through comparing their situation with relevant reference points in the market-place – such as what others in similar jobs are being paid or rewarded and what hours they tend to work. His theory is represented in Figure 9 above.

Many people now feel that the whole work equation is completely awry and it's not hard to see why. With the concertina-ing of job roles – collapsing what was once two or even three jobs into one – the cutting of overheads and the ever-increasing demands for shareholder return, people are being asked to give more and more of their time, effort, skill and emotional energy to bolster business performance. Yet, the tangible and intangible returns for most people on their work investment have not continued to match these increasing expectations.

The key issue here is balance. This can be achieved by adjusting either end of the spectrum. Meaning Inc. companies look at both and recognize differences in individual need. The work–life balance question can, however, be something of a red herring; in reality, when organizations have an invigorating sense of purpose, or people feel that their work is meaningful, work–life balance often does go out the window. This was the case at Sony in its early days, when people were prepared to work monstrous hours and would even get locked in the department store where their office was located because they were so engaged in the company's core purpose: to restore Japanese national pride through bringing technological innovation to the world.

However, working intensely long hours over a prolonged period will ultimately be a health hazard. Both China and Japan have words for death from overwork: *karoshi* and *guolaosi*. By demanding so much of people, employers are not only in danger of damaging their employees' well-being but also of destroying meaning for them.

An executive at a top London law firm once described to me how, when he was working late on a Saturday night/Sunday morning, a fire alarm went off in the building. To his amazement about 250 people piled out of the building. "Everyone, including me, was embarrassed to be caught there so late. We were all thinking 'How sad do I look?' We all gazed at our shoes and tried to be invisible."

Numerous studies confirm that people are increasingly dissatisfied with their work–life balance. In an international study into people's attitudes to work, the National Opinion Research Centre and the University of Chicago found that most people in full-time work want to spend more time with their families.[7] The results were particularly potent in the US, where 85 per cent expressed this view. It was also an issue in Germany, the UK, Italy, Sweden, Canada and the Netherlands, where the figure ranged from 60 to 74 per cent.

A case of poor balance

Claire (whose name has been changed for confidentiality) is a lecturer at a business school. The daughter of an international businessman, she grew up assuming that she would follow her father into business. Claire graduated from university and joined a blue-chip organization's graduate training programme. She progressed rapidly through the organization before moving to INSEAD, the graduate business school at Fontainebleau near Paris, to complete her MBA. On leaving, she joined one of the world's leading strategy consultancies. Her sense of satisfaction reached a new level at this point. She felt she had arrived.

In her time with the consultancy, Claire worked on global assignments. Projects included establishing new brands as well as restructuring international organizations. She loved her work and felt it was having impact on a global scale. Yet the job demanded that she work 16-hour days. Between Monday and Friday, Claire's waking hours were dominated by her work and increasingly she found that Friday night and Saturday morning were focused on recovering from the efforts of the week.

After four years, Claire left. She loved the job and continues to feel it was the best organization she has worked for, but she could not accept the negative impact it had on her broader life. While she does not regret her decision, she resents having to choose between having the job of her dreams and having a home life.

A 10-year study which was begun in 1992 by the London School of Economics (LSE) and the University of Westminster found that people were much less satisfied with their work than they were ten years previously.[8] The area with the most significant fall in satisfaction and happiness revolved around the amount of work people had to perform and the hours they needed to spend doing it. This trend was found to apply across both genders, at virtually all levels of seniority.

Young people want a life outside work too. Charlotte and Laura Shelton in their recent book report their findings that there are two common features of companies who have learned how to keep Generation X-ers satisfied:[9] first, having extremely egalitarian company structures and, second, being super-supportive of employees' desire to get a life outside work. A total of 61 per cent of female Generation X-ers say they would leave their current jobs if they were offered more flexible hours elsewhere.

The sheer number of books, commentators and articles covering this particular subject is overwhelming and indicates that it is an issue that is unlikely to go away very quickly or easily. Resentment in the workplace is reaching crisis levels and people are increasingly planning their exit strategies. Indeed, work–life balance looks increasingly likely to be the lens through which people will judge companies and how they want to live.

What is driving the imbalance?

Before companies or individuals can begin to understand how to deal with work–life imbalance, they first need to understand the issues that are driving it in the first place. These include: leaders and individuals paying lip-service to the notion; people not really knowing what will make them feel successful and fulfilled; and, finally, the vicious cycle that comes from people not investing equally in both their work and their personal lives.

Paying lip-service

The question of balance is an area that businesses cannot ignore. Yet it is one, perhaps more than any other, to which leaders often pay mere lip-service. While virtually every major organization now has a work–life balance policy, and it is a legal requirement for employers to give consideration to part-time work, it is still the area where there is perhaps the greatest difference between stated policy and actual practice. Intellectually, most people appreciate the need for employees to have a functioning home life. Yet in many cases the actions of leaders do not support the ideals they aspire to. In truth, there are powerful forces which limit the motivation of leaders to address work–life balance issues.

First, leaders are under incredible pressure to deliver growth rapidly and consistently, and they are now also heavily incentivized to do so. Increasingly, directors of organizations can receive huge financial rewards if they are successful – or sometimes, even if they are not. Because of this, any work–life imbalance they may experience seems worthwhile.

Second, the psychological make-up of many leaders is such that they don't fully appreciate others' need for balance. Our work with leaders has led us to believe that many of them frequently place a considerably higher value on competence and success in career terms and a corresponding lower value on success in relationships and other facets of life than the majority of their employees.

Third, many leaders have had to work extraordinarily hard to get where they are and they don't see why others should have to do anything less. While they might acknowledge that excessive working hours are not great for people, their own experiences often make it difficult for them to generate real sympathy for others.

And it is not just leaders who are guilty of paying lip-service to the need for balance. All types of employee have been prepared to tolerate the fact that work erodes so much of their personal lives because of the lure of the potential jackpot. Increasingly, however, people are beginning to realize that only a few ever reach the summit. This has led them to questions whether it is worth such strenuous effort when the odds are so stacked against them.

People don't know what they want

We once worked with a senior leader who would fervently bemoan the effect that his long working hours were having on his health and family life. He would talk incessantly about the fact that the situation had become untenable and how committed he was to doing something about it. Yet he never did. Two years after his initial discussions with us, he was still continuing to work just as hard and just as long. The truth was that, deep down, he really didn't want to change things. His approach was based on the belief that hard work had got him to where he was and, no matter how much he recognized the logic of working in a different way, he just did not accept it at an emotional level. Being honest with himself was the only way he could reconcile the whole situation.

A major reason behind the ubiquitous sense of work–life imbalance is that people don't really know what they want. For instance, there is a collective belief shared in many parts of the world that more money and career success will lead to happiness and fulfilment. As human beings, we feel confident in our ability to know what gives us this sense of fulfilment. If asked, most people would feel fairly certain of their ability to write a list of things that make them happy. Many would include more money and a promotion in such a list. Thousands enter their nation's lotteries in the hope of becoming millionaires.

Yet research would suggest that human beings are surprisingly poor judges of what fulfils them and, as a consequence, they find it hard to make good choices about how to spend their time. Consistently, both economists and psychologists have been unable to find any link between increasing wealth and significantly improved levels of happiness. Poverty has equally consistently been found to have crippling effects, but researchers have found that increasing wealth only results in the smallest increase in happiness. So while many believe that earning more money will improve the quality of their life, the reality is that once people in the US and UK earn over the threshold of £12,000 ($25,000), there is a virtually no relationship between their salary and their happiness.[10] The cliché that money can't buy happiness seems to be true.

Even the ultimate prize, winning the lottery, only has a fleeting impact. Social psychologists Philip Brickman, Dan Coates and Ronnie Janoff-Bulman tracked lottery winners to investigate how they reacted to their new-found fortunes.[11] While a big win initially led to a feeling of euphoria, overall levels of contentment returned to pre-lottery win levels within just a year.

Likewise, securing the next promotion frequently leads to no change in long-term happiness levels. In a study of academics looking to secure tenure, psychologist Daniel Gilbert and his colleagues found that those lecturers who reached tenure were no happier than those who failed to achieve this important step on the academic ladder.[12] Despite all the advantages of tenure – increased job security, greater freedom to set their own research agenda and heightened status – tenured professors were no happier than assistant professors.

The danger is that people end up pursuing activities that they think make them happy. These are invariably defined by prevailing societal norms rather than what is meaningful and important to them. The result is a life defined by stereotypes of success rather than the factors that genuinely lead to fulfilment. Over the last thirty years, these commonly held definitions of success have broadened significantly. The most obvious example is the change in expectations for both men and women. While once, women were expected to be homemakers and men the wage earners, today both are expected to fully participate in the economy and be active parents.

But that is not where the expectations stop. The definition of success is also broadening in more subtle ways. More than ever, success is measured on multiple scales, from earning money to exercising regularly, from eating properly to having a broad group of friends, from actively participating in your community to being well read and having a rich cultural life. As our definition of success expands, our chances of meeting the benchmark in all domains decreases. The result is that people feel guilty about the impact their work is having on significant relationships, and at the same time a nagging feeling of underachievement in their work. Men and women try to live up to these norms and perform on all fronts. They don't know what to stop doing to improve the quality of their life. They run the risk of continuing to strive for goals that will have little impact on their overall happiness but put intense pressure on their work–life balance.

Another, more recent, addition to the stereotype of what makes you happy is the idea of early retirement or no job at all. As many as 35 per cent of Generation Y[13] apparently aspire to this. Yet the reality for those who leave the rat race is that unless they replace their lives with other engaging or meaningful roles, they frequently end up feeling empty inside.

The key point is that people often misjudge themselves and, as a consequence, can end up making poor decisions about how to live their lives. Many need time, and sometimes support from others, to help them really figure out what it is they want and what ultimately constitutes both success and fulfilment for them.

Vicious cycles

Work–life balance is often compromised when people get themselves trapped in vicious cycles. A marketing executive we worked with is a good example. When her personal life atrophied she placed great emphasis on advancing her career. Striving for more money and a prestigious job title became paramount. She worked obsessively to manage the best campaigns and to raise her profile across the business. In an effort to compensate for what was missing in her personal life, she bought an expensive inner-city property and spent heavily on exotic holidays. This increased the pressure to earn a larger salary and, in turn, led to her working even longer and harder. The energy and time she invested in her work made it all the more difficult for her to rebuild her personal life. People described her as a classic workaholic. She was caught in a cycle with no clear way out.

A similar, but opposite, pattern to the workaholic frequently occurs with mothers who choose to return to work part-time after having children. Having been used to performing a critical and central role before their child was born, they frequently find that the work considered suitable for a part-time role is similar but not as high profile or as important as their previous work. This results in them getting less from their work, which leads to a greater investment in their life outside work and in their children. Others notice this withdrawal, and they get offered less sexy work which only leads to the cycle repeating itself.

In possibly the most extensive and significant series of studies in the area of work–life balance, Stewart Friedman and Jeffrey

Greenhaus looked at the lives and careers of 860 business professionals.[14] One of the main findings was that people who feel in balance are able to respond more resiliently to setbacks in either work or home. When problems occurred at home, those with balance were able to continue more effectively at work, and when major issues, such as possible redundancy, occurred at work, those with a strong supportive personal life were much more able to withstand the pressures.

The reward gap

The tangible rewards that people receive in a company are an important aspect of rebalancing the work equation and creating a sense of equity for them. Yet, over time, some significant asymmetries have developed around how people are compensated for their work and this has contributed to the growing sense of unfairness that people experience.

Pay imbalances

The difference between the earnings of the most senior leaders and their workforces is growing. The extraordinary increases in compensation bestowed on people at the top of organizations has captured the attention of the business world for some time, yet median salary levels, certainly in the US, have remained virtually stationary. According to *Fortune* magazine, CEO salaries for the top firms in the US rose from being 39 times that of the average worker in 1970 to a skyrocketing 1,000 times more by 1999.[15] Something is definitely amiss. The benefits of working hard have significantly increased for those at the top. It is no wonder, then, that they are considerably more motivated to put up with a work–life imbalance than others, particularly youngsters and our leaders of tomorrow. Excessive leadership compensation also leads to destructive behaviour inside organizations because people are no longer prepared to accept the pay differentials that so separate the top earners from the rest.

Poor stock option performance

Stock options have failed to effectively right the scales. In the 1980s and 1990s, the stock market performed exceptionally strongly and price/earnings ratios hit historical highs. Such a boom led to big jackpots for business leaders. In order to continue to deliver such price/earnings ratios, however, companies have to produce the profit growth that is implied by them. Not surprisingly, this has become increasingly difficult to achieve. Even if companies do hit their sky-high targets, the share price often stays the same. This has led to disgruntled bosses trying to rebase their bonus packages because they compare themselves to what the leaders of the 1980s and 1990s were getting. However, today's leaders need to realize that those tremendous jackpots were an aberration and are no longer achievable in today's world.

Let's now turn to how organizations and leaders can begin to create the right balance for their people.

Providing meaning through balance and fairness

Powerful and understandable forces mean leaders want their businesses to perform successfully. It is therefore unrealistic to advocate work–life balance strategies which endanger this. A much more pragmatic and potentially fruitful route is to identify solutions that improve both the performance of the business and an employee's capacity to have balance.

At present, business performance and work–life balance tend to be considered separately. Businesses spend much of their time looking for ways to improve their performance and raise profitability. Simultaneously, employees and, to some extent, HR functions are searching for solutions to tackle their own individual work–life balance challenges or those faced by the organization. Rarely are the two activities joined together. As a result, organizational change frequently leads to a deterioration of people's balance, and HR functions propose work–life balance policies which cause a decrease in efficiency or are positioned as perks that constitute part of an employee's remuneration.

The most sensible way forward is to bring these two streams of activity together. By encouraging managers to consider balance as well as business improvements, leaders are likely to find considerably more commitment from their employees to the initiative. By supporting employees to develop solutions that help them achieve their balance and improve performance in their area, they are likely to find managers considerably more receptive to the solution.

So, if businesses want to improve the balance of their employees' lives, what can they do?

Be flexible

A fundamental step in tackling the whole work–life balance crisis is to be flexible and prepared to adapt people's working contracts in a way that will ultimately work for both the individual and the company. One of the real challenges in creating better work–life balance is that everyone wants and needs something different. What's more, the differences don't just occur between individuals but also across time, as individuals go through different phases of their life.

What people want above all else is a real sense of control over their work. They want to have a dialogue with their employers about their jobs and how they engage with their work rather than feeling it is all a one-way street. Entering into an open dialogue with people in this way and creating the flexibility to custom-design their jobs can ensure that both the individual and the business get what they want. Central to making this work is the whole issue of fairness and equity. Employees are not going to be happy if they see other colleagues working on more favourable contracts than they are, particularly if the amount and quality of work demanded is the same.

Consequently, flexibility has to be balanced with laser-sharp focus on performance and delivery if it is to be a successful long-term strategy for a business. For some companies, there is a very clear focusing mechanism around what is required of people. With salespeople, it is around the volume of stock or services they sell and therefore the amount of commission or revenue they are able to generate for the company. Taking a Friday afternoon off or having an extended holiday may be an acceptable form of flexibility if a salesperson has exceeded all of their targets. Other departments often have to work harder at defining the outputs and expectations they have of their people so that the level of flexibility offered is fair and equitable.

Achieving work–life balance does not have to be a matter of either having a job or not. Rather, approaching the whole situation with greater flexibility and open-mindedness could be a way of retaining talented people. For example, we have talked about people harbouring escape plans and wanting to leave their job roles to pursue other things. Businesses could usefully explore these desires with their people and work together to agree a plan which allows them to delve into other interests gradually while continuing to work. In this way, businesses can continue to benefit from the years of experience and knowledge that people accumulate, while the risks for individuals in leaving the security of their jobs before venturing into other areas are reduced.

If flexibility is really going to work, leaders also need to ensure that people who are prioritizing their home life, for whatever reason, continue to receive opportunities within the workplace. If people do wish to work part-time, they are frequently given less high-profile work, fewer training opportunities and are expected simply to be grateful for the perk of working part-time. As a consequence, they can end up putting less into their work and more into their home life, with the cycle becoming more pronounced. If this cycle is to be broken, leaders need to think about how they can involve and fully engage people.

A specific form of flexibility that can help people to achieve greater balance is to rely on the cooperation and support of teams. If someone needs time off, other members can cover for them and vice versa. In the notoriously tough environment of investment banking, where work–life balance is notoriously out of kilter, Goldman Sachs may not have entirely cracked the problem, but they have made some real inroads. The company has a very strong cultural orientation around teams, where work responsibility is shared among members. Therefore, when someone wants or needs to take some time off, the team can compensate for their absence and still deliver.

Hand in your knives!

In November 2004, London's Metropolitan Police launched a national anti-knife crime campaign called Operation Blunt.[16] They made an appeal for people to hand in their knives and other weapons. A number of initiatives were launched, including the installation of metal detectors in some of the busier London train stations. The initiative resulted in almost 2,000 surrendered knives in amnesty bins, 533 arrests and hundreds of knives seized.

Guinness (now Diageo) latched on to this idea and introduced a similar approach in an effort to stamp out wasted effort. Managers were asked to let the business know of any projects they felt should be scrapped because they were going nowhere, not adding value to the business or taking up valuable time and resources which might otherwise be more effectively harnessed. In response, no one would be reprimanded, demoted or shamed in any way. This led to a mass dumping of projects across the business. It allowed people to inject more focused energy and time into the projects that were really going to make a difference to business performance. As a consequence, managers and their people felt much more productive and there was a huge increase in the number of projects that had a successful impact on the business.

Help with the chores

Work and life each have their own two sub-categories: quality time and chores. Taking some of the drudgery out of life and work chores helps increase the time that people can spend enjoying themselves in "quality time".

Genentech's Lifeworks department is dedicated to making people's lives outside of work easier. It provides near-site child care – instantly reducing the time and irritation of being stuck in traffic. It has an on-site dry-cleaning facility and a concierge service which will run all sorts of errands for employees from postage to gift collection and wrapping. On-site health and fitness programmes also remove the chore of travelling after work.

Similarly, Google provides numerous convenient ways of helping Googlers reduce the time they spend on chores outside of their working time. There's an on-site laundry, hair styling, dental and medical care, a car wash, day-care, fitness facilities with personal trainers and a professional masseuse.[17] Meaning Inc. companies like Google and Genentech think creatively about the kind of support they could provide for their people in order to create a more satisfactory and sustainable work–life balance. In this case, a little goes a long way.

Dull but necessary chores don't just exist outside work, they are an integral part of most people's working lives as well. A Microsoft technologist offers a different take on Google's 10 per cent rule: "The thing is, I need 10 per cent of my time to do all the work I hate to do, like expense reports or other corporate procedures and processes. Now if someone could take those kinds of chores away, then *that* would be an employee benefit I'd really like."[18] There is clearly an opportunity for organizations to think carefully about this in an effort to maximize the quality time people have at work.

Create space for reflection and new experiences

Given that most of us are relatively poor at making judgements about what will make us happy, taking time out to do something completely different can help to uncover hidden passions or capabilities.

A BBC television programme, "The Week the Women Went", gave some families a unique opportunity to see life from a different angle. Men who typically spent much of their time out of the home and had relatively little involvement in the raising of their children were left in sole charge of the family as their wives left for a week of relaxation with friends.

Before the exercise, the men are confident in their ability to look after the children. Yet they quickly learn that caring for children is hard, demanding work and by mid-week they are tired and fractious. But it is at the end of the programme that things get really interesting. The fathers learn how to look after the children and start to see the rewards of their labours. They are touched by their children's pleasure in spending time with them, they start to understand how to entertain, educate and care for the children and find satisfaction in their new skills. They have a new-found respect for their wives and their relationship with their spouse improves. In short, they begin to enjoy this life they had been missing out on.

Some companies try similar experiments by sending people on secondment programmes where they work for a period of time in another business. This allows individuals to experience different environments, interpersonal relationships, challenges and operating models without having to actually leave and work for another company. They typically return to their own businesses with new ideas and a broader perspective – all of which can make for more effective performance. Often such secondments, however, are reserved for specially selected high-potential groups of people and opportunities can be missed to expose others to the same sorts of experiences. The downside? They typically return to a mountain of work that has piled up, and all the benefit is lost. Companies could deal with this by getting temporary cover, for example.

Sabbaticals

All of our work tells us that people feel they don't have sufficient reflection time or adequate room to really grow and develop personally. Many people also harbour escape plans because of the effects of their jobs on their health and levels of physical and emotional energy. Embedding sabbatical policies, whereby after a given period of service to their company people are allowed to take a designated period of time off to recharge their batteries without having to leave the business, is one way of addressing these issues. Indeed, retaining talented people with all of the experience and unique skills that they bring to a business is a real form of competitive advantage.

Genentech offers a generous and egalitarian sabbatical programme: every employee gets six weeks' paid leave after they have worked there for six years. There is no implicit obligation to use the time to further your career and many people use the time to travel.

Sabbaticals can be equally as effective for CEOs and business leaders. By deliberately removing themselves from the business, not only can they replenish their own energies, but they can also create room for others to step up into higher areas of responsibility in a relatively risk-free way – i.e. with the CEO being on hand to advise if necessary. While a brave move for any CEO, what better test of the sustainability of the processes and practices that you bring to an organization and what better confirmation of the faith you have in the talents of your people?

Providing meaning through special rewards and recognition

Addressing work–life balance is only part of the process in rebalancing the work scales. Companies also need to think broadly and creatively about the whole package they offer people in terms of rewards and recognition.

Create special work environments

One of the most palpable ways in which companies can make their people feel special is by creating special work environments for them. Earlier in the chapter, we saw how Google has achieved this at Googleplex, but there are opportunities for companies to put their own unique twist on things. The important focus must be on how the environment makes people feel and the extent to which it signals that they are valued. There is a big difference between an environment that sufficiently meets work health and safety standards and one which sets the company apart as something different and special. Looking after people's sustenance needs through employing a fantastic chef was important at Google because of the lack of positive alternatives in the immediate locale, but even having fresh apples available can add significantly to people's experience of work.

Rebalance executive compensation

From the international surveys quoted on page 262, it is clear that a good work–life balance occurs most frequently in egalitarian set-ups where there is less of a difference between the earnings of the most senior people and those in the rest of the organization. As we have mentioned, in many parts of the world the gap between CEO compensation and average earnings has grown enormously. Because they are rewarded so generously, CEOs only have to endure the tremendous hours and pressures of work for a few years in order to set their families up financially for life – a very attractive end goal. For others, working extraordinary hours becomes part of the struggle to win that jackpot and get to the plum, high-paying positions that will provide them with broader financial options. However, as the competition grows ever fiercer and the funnel ever narrower, people have started to challenge the point of those long hours and the unfairness of how the jackpot is divided.

At Whole Foods Market, the largest natural foods grocer in the US, no executive is paid more than eight times the average wage.[19] CEO and co-founder John Mackey says: "There's a notion that you can't be touchy-feely *and* serious. We don't fit stereotypes. There's plenty of managerial edge with this company – the culture creates it."

Achieving balance through individual responsibility

A female senior executive we worked with complained constantly about how difficult it was to manage her workload and how much of a strain it put on her life. Bizarrely, when she did go on holiday, she often hated it. No matter how much she needed to relax or how wonderful or interesting the holiday destination was, after a day or two she would be feeling utterly bored and eager to get back to work. At the heart of her problem was the fact that she didn't really know what would make her happy.

The first strategy for people in managing their work–life balance effectively is to take responsibility for discovering what gives them personal fulfilment rather than relying on commonly held beliefs and views about what leads to this fulfilment. In analysing this issue, people need to think both about their present and their future fulfilment. They need to project themselves into the future, think forward in time about what they want to achieve, and plan accordingly. We often ask people: "If the next year of your life was to be truly amazing, what would have happened? What would you have achieved? How would you have spent your time and what would you have needed to compromise?" Similarly, looking back at the kinds of achievements and activities that have created real joy in their lives in the past helps people gain clarity about what is important to them. By doing this, they are able to make better decisions about how to invest their energy.

It is not only work that people need to think more deeply about, but also how they spend their time outside work. Despite the whole work–life balance debate, recent research shows that people's leisure time has actually increased. Technology and a rise in the number of machines that do our work for us, such as washing machines, dishwashers, and dryers, as well as the prevalence of various services like home secretarial support, have enabled this. Yet people continue to experience dissatisfaction with their leisure time. The reason is that they don't really know how to use it effectively. Recognizing this is a first step in creating a positive work–life balance.

Another worthwhile strategy is to learn more about the impact potential jobs may have on their lives. When weighing up whether to apply for a job, it is useful to talk to people who are currently performing that role to find out what the job entails. By gathering more information about the options and then thinking through whether the position suits them, rather than basing decisions on perceptions, people are likely to make better decisions as to how to spend their time and to eliminate the guilt that can potentially be attached to any decision which may emphasize work over life or vice versa.

While some people do make informed decisions about how to organize their time, it can all fall apart when the reality of work takes hold. That promise to leave work at 6pm every Wednesday to watch your son's football practice or to delegate that project instead of getting involved can all be forgotten when a crisis arises with an important proposal or deal. Consequently, one of the most common symptoms of a life imbalance is a chronic sense of guilt. Often, the guilt that people experience is the biggest issue and if the person involved can remember that they very carefully and consciously made the choice to stay and work on the deal, they can move on again. Putting time boundaries on themselves can also be a useful mechanism for sticking to decisions.

In summary:

- A lack of work–life balance and what people get in return for their work efforts is a critical issue for businesses and one to which leaders can no longer pay mere lip-service. While many people used traditionally to accept the long hours and the empty concern of their leaders, now the scales have shifted and people are feeling cheated. It matters because the jackpot that used to lure people into working so intensely is so unattainable for most that they are just not prepared to put up with it any longer. As a consequence, employees, particularly the younger generation, will severely judge those businesses that get the balance wrong. Lawsuits could well be on their way.

So, companies will need to come up with some real and genuine responses to the problem. We propose the following:

- Balance means different things to different people. Therefore, companies need to be flexible in what they offer and be prepared to have an open dialogue with individuals in order to negotiate a format that works for them. The dialogue needs to be an ongoing process and people should also be allowed to change their deal over time. A key issue in getting balance right is to make work more meaningful for people.

- There are huge amounts of wasted energy and effort inside many businesses that exacerbate the imbalance people experience. This can be addressed by embedding a zero-based activity approach whereby effort is directed toward what needs to be achieved and anything that does not align with that is thrown out; people genuinely hand in their knives. It requires a shift to rewarding and measuring outputs rather than inputs. Much more attention needs to be given to understanding how to judge outcomes if companies are to get this balance right.

- Rebalancing the scales needs to be a mutual process whereby companies identify solutions that benefit both the individual and the business. People need to have time for reflection and refreshment. Allowing sabbaticals, time and space for such reflection and new experiences can be a real opportunity for the business as well. It is a strategy that can drive innovation, recruitment, retention and loyalty as well as rejuvenate people, prevent burn-out and avoid the expense of stress-related illness.

- Companies need to create distinctive stories around the benefits they offer. Creating invigorating work environments and offering special services that help make people's lives easier – dry-cleaning, fitness facilities, child care or even holidays in the company castle – all make a huge difference. People need to feel special and being able to talk to others about the perks of their jobs is one way this can be achieved.

- Top leaders' behaviour needs to change because people take their cues so strongly from them. Ensuring leadership compensation levels are fairly calibrated against others in the business, managing to keep a check on their own work hours and being prepared to take time for sabbaticals or reflection all send the right signals. These behaviours serve to create alignment around expected levels of balance and help people to relax more about their work in a way that benefits all parties.

- Individuals are partly to blame for work–life imbalance. They are prone to getting caught up in vicious cycles and can blame the situation rather than take responsibility themselves for breaking the deadlock. People need to start by focusing on what is meaningful to them as individuals as opposed to being driven by societal norms and expectations. Such honest self-understanding is a critical step in rebalancing the scales.

- Individuals also need to be prepared to enter into open dialogue with their companies so that effective solutions can be jointly identified and agreed. Having decided on their preferred life design, individuals need to put sufficient boundaries in place to ensure they stick to it and not waver when their plans clash with their work demands.

The suggestions presented in this chapter for creating that feeling of specialness are just a start. Our hope is that they will trigger the imagination of organizations and their leaders and enable them to discover their own unique ways of balancing the work equation, thus ensuring that both the organization and the individual enjoy a positive and sustainable partnership.

Conclusion

L et's now summarize some of the key themes that we have covered in this book and consider some questions that might naturally arise from this. We would also like to place what we have written in the context of other management literature.

Become psychologically minded

A key thread that runs through this book is the importance of ephemeral, psychological concepts for the success of individuals, companies, and even nations. Whenever you look deeply at the roots of success and failure, psychological factors play a key role.

In the physical sciences one can follow a reductionist logic which reduces everything to mathematics. Biology can ultimately be reduced to chemistry; which in turn can be reduced to physics. Physics itself can essentially be reduced to mathematics. An understanding of mathematics, therefore, lies at the root of understanding all physical phenomena.

Similarly, we believe that disciplines such as sociology, politics and economics all reduce ultimately to the science of psychology. In the social world, ultimately it is only people's behaviour that is the agent for anything. John Maynard Keynes once remarked that every politician is the prisoner of some "defunct economist". Our view is that every commentator on business, economics, politics or any other social science follows either a valid or a defunct implicit theory of psychology. Core to all theories in the social world is an implicit model of what makes people behave in particular ways.

When we say that everyone needs to become psychologically minded, we do not mean that people need to become versed in the technicalities of the discipline. Rather we mean that people have to work hard to get into the minds and hearts of others. One needs to really understand how actions, initiatives and messages are being experienced by people in order to co-opt them to a course of action. To do this requires clear mental models of what makes people tick but also an openness and flexibility in applying these concepts to each and every person. In short, this means getting into the unique headspace of every individual that you deal with.

● See things through the lens of meaning

In the introduction to this book, we quoted Stuart Crainer and Des Dearlove's article "Whatever Happened to Yesterday's Bright Ideas?" There has been a tendency in management literature to dump what has gone before in order to claim originality for one's ideas. Within companies this is exactly the process that leads to attention deficit organizations.

We have tried to avoid this trap and throughout this work have recognized and paid homage to ideas that we feel are valid. Our conclusions are consistent with those reached in works like *In Search of Excellence*, *Built to Last*, *The Learning Organisation* and *The 8th Habit*. However, this is not to say that our views are identical with these perspectives. We have tried in an honest way to identify which themes from earlier writings are still relevant in the 21st century.

However, we would like to make a potentially broader point which risks being somewhat grandiose. Much of this earlier writing we feel can be subsumed under the meaning rubric. The reason that a lot of the ideas mentioned in the above works are either relevant today or not relevant is the extent to which they create or destroy meaning in the new world. So, for example, if we take *Built to Last*, we agree with the theme that having a clear set of corporate values is vital for business success. However, another theme from that work – that highly successful organizations tend to be somewhat "cultish" – we would question. Quite simply, in today's world cult-like organizations are a turn-off for people because they destroy meaning by eroding an individual sense of uniqueness.

We believe that meaning is a lens through which much management writing can be reviewed. More importantly, we believe that meaning provides a compass for navigating one's way through a complex and turbulent organizational world. In work environments where people want changes, it is also important to remember that the specific ways in which meaning may or may not be created for others will shift. However, the drive for meaning is fundamental. It just expresses itself in different ways in different situations. We believe leaders cannot go far wrong if they use the concept of meaning as a compass and navigational tool. This also means recognizing that you will never arrive at the end destination as the meaning goalposts are ever shifting and changing.

Reconcile contradictions

In reflecting upon what we have said, the reader might identify a number of ideas that on the surface seem to be contradictory. However, we believe that many of these apparent contradictions are actually concepts that enforce each other. Let's look at some of these briefly.

Being long term versus driving short-term results

Much of what we say could be interpreted as encouraging leaders to show courage in doing what is right long-term for a business. Get some core things right and long-term success will follow is the message. There is much truth in this. However, this is not the reality that most leaders inhabit. Frequently, leaders need to fix the basics and get short-term results moving in the right direction before they can pull the meaning levers to drive further success. Ultimately, organizations exist to succeed in the world of business. If they do not do this their existence is to some extent meaningless, as well as somewhat brief, however nice or worthy they may be.

Meaningful organizations are aggressive about both short-term and long-term goals. They recognize that the aggressive pursuit of positive results is a necessary but insufficient condition for creating meaning in the long term. Leaders in these organizations typically move dynamically between the short term and the long term. More importantly, they are able to show how more immediate initiatives connect with the long-term agenda that is being played out.

● Soft versus hard approaches to managing others

At many points in this book we have talked about the value of believing in people, playing to their strengths and giving everyone a chance to perform. We have also talked about loosening organizational boundaries to allow people to contribute in ways that are individually meaningful for themselves. At other times, we have argued that companies need to become much sharper at judging people's performance. We emphatically believe that these two principles are not contradictory at all. In fact, becoming aggressive at performance management is a necessary condition for much of the loosening of boundaries that we also argue for. Fundamentally, it's about saying that, in the new world, businesses need to give people the freedom to contribute in ways that play to their drives and inclinations. But then companies also have a duty to sharply differentiate between people in terms of the outputs they deliver. In the absence of this, some of the meaning themes we have talked about risk destabilizing organizations or creating confusion and a sense of inequity.

Looking inside/to the past versus looking outside/to the future

We have argued that leaders need to look deeply at the core values of their organization and the history that lies behind their current reality. At other times, we have suggested that leaders need to be thinking much more deeply about the outside world and what is over the horizon. Again, we do not see a contradiction between these things. You can only make sense of what you have internally and your history if you are aware of what's happening out there and what may be coming next. The understanding of one area provides the context for understanding the other. Similarly, any sensible response to the external environment and future trends needs to be anchored in a deep understanding of a company's core strengths and its DNA.

We see most leaders inhabiting the world of the now and being preoccupied with their current realities. Becoming more reflective about one's past, as well as being alive to the external environment and the future, is a key condition for the creation of meaning. The ability to contextualize, frame and create coherence for people requires leaders to move with versatility between the past, present and future and make the relevant connections between them.

Applicability at all levels

A key theme running through the book is that the creation of meaning can drive success at all levels. We are confident that if you are working on your own, or have no job at all, you will still benefit from thinking about much that we have written about. We also believe that the creation of meaning, apart from being critical to the success of business, applies at a national level as well.

Another important point is that you can create meaning in your part of the organization – you don't have to wait for your top leadership to get it right. A recent study found that engagement levels varied more within companies than between companies. This graphically illustrates the point that the creation of meaning is a local task. In this sense, one could argue that there is no such thing as company culture but a variety of sub-cultures which may or may not be strong on Meaning Inc. attributes. We would encourage leaders of units or small teams to think hard about the different dimensions of meaning that we have articulated and how these ideas can be embedded in their part of the business.

Push the world around one more time

At a recent lunch, when I was describing this book to a colleague who works as a coach in investment banking, I said that we felt it was important for two reasons. First, as we suggested in the introduction, because corporations are arguably now the most powerful institutions in the world. Trying to shift their focus and behaviour in a positive direction is therefore an incredibly important endeavour. Second, work is where most people spend the majority of their waking lives. Trying to make this time more meaningful and worthwhile is therefore also not a negligible goal. "In investment banking terms, we would call that massive leverage," he said. Reflecting on this, I believe he is right. Just inching forward in some of the areas we have identified is likely to yield enormous dividends both in terms of people's experience of work and the impact companies have on the world around them. Both are goals that would be high in just about anyone's meaning hierarchy.

But there is no magic wand that can be waved to move things forward. Mahatma Gandhi once said, "We must become the change we want to see." Ultimately, it all boils down to individual responsibility. We hope, through this book, to have encouraged you to do your bit to push the world around one more time.

Appendix: Diagnosis tools

There are a variety of tools for diagnosing where an organization is with respect to Meaning Inc. attributes. A combination of surveys, deep-structure interviews and focus groups is required to flush out the issues. To this end, YSC has developed the following:

- The YSC Meaning InQ measure: This is a short survey instrument which has its roots in the Meaning Inc. model outlined in this book. The instrument allows an organization to quickly assess where it is on the Meaning Inc. attributes. It also allows different areas to assess their strengths and weaknesses relative to other parts of an organization. A wide variety of external benchmark data is available.

- Deep-structure interviews: YSC has developed an interview process that goes under the surface and attempts to identify what people really think about their work and their organization. This interview process is designed, in particular, to explore differences between espoused and real values. It also helps highlight core underlying assumptions that drive behaviour.

- Internal group investigation: We have found that an extremely helpful technique is to single out a small number of high-potential individuals to go into their organization and collect data on Meaning Inc. attributes. The individuals selected need to be confident and well regarded in the business. In addition, a clear contract has to be established of not "shooting the messenger". Once the group has collected the data, they typically present it back to the senior team, who then take responsibility and ownership for developing solutions.

In addition to the above, there are some commonly available instruments, which look at the alignment between personal and corporate values. A particular tool that we find helpful is called CTT (Cultural Transformation Tool). This instrument formally measures an individual's values and how these map on to company values. The tool produces graphic output which clearly identifies areas of concern. The instrument is extremely easy to complete and the data can be processed rapidly.

Notes

Introduction

1. This quote has been attributed to a number of people including: Sam Goldwyn, Casey Stengel and Yogi Berra.

2. Data tabulated by Rhett A. Butler of Mongabay.com, based on data supplied by *Fortune* magazine, 25 July 2005; and World Development Indicators – World Bank, 2005.

3. World Development Indicators – World Bank, 2006.

4. The Economy; Red Flags. Trust in Business – http://www.publicagenda.org/issues

5. "Trust in Governments, Corporations and Global Institutions continues to decline" – Press Release, World Economic Forum, 2005.

6. *Dilbert* – see www.dilbert.com

7. Andresky Fraser, J., *White Collar Sweatshop: The Deterioration of Work and Its Rewards in Corporate America,* New York, W. W. Norton & Company Inc. (2001); Bunting, M., *Willing Slaves: How the Overwork Culture is Ruining Our Lives,* HarperCollins, London (2004).

8. Maier, C., *Bonjour Paresse,* European Schoolbooks Ltd, Cheltenham (2004).

9. Collins, J. C. & Porras, J. I., *Built to Last: Successful Habits of Visionary Companies,* HarperCollins, New York, 1994.

10. Crainer, S. & Dearlove, D., "Whatever Happened to Yesterday's Bright Ideas?" *Across the Board,* Vol. 43, No. 3, May/June 2006.

1 Back to the future

1. Maddison, A., *The World Economy: A Millennial Perspective*, Economic History Services (2001).

2. "The giant who touched tomorrow – A brief story of Jamsetji Tata" http://www.tata.com/history

3. Ibid.

4. Lala, R. M., *The Creation of Wealth*, Penguin Books Ltd, Harmondsworth (1981).

5. For example, in the Hewitt Associates Awards for India's Best Employers in 2004, three Tata companies (Tata Steel, Tata Motors and Tata Consulting Services) were in the top 25, with TCS coming first.

6. "The giant who touched tomorrow" – see note 2.

7. "The World's Most Respected Companies", *Financial Times/*PricewaterhouseCoopers (2005).

8. "A New Kind of Company", *Newsweek* (International Edition), 4 July 2006.

9. Lord Browne, "Breaking Ranks", speech to Stanford Business School (September 1997).

10. Shinn, S., "Oil and Water", *BizEd*, November/December 2005.

11. The World's Most Respected Companies – see note 7.

12. "*Fortune* 100 Best Companies to Work For", *Fortune* magazine, 2006.

13. Ibid.

14. Schlosser, E., *Fast-Food Nation: The Dark Side of the All-American Meal*, Houghton Mifflin Company, New York (2001).

15. Cooperative Bank, *Ethical Consumerism Report*, 12 December 2005.

16. More than a third of all consumers boycott at least one brand. GMIPOLLS, press release, August 2005.

17. See *Ethical Consumer* http://www.ethicalconsumer.org/boycotts/boycottsnewsrecent.htm

18. Bakan, J., *The Corporation: The Pathological Pursuit of Profit and Power*, Penguin Books Ltd, London (2004).

19. Ibid.

20. Elkington, J., *Cannibals with Forks: The Triple Bottom Line of 21st-Century Business*, New Society Publishers, Gabriola, BC (1998).

21. *Sunday Times*, survey, March 2006.

22. Scott, P. & Young, D., *Having Their Cake: How the City and Big Bosses Are Consuming UK Business*, Kogan Page, London (2004).

23. *Report on Socially Responsible Investing Trends in the United States*, p. 4, SIF Industry Research Program (2003).

24. Bunting, M., *Willing Slaves: How the Overwork Culture is Ruining Our Lives*, HarperCollins, London (2004).

2 Running on empty

1. Eliot, T. S., *Collected Poems 1909–62*, Faber and Faber, London (1974).

2. Flade, P., "Britain's Workforce Needs Inspiration", *Gallup Management Journal* (Dec 2003).

3. Covey, S. R., *The 8th Habit – From Effectiveness to Greatness*, Simon & Schuster, London (2004).

4. Guest, D. & Conway, N., "Employee Well-being and the Psychological Contract", Research Report, CIPD, London (2004).

5. Workplace Employee Relations Survey, http://www.dti.gov.uk/ (2004).

6. Doyle, T. C., "New Economy, New Culture", *VARBusiness*, July 2000.

7. Roberts, M., "The statistics that shock", *In the Defence of Marxism*, May 2006.

8. "Productivity Growth and Profits Far Outpace Compensation in Current Expansion", Economic Policy Institute, 21 April 2005.

9. Freud, S., *Civilization and its Discontents*, Penguin Books Ltd, London (2002).

10. Jahoda, M., Lazarsfeld, P.F. & Ziesel, H., *Marienthal: The Sociography of an Unemployed Community*, Transaction Publishers, New Jersey (2002).

11. Singer, W., "Neuronal Synchrony: A Versatile Code for the Definition of Relations?", *Neuron* 24, 1999.

12. Ramachandran, V. S. & Blakeslee, S., *Phantoms in the Brain: Probing the Mysteries of the Human Mind*, William Morrow and Company, New York (1998).

13. Frankl, V. E., *Man's Search For Meaning*, Simon & Schuster, London (1997).

14. Maslow, A., "A Theory of Human Motivation", *Psychological Review* 50, pp.370–96 (1943).

15. Maslow, A., *Motivation and Personality*, Harper, New York (1954).

16. Giddens, A., *Modernity and Self Identity: Self and Society in the Late Modern Age*, Polity Press, Cambridge (1991).

17. Blythe, R., *Akenfield: Portrait of an English Village*, Penguin Books Ltd, London (1999).

18. Collins, J. C. & Porras, J. I., *Built to Last: Successful Habits of Visionary Companies*, HarperCollins Publishers, New York (1994).

19. Collins, J., *Good to Great*, Random House Business Books, London (2001).

20. Shrii Prabhat Rainjan Sarkar, *The Place of Sadvipras in the Social Cycle* www.proutworld.org/ideology/leadership/placesadv.htm

21. Chaves, M., "Abiding Faith", *Context, Understanding People in their SOCIAL WORLDS*, Vol. 1, No. 2, 2002.

22. Robisch, A., "Religious Identification in the US; Consultants on Religious Tolerance", Consultants on Religious Tolerance, March 2006.

23. Smith, Tom W., "A Cross-national Comparison on Attitudes towards Work by Age and Labor Force Status", National Opinion Research Centre/ University of Chicago, December 2000.

3   Building a Meaning Inc. culture

1. Gerstner, Louis V., *Who Says Elephants Can't Dance*, Harper Business, HarperCollins, London (2002).

2. Simon, W. L. & Young, J. S., *iCon Steve Jobs: The Greatest Second Act in the History of Business*, John Wiley & Sons, Inc. (2005).

3. Mead, G. H., *Mind, Self and Society*, University of Chicago Press, Chicago (1934).

4. Beckett, S., *Waiting for Godot*, Faber and Faber, London (2006).

5. Seligman, Martin E. P., "The President's Address", *American Psychologist*, S4, 559–62 (1999).

6. Covey, S. R., *The 8th Habit – From Effectiveness to Greatness*, Simon & Schuster, London (2004).

7. Guest, D. & Conway, N., "Employee well-being and the Psychological Contract", Research Report, CIPD, London (2004).

8. Freiberg, J. & Freiberg, K., *Nuts! Southwest Airlines' Crazy Recipe for Business and Personal Success*, Broadway Books, New York (1996).

4   Meaning Inc. leadership

1. Sion, W. L. & Young, J. S., *iCon Steve Jobs: The Greatest Second Act in the History of Business*, John Wiley & Sons, Inc. (2005).

2. Senge, P., *The Fifth Discipline*, Random House Business Books (2006).

3. Frankl, V. E., *Man's Search for Meaning*, Simon & Schuster, London (1997).

4. Dylan, B., "A Hard Rain's A-Gonna Fall", 1963.

5. Winnicott, D. W., *Playing and Reality*, Routledge, London (1991).

5   The power of an invigorating purpose

1. Simon, W. L. & Young, J. S., *iCon Steve Jobs: The Greatest Second Act in the History of Business*, John Wiley & Sons, Inc. (2005).

2. Deutschman, A., *The Second Coming of Steve Jobs*, Broadway Books, New York (2000).

3. Lord Browne, "Breaking Ranks", Speech to Stanford Business School, September 1997.

4. "Ray of Hope" in *The Green Business Letter*, www.greenbiz.com (October 2004).

5. Blythe, R., *Akenfield: Portrait of an English Village*, Penguin Books Ltd, London (1999).

6. Liker, J. K., *The Toyota Way – 14 Management Principles from the World's Greatest Manufacturer*, McGraw-Hill (2003).

7. Silverberg, D., "Sir Richard Branson's Virgin Territory", digitaljournal. com, 22 April 2005.

8. Prahalad, C. K., *The Fortune at the Bottom of the Pyramid: Eradicating Poverty Through Profits*, Pearson Education, Inc., Saddle River, NJ, (2004).

9. Collins, J. C. & Porras, J. I., *Built to Last: Successful Habits of Visionary Companies*, HarperCollins Publishers, New York (1994).

6   Meaning through history, values and continuity

1. Yokoi, G. & O'Reilly, C., "Building the Culture at Agilent Technologies: Back to the Future", *Harvard Business Online*, Case HR–20 September (2001).

2. Charan, R. & Tichy, N., *Every Business is a Growth Business: How Your Company Can Prosper Year After Year*, Three Rivers Press, New York (2000). (Originally published by Times Books, 1998.)

3. Booz Allen Hamilton, "Quest Diagnostics" on www.boozallen.com.

4. Martens, M. L., "Hang On to Those Founders" in *Harvard Business Review*, www.harvardbusinessonline.com (2005).

5. "Overcoming New Hire Derailers", Research paper published by the Corporate Executive Board (2003).

6. Ibid.

7. Liker, J. K., *The Toyota Way: 14 Management Principles from the World's Greatest Manufacturer*, McGraw-Hill (2003).

7   Inside-Out branding

1. *Brands and Branding*, Economist Books, London (April 2004).

2. The superbrand has a powerful external brand image that sets them apart from their competitors, www.bmrb.co.uk.

3. Bunting, M., *Willing Slaves: How the Overwork Culture is Ruining Our Lives*, HarperCollins, London (2004).

4. "A whole new brand of ideas", *Guardian*, 25 June 2005.

5. See customer testimonials at www.lovemarks.com.

6. Roberts, K., *Lovemarks* (2005). Details on global availability at www. lovemarks.com.

7. According to the Interbrand/*Business Week* survey of Global Brands. Further information at www.interbrand.com.

8. De Mesa, A., "How far can a brand stretch?" (2004) www.brandchannel. com.

9. "A worm's eye view", *Guardian*, March 2004.

10. "Hand-to-brand combat", *Guardian*, 23 September 2000.

11. Klein, N., *No Logo*, Flamingo, London (2001).

12. The most up-to-date *Fortune* Lists are posted at http://money.cnn.com/ lists/index.html.

13. Boyle, D., *Authenticity: Brands, Fakes, Spin and the Lust for Real Life*, HarperPerennial (2004).

14. View the many discussion channels at http://discussions.apple.com/ index.jspa.

15. Fournier, S. & Mick, D. G., – "Rediscovering Satisfaction", *Journal of Marketing*, cited on Harvard Business School Working Knowledge, http:// hbswk.hbs.edu (1999).

16. See www.lovemarks.com for further discussion of the difference between blands and brands.

17. http://www.brandchannel.com/start1.asp?fa_id=273.

18. Garrett, J., "The Human Side of Brand", *Gallup Management Journal*, http://gmj.gallup.com (2001).

19. Milligan, A. & Smith, S., *Uncommon Practice*, Financial Times Prentice Hall (2002) or www.pret.com.

8   Having impact

1. Bloom, H., *The Anxiety of Influence: A Theory of Poetry*, Oxford University Press, New York (1973; 2nd edn 1997).

2. Galbraith, J. K., *The Economics of Innocent Fraud*, Houghton Mifflin Company (2004).

3. Bartlett, C. A. & Ghoshal, S., "Matrix Management: Not a Structure, a Frame of Mind", *Harvard Business Review*, July–August 1990.

9   Good to grow

1. Stojanovic, S., "My Vision: Love, Meaning and the Whole Person in Business" in Green, S., *The New Visionaries: Evolutionary Leadership for an Evolving World*, New Visionaries www.evolutionaryinstitute.com (2006).

2. Jacobson, L. & Rosenthal, R., *Pygmalion in the Classroom*, Holt, Rinehart & Winston, New York (1968).

3. Rosenthal, R., "Covert Communication in Classrooms, Clinics and Courtrooms", *Eye on Psi Chi*, Vol. 3, No. 1, 1998.

4. Semler, R., *The Seven-day Weekend: A Better Way to Work in the 21st Century*, Century, London (2004).

5. See http://www.gore.com/en_xx/aboutus/culture/index.html.

6. Csikszentmihalyi, M., *Flow: The Psychology of Optimal Experience*, HarperPerennial, New York (1991).

7. Bossidy, L., Burck, C. & Charan, R., *Execution: The Discipline of Getting Things Done*, Crown Business, New York (2002).

8. Covey, S. R., *The 7 Habits of Highly Effective People*, Simon & Schuster, London (2004).

9. Covey, S. R., *The 8th Habit: From Effectiveness to Greatness*, Simon & Schuster, London (2004).

10. See, for example, Beer, M. & Eisenstat, R. A., "Got a New Strategy? Now Make it Happen" in *How to Have an Honest Conversation About Your Business Strategy*, *Harvard Business Review*, Vol. 82, No. 2, February 2004.

11. History of Diageo; www.diageo.co.uk.

10   Belonging

1. Freiberg, K. & J., *Nuts! Southwest Airlines' Crazy Recipe for Business and Personal Success*, Broadway Books, New York (1996).

2. See the Harris Interactive Survey reported in Covey, S. R., *The 8th Habit – From Effectiveness to Greatness*, Simon & Schuster, London (2004).

3. Guest, D. & Conway, N., "Employee Well-being and the Psychological Contract", research report, CIPD, London (2004).

4. Bowlby, J., "Attachment and Loss": *Attachment* (Vol. 1), Basic Books, New York (1969).

5. Spitz, R. A., "Anaclitic Depression" in *Psychoanalytic Study of the Child*, 2, pp. 313–42 (1946).

6. Harlow, H. F. & Zimmerman, R., "Affectional Responses in Infant Monkey", *Science*, 130, 421–32 (1959).

7. Brown, G. W. & Harris, T., *Social Origins of Depression: A Study of Psychiatric Disorder in Women*, Tavistock Publications, London (1978).

8. http://www.lorenbennett.org/nbelong.htm.

9. http://www.bizjournals.com/dayton/stories/1996/12/16/focus3.html.

10. Csikszentmihalyi, M., *Good Business: Leadership, Flow and the Making of Meaning*, Hodder and Stoughton, London (2003).

11. Quoted in *Financial Times* article by Alison Maitland, 10 August 2006.

12. Covey, S. R., *The 8th Habit: From Effectiveness to Greatness*, Simon & Schuster, London (2004).

13. Marten, M. L., "Hang on to Those Founders", *Harvard Business Review*, www.harvardbusinessonline.com (2005).

14. Branson, R., *Losing My Virginity*, Virgin Publishing, London (2005).

15. Freiberg, K. & J., *Nuts! Southwest Airlines' Crazy Recipe for Business and Personal Success*, Broadway Books, New York (1996).

16. Collins, J. C. & Porras, J. I., *Built to Last: Successful Habits of Visionary Companies*, HarperCollins, New York (1994).

11 Rebalancing

1. De Botton, A., *Status Anxiety*, Penguin Books (2004). De Botton is interpreting Jean-Jacques Rousseau's views in *Discourse on the Origin of Inequality*.

2. Vise, D. A., *The Google Story*, Bantam Dell, New York (2005).

3. Garrett, J., "The human side of brand", *Gallup Management Journal*, http://gmj.gallup.com (2001).

4. Cosmides, L. & Tooby, J., "Cognitive Adaptions for Social Exchange" in J. Barkow, L. Cosmides & J. Tooby (eds.),*The Adapted Mind: Evolutionary*

Psychology and the Generation of Culture, Oxford University Press, New York (1992).

5.   Adams, J., "Toward an Understanding of Inequity", *Journal of Abnormal and Social Psychology* 67: 422–36 (1963).

6.   Ibid.

7.   Smith, T. W., "A Cross-national Comparison on Attitudes towards Work by Age and Labor Force Status", National Opinion Research Centre/ University of Chicago, December 2000.

8.   Taylor, R., "Britain's World of Work – Myths and Realities", ESRC Future of World Programme Seminar Series (2002), available at www.esrc.ac.uk.

9.   Shelton, C. & L., *The NeXt Revolution: What Gen X Women Want at Work and How Their Boomer Bosses Can Help Them Get It* (2005).

10. Brickman, P., Coates, D. & Janoff-Bulman, R., "Lottery Winners and Accident Victims. Is Happiness Relative?" *Journal of Personality and Social Psychology* 36, 917–27 (1978).

11. Ibid.

12. Gilbert, D. T., Pinel, E. C., Wilson, T. D., Blumber, S. J. & Wheatley, T. P., "Immune Neglect: A Source of Durability Bias in Affective Forecasting", *Journal of Personality and Social Psychology* 75, 617–38 (1998).

13. Generation Y refers to those born from the late 1970s through to the 1990s.

14. Friedman, S. D. & Greenhaus, J. H., *Work and Family – Allies or Enemies? What Happens when Business Professionals Confront Life Choices*, Oxford University Press, New York (2000).

15. http://www.pkarchive.org/economy/ForRicher.html. Article by Paul Krugman.

16. http://cms.met.police.uk/news/arrests_and_charges/violence_against_ the_person/knife_crime_arrests.

17. Vise, D. A., *The Google Story*, Bantam Dell, New York (2005).

18. Ibid.

19. www.fastcompany.com.

Index